Ernest Mercier

FRENCH TECHNOCRAT

ERNEST MERCIER IN 1927

Ernest Mercier

FRENCH TECHNOCRAT

by

Richard F. Kuisel

1967

UNIVERSITY OF CALIFORNIA PRESS

BERKELEY AND LOS ANGELES

University of California Press
Berkeley and Los Angeles, California
Cambridge University Press
London, England
Copyright © 1967, by
The Regents of the University of California
Library of Congress Catalog Card Number: 67–22604
Printed in the United States of America

For Johness

Preface

"EN BOUCHE CLOSE, n'entre mouche," was the motto of Jacques Coeur, the famous fifteenth-century financier. Since the late Middle Ages French businessmen have continued to believe that the discreet will be rewarded with success. Historically they have tended to confine themselves to business affairs, to shun publicity and professional organization, and to regard secrecy as a virtue. When it has been necessary to engage in political activity, they have preferred to exert influence behind closed doors. Such behavior has provoked other Frenchmen to view businessmen with suspicion and even apprehension. It has also obstructed the efforts of historians to understand the attitudes and activities of this powerful element of the French Right. Most studies of the Right in twentieth-century France deal with politicians, military leaders, the press, or the intelligentsia and ignore the difficult-to-document entrepreneurial class. Few historians have been interested in the subject because private records are generally unavailable. My study attempts to add to our meager knowledge of the French business community during the crucial decades between Versailles and Vichy.

The majority of French businessmen during the interwar years regarded politics, foreign affairs, social problems, and economic policy with a certain diffidence and were reluctant to translate their private opinions into action. Yet there was a small minority who did not share this reticence and openly expressed their views on such issues. There were even a few employers who actively campaigned for national reform.

One such businessman was Ernest Mercier (1878–1955), who sought to reform not merely the attitudes and practices of the business community but the entire French political and economic structure. This enterprising manager rose to prominence after the First World War as head of the nation's largest utilities syndicate, and he moved from the electric power industry, which he modernized in the Paris region, to the creation of a native petroleum industry. At the peak of his career this industrial magnate acted as a spokesman for the managerial cadres from the dynamic sector of the economy. He also enjoyed the confidence of the Third Republic's right-wing political and military elite. Marshals Foch and Pétain, Presidents Poincaré and Lebrun, and Premiers Tardieu, Flandin, and Laval were his personal friends. To win the French economic and intellectual elite to the cause of modernization, Mercier organized a pressure group, the Redressement Français (1925–1935). This movement proposed to overhaul the Third Republic along technocratic lines; its slogan was "Enough politics. We want results!" Mercier also participated directly or indirectly in most of the major domestic crises of the interwar years. He helped foment the antiparliamentary riots of February, 1934, and actively assisted in the execution of foreign policy in the mid-1930's. The ordeals he faced after the fall of France in 1940 reflected the rapidly changing fortunes of big business from Vichy to the liberation. His biography thus illuminates the character of the French business community, especially the ideas and activities of the modernizing managerial elite, in the first half of this century.

The career of Ernest Mercier also discloses a development of great significance for contemporary France as well as for other advanced industrial societies—the rise to power of the technical-managerial class. He was one of the "new men" or "technocrats" in business and government who envisaged a new France equipped with a dynamic economy geared to mass production and a government directed by apolitical experts. In their day Mercier and his fellow managerial technocrats made little headway in streamlining either their nation's economy or its political system, but their efforts marked the beginning of a movement which gained strength during and after the Second World War.

The term "technocracy" has a different popular connotation in France than in the United States largely because of contrasting past experiences. Our view is strongly marked by the fanciful scheme popularized by the eccentric intellectual, Howard Scott, during the depression. Although the French imported the term "technocracy" from Scott's movement, they grafted it on to an older and more respected tradition of thought and practice. Modern technocratic doctrine in France dates back to the Comte de Saint-Simon, the early prophet of industrialism. From Saint-Simon on French technocrats have sought a sweeping reorganization of society and thus have gone beyond the narrow definition usually assigned technocracy by contemporary political scientists: "the transfer of [governmental] power from 'political leaders' to the 'experts.' " [1] The heirs of Saint-Simon, who gained important influence in the French business community during the

[1] Roger Grégoire, "Technocracy and the Role of Experts in Government," report submitted to the Fifth World Congress, International Political Science Association, Paris, 1961.

nineteenth and twentieth centuries, believed that advancing technology required economic and, to a degree, social change, as much as it did the elevation of experts to positions of authority in government. The typical French technocrat seeks economic modernization—meaning economic expansion, the scientific utilization of resources, and an organized national economy directed by technicians. Yet economic and political streamlining alone does not satisfy him for he also wants to see society infused with the values of efficiency, productivity, and expertise, and in this way urges a radical transformation of traditional values.

Mercier may be considered as a prototype of this new technical-managerial class which today hopes to remodel France into a technocracy. His biography is a study in the deficiencies and merits of the technocratic mentality. His elitist and antidemocratic tendencies, for example, led him to join an authoritarian veterans' organization, the Croix de Feu, and to encourage violence against the Third Republic. Yet he also embodied the finest ideals of the Saint-Simonian tradition and selflessly dedicated his life to the creation of a richer and more humane France.

There are two points that the reader should hold in mind. First, I have raised a few questions that I have not fully resolved, because of a lack of adequate evidence for certain controversial issues. It seemed far better, however, to relate what was known about such problems than to ignore them altogether. Second, I have not bound my presentation to a strict chronological order. Thus Mercier's industrial achievements are discussed at the beginning of this study, but with the fourth chapter the focus shifts to his political career. Perhaps there is some sacrifice in narrative continuity by separating his two roles. Yet the organization I have selected has the benefit of heightened topical coherence.

The documentation for the career of Ernest Mercier is relatively complete in comparison to the general dearth of materials for modern French business history. He expounded his ideas, of considerable breadth and influence, in numerous books, articles, and lectures. His political activities, which were always rather sensational, and his monumental industrial achievements attracted widespread contemporary comment. But the most important source of information for my biography was his widow, Marguerite Dreyfus Mercier. Not only did she spend long hours relating her memories of her late husband but also she generously allowed me to read his private papers. Largely through the aid of Mme Mercier, I also interviewed and corresponded with many of his former friends and business associates. Their recollections were invaluable for this study. I owe a special debt of gratitude to the following gentlemen: MM. Roger Boutteville, Alfred Lambert-Ribot,

Jean Buisson, Pierre Massé, Raphaël Alibert, François Legueu, Ludovic Barthélemy, Joseph Thuillier, Guillaume de Tarde, Henry Davezac, René de Montaigu, Victor de Metz, and René Mayer.

This book has had the great advantage of the close attention of one of the most learned and perceptive historians of modern France, Professor Gordon Wright. He directed the first version of this work as a doctoral dissertation and later generously devoted much time and energy toward its improvement. I am also deeply indebted to Professor Raymond J. Sontag who stimulated my interest in interwar Europe and profoundly influenced my thinking about history. Mention must be made further of the valuable criticism and suggestions given me by Professors René Rémond, David S. Landes, and Paul Schroeder.

Research for this study required two trips to France: in 1960–1961 and again in the summer of 1964. My thanks go to the Danforth Foundation and to the University of Illinois Research Board for sponsoring these visits. The latter institution also sustained my project with numerous supplemental grants. Only those who have published a historical monograph are fully aware of the enormous assistance, tangible and intangible, given by the author's wife: my deepest thanks to Johness.

Champaign, Illinois   R. F. K.

Contents

The Young Polytechnician

NONCONFORMITY, an interest in politics, and above all an urge to build and to reform were traits of the Mercier family. Three generations of Merciers were distinguished by a bold, enterprising spirit. Ernest's grandfather was a pioneering Algerian *colon*, and his father was a zealous municipal reformer. But Ernest himself was to be one of the great builders of modern France.

The Merciers were from the rugged region of the Doubs. Ernest's grandfather, Stanislas Mercier, was born in a small town outside Montbéliard in the early 1800's.[1] He was a sturdy, robust, rather uncomplicated man, who had a thirst for independence. He rejected Catholicism for Protestantism (which subsequently became the religion of all the Merciers), and under the Second Empire openly paraded his republicanism. As a military health officer he resigned rather than shave off his beard to comply with an army regulation. In 1854, soon after leaving the army, he took his family to settle in Algeria. He tried homesteading, and then moved to the town of Aumale, southeast of Algiers, where he opened a small pharmacy.

Ernest's father, Ernest, Sr. (1840–1907), began his career by mastering Arabic and becoming an official interpreter. At the age of thirty-one he moved to Constantine, and soon, despite a rudimentary formal education, he became engrossed in historical research, specifically about Algeria and the role of France in civilizing North Africa. He eventually became one of the most eminent historians of North Africa, the author of numerous works considered classics in the field. He also entered politics. He became head of the local Radical party and was elected mayor of Constantine. He served as mayor for nearly twenty years, during which time he initiated a number of public works programs to transform Constantine into a modern city. His achievements as scholar and civic leader won him fame as one of the "Fathers of Algeria."

[1] Most of the background material on the Mercier family is from a volume commemorating the centennial of Ernest Mercier, Sr., *L'Afrique à travers ses fils: Ernest Mercier* (Paris, 1944). More intimate details are contained in a special summary prepared by Ernest Mercier for his children in 1940. This document is part of the Mercier papers which are in the possession of Mme Ernest Mercier in Paris.

On his maternal side, Ernest Mercier had a background of cultural sophistication. The Lecomtes, too, were Protestants from Montbéliard, but they were urbane, academic people. Ernest's grandmother, whom he worshiped, was a highly educated woman with an exotic past. As a girl, she went to Russia to act as governess for a prominent family. She was married to a doctor named von Styx, who died within a few months of their marriage while combatting an epidemic of typhus in Astrakhan. The young widow took up residence in the household of her father-in-law, who was rector of the University of Dorpat, and it was there that her daughter, Marie, was born in 1849. When Marie was seven she and her mother moved to Montbéliard. Marie became fluent in English and German, and she studied music in Paris; for a time she thought of a career in singing. In 1873 she married Ernest Mercier, Sr., whom she met on one of his visits to his parents' former home, and they moved to Algeria. They had five children, of whom the third was Ernest Frédéric Honorat Mercier, born February 4, 1878, in Constantine.[2] Ernest's mother filled the household with music and culture, while grandmother de Styx (the change from von was made in France) enchanted him with stories about the strange customs of Russia. The boy tried to emulate his mother's interests, but when he found that he lacked musical talent he turned to drawing and literature, especially the classics. In later years he always kept an edition of Homer on his desk and took great pride in his ability to read the original Greek text.

From his father, who was absorbed by scholarly research and political struggles, Ernest at an early age learned something of the hatreds and polemics of partisan politics. Since neither of his parents was a practicing Protestant, he also grew up with no strong commitment toward religion. His three brothers imitated their father and learned Arabic. Gustave, the eldest, was a military interpreter before entering municipal government; Louis became an assistant to Marshal Lyautey in Morocco; and Maurice eventually followed Ernest into the business world. His only sister married and later helped Ernest through difficult years raising his family for him.

Like many another small boy, Ernest made model boats and spent

[2] The principal source of information for the youth of Ernest Mercier is his private papers. These include a short autobiography, entitled "Notes," written in 1941, which deals only with the more controversial side of his career, and also a brief biography written by his brother Maurice, called "Mon Frère Ernest Mercier." Parts of "Mon Frère" as well as a great deal of other material are available in a memorial volume prepared by Mme Ernest Mercier, *Ernest Mercier: une grande destinée* (Paris, 1958). This work is the major published source for Mercier's career; it contains essays by his friends and colleagues, excerpts from his writings, a few documents, and many testimonial letters.

holidays on the shore of the Mediterranean; and as he grew a little older, he began to dream of a career in the navy. When his teacher in Constantine told him that such a career required education at one of the *grandes écoles* such as the Polytechnique, Ernest concentrated on mastering mathematics and trying for a scholarship, for his father's finances would scarcely have allowed him an education in Paris. He won a scholarship, to the *lycée* Louis-le-Grand, and did so well there that he was awarded not only the physics prize in the *concours général* but also the unusual opportunity of entering either the École Normale Supérieure or the École Polytechnique. Ernest at nineteen was still bent on a career in the navy, so the choice was a foregone conclusion. He was an excellent student at the Polytechnique, where he majored in naval engineering, and was graduated thirteenth in his class in 1899. But almost as important as his studies were the lifelong friends he made at this venerable school of engineering, which, like Saint-Cyr and the other *grandes écoles,* was pervaded with a strong air of self-conscious elitism.[3] In later life Mercier surrounded himself with comrades from "X," as they called the Polytechnique.

As an honor graduate, Ernest could easily have gone into industry, but he remained true to his dreams and entered the navy. His first post, Toulon, was something of a revelation. He had not known that his country was so backward technically. The electrical facilities of the arsenal, in particular, seemed grossly inadequate. He convinced his superiors that renovation was necessary, and they sent him back to Paris for advanced study at the École Supérieure d'Électricité.

During his stay in Paris from 1905 to 1908, Ernest met and married Madeleine Tassin, the daughter of Senator Pierre Tassin,[4] an anticlerical republican, and through this connection was introduced into the political salons of the Third Republic. For a short time he worked in the Ministry of the Navy supervising the modernization of radio-telegraph equipment. Then, filled with enthusiasm for the future of electricity, he returned to Toulon, in 1908, to begin his first major task—the construction of a new power plant and the electrification of the arsenal and the port. His modern design was a brilliant success.

This accomplishment plus Mercier's fine record at the Polytechnique attracted the attention of Albert Petsche, also a Polytechnician and, as top manager of a public utility syndicate, one of the most powerful men in the newly emerging electrical industry.[5] Petsche needed a

[3] For a survey of the school's colorful history, see Jean-Pierre Callot, *Histoire de l'École Polytechnique, ses légendes, ses traditions, sa gloire* (Paris, 1958).

[4] Madeleine Tassin was born in 1881 and died in 1924 after a long illness.

[5] For Petsche's career, see the memorial biography written by Ernest Mercier, *Albert Petsche, 1860–1933* (Paris, 1933). A critical, though not always accurate,

specialist to direct the construction of a new power plant in suburban Paris, and it was natural for him, like many other French businessmen, to look for candidates among the list of high graduates of the Polytechnique. It is, indeed, still the practice in French industry, especially in electricity, for Polytechnicians to monopolize the highest managerial posts.[6] Petsche's offer to enter private industry, where opportunity and reward were greater than in the navy, was of course an attractive one to Mercier, who had a growing family to provide for,[7] and in 1912 he left the navy to try his hand with Petsche. The association developed into a personal friendship which would in time help Mercier to the top of the business world.

The public utility syndicate of which Petsche was director very shortly came to be known as the Messine group, from the address on the rue de Messine which was the location of the general offices of the Société Lyonnaise des Eaux et de l'Éclairage and its numerous associated companies. This firm had built a strong position in public utilities throughout central France and also acted as a holding company for the Messine group. Petsche made Mercier chief engineer for the group's main electric power company in suburban Paris. After a number of rapid promotions in 1913–1914, Mercier was given the job of representing the Messine group in a new company organized for the purpose of electrifying the government railways. The head of the enterprise was Louis Loucheur, a fellow Polytechnician (and, like Petsche, a Protestant). Thus began the second key friendship in Mercier's rise.

When war broke out, Mercier, now thirty-six, was immediately called back into the navy. The next three years proved to be a catalyst to his career. He emerged as a hero, and he also acquired valuable experience within his technical field, and gained many lasting and important friendships. For the first three years of the war he performed so many dangerous missions for the navy that he compared his adventures to those of Ulysses. His war letters provide rich evidence for this period.

He was first sent to the coast of Montenegro to erect a fortified ra-

---

study of the Petsche family is by Roger Mennevée: "M. Maurice Petsche, ministre des finances, biographie familiale," *Les Documents politiques, diplomatiques et financiers,* January, 1950, pp. 3–22. (Hereafter this periodical will be cited as *Les Documents politiques.*)

[6] See Nicole Delefortrie-Soubeyroux, *Les Dirigeants de l'industrie française,* Collection "Recherches sur l'économie française," No. 6 (Paris, 1961), pp. 58, 107, 166–169; Jacques Billy, "Les X dans les affaires," *Entreprise,* Nov. 24, 1962, pp. 47–61.

[7] At the time Mercier had three children: Robert, Christiane, and Pierre. A fourth child, Francette, was born in 1914.

dio-telegraph installation which would serve as an observation station on the Adriatic and establish communications with Serbia and Russia. He completed the assignment, though under bombardment, and received the medal of the Legion of Honor for his effort. His next assignment, early in 1915, was to cross the Balkans to Sebastopol and collect technical data on the Russian fleet. The journey was hazardous, but successful. By the time he returned to France the Allies had begun their ambitious campaign in the Mediterranean, and Mercier was sent to the Dardanelles, thence to Salonica, to install shore batteries and organize port facilities. He even doubled on occasion as a sea diver to clear sunken ships. Mercier always preferred front-line duty, and it was in these experiences that he became inspired with the "spirit of the Front," which was to play so important a part in the mystique of the Redressement Français. He was wounded at Gallipoli, and received a second decoration.

With the entry of Rumania into the war on the side of the Allies in 1916, Mercier was sent to the Balkans as a technical adviser to the staff of the Rumanian army, with the rank of colonel. Rumanian preparations for the defense of the Danube were haphazard, at best, and Mercier in alarm took the bold step of contacting King Ferdinand and persuading him to bolster the defenses by placing a Russian in command. On the eve of the battle, the Russians abruptly withdrew. The King personally rebuked Mercier: "I was wrong to let myself be convinced; you must be punished. I am giving you command of the defense of the Danube." [8] Mercier, untrained in tactics, and with pitiful equipment and a handful of apathetic Rumanian militia, faced a powerful German-Bulgarian army. The results were foreseeable: when the enemy crossed the river at dawn, the Rumanian troops began climbing out of the trenches and departing like flies.[9] Mercier tried to rally the remnants of his men for a counterattack, but in so doing he was injured in the foot by an exploding shell. He was helped to a horse and fought on till dusk, and was then evacuated to Jassy where the Rumanian government had taken refuge.

The wound proved to be a bad one, which kept him on crutches for nearly two years and away from the Front for the remainder of the war. For a few months he stayed on at Jassy, as an unofficial agent for the French government. He had continued to maintain close contact

[8] From "Vita" (Mercier papers), an outline of Mercier's career which he prepared around 1950.
[9] See Mercier's letter to Madeleine Tassin Mercier, Nov. 28, 1916, in *Ernest Mercier*, p. 126.

with both Petsche and Loucheur, who now held high positions in the Ministry of Armaments,[10] and from Jassy he was able to report to them on the condition of the Rumanian munitions industry.[11]

The dashing young French officer, whom everyone recognized as a confidant of the king, soon made many friends in the ruling circles of the Rumanian government. He had striking blue eyes and an enormous blond moustache which he could wind about his ears, and he seemed a happy combination of charm and unusual intelligence. King Ferdinand himself came to see him in the hospital and presented him with Rumania's highest military decoration. He met the Francophile Brătianu brothers, the elder of whom was also a Polytechnician, and General Averescu; these men were to rule Rumania in the 1920's.

In February, 1917, Mercier was evacuated across Russia and thence to France. He was promptly given a post in the armaments ministry and a promotion to the rank of colonel in the French army. When Loucheur was appointed Minister of Armaments, Mercier became his chief technical adviser, and from then on he acted as the ministry's representative to both the military and industry, handling problems of armaments manufacture. He became Loucheur's personal liaison with Generals Foch and Pétain. This marked the beginning of Mercier's friendship with France's highest military leaders. Another of his tasks was to help provision the fresh American troops.[12] His liaison services at the ministry so marked him in the eyes of the Allied staffs that ever after his Anglo-American friends referred to him as "Colonel Mercier."

Mercier's efforts to supply the Front made him acutely aware of the backwardness of the French industrial plant. In the last winter of the war, especially, there was a severe lack of gasoline and oil for the army, and he was also handicapped at every turn by the feeble capacity and general disorder of the electric power industry. There was so little power that some munitions plants were forced to operate only at night, when the drain was less heavy. Under Loucheur's ministry, Mercier un-

[10] Émmanuel Beau de Loménie, *Les Responsabilités des dynasties bourgeoises* (Paris, 1947–1963), III, 65–66, argues that Loucheur rose to power as a crafty munitions profiteer. But this interpretation is based on the unfriendly account of the banker Octave Homberg, *Les Coulisses de l'histoire: souvenirs, 1898–1928* (Paris, 1938), pp. 149–150, who even questions Loucheur's integrity. This view seems unfair in the light of Loucheur's later career. For a partisan study see *Louis Loucheur, Carnets secrets, 1908–1932*, ed. Jacques de Launay (Brussels, 1962).

[11] See Mercier to Petsche, Dec. 21, 1916, Papers of Louis Loucheur, Bundle XI, Hoover Institution on War, Revolution, and Peace (hereafter cited as Loucheur papers). Much of Mercier's wartime correspondence with Petsche was relayed to Loucheur and thus can be found in the latter's papers.

[12] One American officer wrote: "I know of no one who did more to assist the AEF in its armament and supply program than he." See Nelson Dean Jay to Philip Cortney, Mar. 9, 1959, Mercier papers.

dertook the reorganization of the electric power industry in the Paris region, beginning with the decision, in 1918, and largely at his urging, to standardize the frequency of electrical current.[13]

The end of the war did not immediately terminate Mercier's government service. Loucheur had moved from the Ministry of Armaments to the Ministry of Liberated Zones and was thus empowered with the administration of sanctions against Germany after the breakdown in reparations negotiations. When the French moved into the Rhineland in the spring of 1921, Loucheur gave Mercier the task of organizing the operation of German factories under the Military Control Commission.[14]

The war was thus a boon to Mercier, who became a military hero and expanded his friendships in government, business, and the military on both sides of the Atlantic. Yet he also emerged from the victory keenly dissatisfied with his nation's industrial performance. In the midst of the war while far from home he had frequently pondered the economic reconstruction of France—a goal that was to become his overruling passion.

[13] Roger Boutteville, "L'Oeuvre d'Ernest Mercier dans l'industrie électrique," in *Ernest Mercier*, p. 61.
[14] Loucheur to Mercier, May 21, 1921, Mercier papers.

2

The Messine Group:

THE MODERNIZATION OF THE ELECTRIC POWER INDUSTRY

AFTER THE SIGNING OF THE ARMISTICE, Mercier returned to his position with the Messine group, more aware than ever of the need for revamping the electric power industry in the Paris region. Only in the city itself had there so far been any attempt at modernization, through the newly created Compagnie Parisienne de Distribution d'Électricité (CPDE). In the suburbs a welter of local and fiercely competitive power companies, using obsolete equipment, made electricity expensive and undependable. Current was produced at diverse frequencies and tensions, making interconnection impossible; there was duplication of power lines, lack of reciprocal interconnection, and frequent rate wars.[1] To add to the confusion, some of the distributors did not produce their own power but bought it from special producers or from other distributors. Mercier believed that he could bring order into this chaos, and at the same time expand the influence of the Messine group in France and her overseas possessions.

The plan was simple but bold, and it required enormous capital. If the suburban power industry could be persuaded to buy its current from one common source, the whole suburban area could be supplied with power by a few huge supercenters utilizing a single high-tension system. Admittedly, the plan demanded skillful negotiation. The funds, though enormous, were available, largely because Lyonnaise des Eaux, the kingpin of the Messine group, had liquidated some valuable holdings in Spain and was prepared to expand its activities.[2] The technical and managerial genius necessary to realize this scheme was provided by Mercier.[3]

The negotiations went rapidly, and in 1919 six suburban producers merged to form a new company, the Union d'Électricité, under the

---

[1] See Charles Malégarie, *L'Électricité à Paris* (Paris, 1947), p. 286; also Gaston Girousse, "Ernest Mercier au Triphasé," Mercier papers.

[2] *Groupe Cortambert, Bulletin de liaison*, No. 1 (June, 1959), p. 3.

[3] For an excellent analysis of Mercier's achievements see Roger Boutteville, "L'Oeuvre d'Ernest Mercier dans l'industrie électrique," in *Ernest Mercier: une grande destinée*, pp. 59–81.

control of the Messine group. Petsche became president, and Mercier managing director. The company at once proceeded to buy up plants of those distributors who produced their own power. Some of these it closed. The next step was the building of a new supercenter at Gennevilliers, north of Paris. The Gennevilliers station, constructed at Mercier's insistence according to the latest techniques, was placed in operation in 1922. It was the most powerful single thermal center in the world (400,000 kw. capacity), and its technical innovations earned Mercier an international reputation.[4] A subterranean high-tension system (60,000 volts) far in advance even of those used in London and New York, soon connected Gennevilliers with all the suburbs, beginning the vast interconnection system of the Paris region. The scheme was almost too daring for its day, and the first years of operation were marred by numerous power failures owing to defective equipment. At one point when the entire system seemed on the verge of breakdown, Mercier worked day and night for weeks until new cables were devised which solved the problem. The Union d'Électricité survived its initial setbacks, and by 1924 even the most skeptical had to acknowledge that the revolutionary plan was a success. By then the Messine group had gained control over the distribution of electricity in the greater Paris area.

Mercier's triumph with the Union d'Électricité made him definitely the number two man in the syndicate, which could now set about expanding its influence throughout the French public utility industry. Lyonnaise des Eaux already controlled a number of small public utility concessions in central France, and in the '20's it attempted to create a gas and water monopoly in the Paris region by absorbing companies and acquiring concessions. It had such success that it was denounced as "the precursor of a general utility trust." [5] Together Petsche and Mercier also developed new public utility concessions throughout North Africa, especially in Morocco. But most significantly Mercier prepared a master plan to introduce hydroelectric power to the Paris region.[6] In association with the state Paris–Orleans railway the Union d'Électricité formed a new hydroelectric subsidiary which constructed a station on the river Creuse. By 1926 the Paris area and the railroad were receiving hydroelectric energy for the first time over an aerial high-tension system from the Massif Central.

[4] See Ernest Mercier, The "Union d'Électricité" and the Gennevilliers Station, trans. C. M. Popp (Paris, 1922) ; Electrical World, Nov. 28, 1925, p. 1104.

[5] Bertrand de Jouvenel and René Rotter, La Flèche, Feb. 1, 1936. For the activities of Lyonnaise des Eaux see also Mercier, Albert Petsche, pp. 21–32, 43–45.

[6] Mercier, "Participations hydroélectriques de UDE," Jan. 23, 1946, Mercier papers.

The drive for modernization and centralization led by the Messine group was culminated in 1930 when the Union d'Électricité reached an agreement with its only remaining competitors in the Paris region, the CPDE and the Société d'Électricité de Paris (SEP). In the '20's, these three companies were the sole producers of electric power in the area: the CPDE supplied the city of Paris, the Union d'Électricité supplied the suburbs, and the SEP, a member of a Belgian syndicate and archrival of the Messine group, furnished power for the Métro and the trams. By the late '20's, the advantages of a merger were too great to ignore. The three groups agreed that the Union d'Électricité and the SEP would assume control of the CPDE's plants, limiting the latter to distribution. They agreed to cooperate in developing new supercenters, a high-tension system, and a dispatching center to allocate power more efficiently. This system interconnected the transmission lines of the Paris region and also linked them with the most important sources of power in France. As a security measure, the modern dispatching station which became the nerve center for the electric power grid in Paris was constructed beneath the rue de Messine.

By the early '30's the Messine group was the nation's pre-eminent electric power enterprise.[7] It was producing two-thirds of the energy for the mighty Paris complex, and it monopolized production and distribution in at least ten departments of central France. It had also gained ascendancy over the development of hydroelectric power in the Massif Central and held similar ambitions for the resources of the Pyrenees. Furthermore, the group was in the process of expanding its interests west and south, toward the Loire and the Midi. So powerful, indeed, was the group that the Left called Petsche the "emperor of electricity" and Mercier "the king." [8] One authoritative study designated the group as the most likely candidate for the unification of the entire French electric power industry.[9]

In the '20's, throughout France, however, there was a general tendency toward centralization and modernization which the Messine group only typified. Everywhere small producers and distributors gave way to large syndicates, local companies were replaced by regional firms, and hydroelectric power made its debut. Superpower plants and high-tension systems were built to meet increased demand and the wide fluctuations in consumption. Even farmers began to receive the

[7] See Albert Renaud, *Les Entreprises électriques et les collectivités* (Bordeaux, 1935), pp. 185, 213–216; Charles Dantin, *Le Réseau de distribution de l'Union d'Électricité et la centrale de Gennevilliers près de Paris* (Paris, 1931), pp. 3–8; *The Electrician*, Dec. 21, 1945, p. 690.

[8] *Commentaires*, Nov. 1, 1931.

[9] Renaud, pp. 223–234.

benefits of electricity. It is significant that the French power industry grew more rapidly during the decade of the '20's than did its European counterparts. In 1920 France, in terms of total energy produced, was far behind both Great Britain and Germany and roughly on a par with Italy. By 1930 France had outstripped Italy, was abreast of Britain, and had closed the gap with Germany.[10] The expansion came to a halt only with the onset of the depression.

In all these years of growth, the achievements of the Messine group were very largely Mercier's. Petsche continued as president until his death in 1933, but Mercier was in sole charge of the electric power holdings of the syndicate. He was a superb technician, especially in thermal power, and an effective business manager. He also knew how to find dynamic young engineers—men like Arrighi de Casanova, who designed the modern supercenter at Vitry-Sud—and he had a gift for instilling an esprit de corps among all his personnel, from engineers to workers. Sometimes he would don blue coveralls and go out to examine equipment, and he took an interest in the smallest details.

Mercier always looked on his work of bringing better service and cheaper power to consumers as a public service. He regarded the Messine group as a triumph of team spirit, which ultimately brought economic strength to France. The Union d'Électricité was, he wrote in 1922, "a living example" of a new spirit of "organization and cooperation" that had made headway among the individualistic French since the war.[11] Some have questioned Mercier's altruism, but there is no doubt of his energy and imagination, particularly during the first postwar decade. A colleague compared his work in scope and vision to that of Baron Haussmann, who had remodeled Paris some fifty years earlier: "Ernest Mercier conceived and put into operation the grid system of Paris—the dispenser of energy—which is indispensable for the city's development, its prosperity, and its very life in the twentieth century. In his domain, he introduced order, opened such broad perspectives, and established such solid foundations that a quarter of a century later no changes have to be made in his plans. One needs only to follow the path that he has traced." [12]

At its height during the early '30's the core of the Messine group

---

[10] Data for these comparisons is from three different sets of statistics: Organization for European Economic Cooperation, *Industrial Statistics, 1900–1959* (Paris, 1960), p. 84; Institut National de la Statistique et des Études Économiques (INSEE), *Annuaire statistique de la France, rétrospectif* (Paris, 1961), pp. 68*–69*; INSEE, *Études et conjoncture,* numéro spécial: *L'Industrie française* (1953), p. 142.

[11] Quoted in *Bulletin de la Société Française des Électriciens,* No. 62 (February, 1956).

[12] Boutteville, in *Ernest Mercier,* p. 69.

consisted of two corporations: Lyonnaise des Eaux and the Union d'Électricité.[13] Mercier candidly admitted that the Lyonnaise des Eaux "controls the Messine group in practice." [14] A special holding company, the Union Financière pour l'Industrie Électrique (UFIE), concentrated capital for the syndicate. Numerous companies were clustered about this nucleus. First there were direct subsidiaries in which, according to Mercier, the Messine group held "the preponderant interest" and "completely controlled the management." [15] These corporations were tied to the syndicate through interlocking directorates, the exchange of capital stock and technical and financial advice, and common financial interests.[16] Most of these fifteen or more subsidiaries were electrical utility companies located mainly in the Paris region, in central France, and in North Africa.[17] Further removed were some ten companies in which the syndicate "possessed important interests" and "shared . . . in the management." Included in this category were some of France's most important power companies, such as the CPDE.[18] On the periphery of the group were a host of diverse enterprises loosely affiliated by the presence of top Messine managers on their boards of directors. Mercier himself held directorships in many companies in the fields of electrical equipment manufacturing (such as Alsthom), shipbuilding, and banking.[19] In short, the Messine group was primarily an electric power combine with interests in other public

[13] The evidence for this analysis of the syndicate is a confidential memorandum prepared by Mercier about 1941 entitled "Structure du groupe Messine" (hereafter cited as "Groupe Messine"). For details on the prewar holdings of Lyonnaise des Eaux, see *Groupe Cortambert, Bulletin de liaison,* No. 1 (June, 1959), pp. 7–9.

[14] "Vita," Mercier papers.

[15] "Groupe Messine," Mercier papers.

[16] This was the typical pattern for combines in the European electrical industry, according to the British Electrical and Allied Manufacturers' Association (BEAMA), *Combines and Trusts in the Electrical Industry* (London, 1927), p. 55.

[17] Mercier lists the following companies as Messine subsidiaries: Nord-Lumière; Ouest-Lumière; Sud-Lumière; Électricité du Nord-Est Parisien; Union Électrique du Centre; Union pour l'Industrie et l'Électricité (and its affiliates); Bonne et Drac; Cie. d'Électricité Industrielle (and its affiliates); Sté. d'Électricité du Littoral Normand; Énergie Électrique du Rouergue; Sté. Marocaine de Distribution d'Eau, de Gaz et d'Électricité (and its affiliates); European Gas Company (formerly British, now French); Union Électrique du Sud; Union Hydro-Électrique. See "Groupe Messine," Mercier papers.

[18] Mercier (*ibid.*) mentions the following companies: CPDE (in association with the Sté. d'Électricité de Paris and the Cie. Générale d'Électricité); Est-Lumière (in association with the Cie. Générale d'Électricité); Sté. de Distribution de l'Ouest (in association with the Cie. Générale d'Électricité and the Sté. d'Éclairage et Force); Sté. d'Éclairage et Force (since 1941 only, in association with Saint-Gobain); Sté. Hydro-Électrique de la Cère (in association avec l'Énergie Industrielle); Sté. d'Électricité de Caen; Sté. d'Applications Industrielles; Sté. Régionale de Distribution du Gaz.

[19] See the Appendix for a complete list of Mercier's managerial positions.

utilities and related industries. All the principal subsidiaries had their general offices at 3 rue de Messine and after 1933 Mercier presided over all of them.

This analysis of the structure of the Messine group has not yet touched on the critical question of whether or not it was a "trust." As this derisive term was used in interwar France it meant simply control by finance capital. Mercier detested the epithet "trust" and attempted to show how inapplicable it was to the Messine group: "The Messine group is a collection of companies joined by technical ties; in this case all the electrical distributors in the Paris region are linked in order to organize their means of producing and distributing energy. . . . The managers of the group, and in particular the president, are chosen for their technical and moral qualities, and not for their financial power which is nonexistent in view of the fixed assets of the group." [20] This explanation is sound up to a point, but it leaves several questions. Who determined company policy: Mercier or his board of directors, the manager-technician or the representatives of the banks and other stock holders? Is it possible that Mercier himself owed his position to certain anonymous financiers? The answers to these questions lie in the tangled morass of corporate finance and in the role of the president in French corporations.

The Left (and certain segments of the extreme Right) claimed that corporation managers were the pawns of the "two hundred families" who controlled the world of French finance. During the '30's, detailed studies traced the labyrinth of kinship which bound these wealthy two hundred together, and designated managers like Mercier as agents or "trustees" of particular families which secretly controlled the corporations. There were, indeed, as these critics charged, some corporation managers who were the financial agents of powerful banking families, such as René Mayer of the Rothschilds and Marcel Champin of the Mirabaud family. This was not the case with Mercier, however.

One rumor, widely circulated in the '30's and still current today, views Mercier as a pawn of the Rothschilds; this canard almost cost Mercier his life during the German occupation, and it requires explicit refutation. The source of the rumor seems to have been the Socialist Augustin Hamon, who in his book *Les Maîtres de la France* revealed incriminating "facts" about Mercier.[21] Hamon showed that the Roths-

[20] "Groupe Messine," Mercier papers.

[21] Augustin Hamon, *Les Maîtres de la France* (Paris, 1936–1938), I, 284–286. See also Henry Coston, *Les Financiers qui mènent le monde* (Paris, 1955), pp. 117–120; Beau de Loménie, *Les Responsabilités des dynasties bourgeoises*, IV, 40; Claude Willard, *Quelques Aspects du fascisme en France avant le 6 février 1934* (Paris, 1961), pp. 215–216.

childs had petroleum interests in Royal Dutch Shell, a firm that helped organize the Compagnie Française des Pétroles. Since Mercier presided over the latter oil company, Hamon thought that he must be a Rothschild agent. The Rothschilds never controlled Royal Dutch Shell, however, and they had no special influence in the Compagnie Française des Pétroles, which was backed by a potpourri of interests. In an effort to buttress his argument, Hamon also contended that the rise of Petsche, and thus Mercier, could only be accounted for by Rothschild aid. He pointed out that Petsche was a manager of the Nord railways, the famous "Rothschild fief." Although admitting it was an "obscure point," Hamon argued that Mercier, Petsche's successor in the Messine group, must accordingly owe his position to the Maison Rothschild. The final proof, he suggested, was that "two Rothschild agents," Paul Eschwege and René Mayer, were Mercier's colleagues, and that Mercier's second wife was the wealthy Jewess, Mme Adolphe Reinach, the niece of Captain Alfred Dreyfus.

Mercier was quite explicit in denying that the Rothschilds had any special influence in the Messine group.[22] The only Rothschild interest stemmed from sharing the ownership of Nord-Lumière, a suburban electrical distributor, with the Messine-held Lyonnaise des Eaux. Through Nord-Lumière, the Rothschild bank held two of eighteen seats on the board of the Union d'Électricité. Petsche accepted an offer from Baron Édouard de Rothschild to sit on the board of his Nord railroad, but in 1933 when Mercier succeeded to the presidency he refused to assume Petsche's position on the board, and during the '30's he significantly reduced Rothschild interests in Nord-Lumière. As for Mercier's friendships with Rothschild representatives like Eschwege and Mayer and his second marriage, which occurred in 1927 after he was Petsche's acknowledged successor—these can scarcely be taken as proof that he was a pawn of the Maison Rothschild. It is worth pointing out, also, that Mercier was a member of the famous "H.S.P." (haute société protestante), and associated primarily with Protestant rather than Jewish business society. One must, I think, accept Mercier's statement that "neither the Rothschild bank nor any member of the Rothschild family played a role in my entry into business or in the development of my career."[23]

There have been various other guesses as to which financial group had the controlling interest in the Messine syndicate.[24] In fact, the

[22] See "Groupe Messine," and "Notes," Mercier papers.

[23] "Notes," Mercier papers.

[24] BEAMA (Combines and Trusts, pp. 62–65) thought it was Thomson-Houston. Mennevée favored the Banque de Paris et des Pays-Bas or the Morgan bank (Les Documents politiques, June, 1927, pp. 243–244, and September, 1937, pp. 401–419) .

principal financiers of the syndicate were the investment and deposit banks which supplied credit, represented stockholders, or owned shares directly. Legal ownership thus rested in the hands of the public and was relatively free of family control. The most important bank was the Crédit Lyonnais, which had founded the Lyonnaise des Eaux.[25] In the words of a president of the latter company, Crédit Lyonnais was "the foundation" of the syndicate.[26] As a deposit bank (banque de dépot) it provided credit, issued new stocks and bonds, and voted the proxies of its depositors through its representatives on the boards of directors. Investment banks (banques d'affaires) duplicated these sources of control and also directly owned stock, augmenting their power. The Banque de Paris et des Pays-Bas and the Union Parisienne belonged to this category and held large blocks of stock in the Union d'Électricité.[27] There were also many private banks (la haute banque), particularly those representing Protestant and Jewish families, which supported the syndicate.[28]

Besides the banks, certain electrical manufacturing concerns were important financial backers of the Messine group. The Société Alsacienne de Constructions Mécaniques, and its partner Thomson-Houston, a large holding company associated with General Electric, helped finance the establishment and expansion of power companies in order to create markets for their products.[29] There were, lastly, special power finance corporations designed to support the development of electric power. Thus the UFIE, for example, functioned like a private bank for the syndicate.

All these banks, electrical manufacturers, and power finance companies theoretically participated in managing the Messine group by placing representatives on the corporations' boards of directors. For example, Baron Brincard, president of Crédit Lyonnais, sat on the board of

[25] Crédit Lyonnais was still one of its two strongest stockholders in 1946, the other being the UFIE (Les Documents politiques, July, 1946, p. B.F.ª). Other deposit banks which financed the syndicate were the Crédit Commercial and the Comptoir National d'Escompte.

[26] Interview with Joseph Thuillier, July 10, 1964.

[27] For the electrical interests of these banques d'affaires see BEAMA, The Electrical Industry in France, Industrial and Economic Progress (London, 1925), p. 15; and Edmond Baldy, Les Banques d'affaires en France depuis 1900 (Paris, 1922), pp. 151–153, 160–161, 298, 304.

[28] Banque Mirabaud, Lazard frères, Banque Odier Bungener, Rothschild frères, Banque Renauld, and the Morgan bank.

[29] In 1889 Auguste Lalance (Mes Souvenirs, 1830–1914 [Paris, 1914], pp. 57–58), representing the Sté. Alsacienne de Constructions Mécaniques, created Le Triphasé, the electricity distributor that became the keystone of the Messine group's interests in suburban Paris. Although the Sté. Alsacienne and Thomson-Houston promoted the development of the power industry, they did not control it as their British manufacturing rivals believed (BEAMA, Combines and Trusts, pp. 62–65).

Lyonnaise des Eaux. Often representatives of the Messine group's financiers held half of the positions on a given board. Their presence on the boards did not mean, however, that they determined policy for the syndicate. In French corporations, the president generally has immense authority and exercises almost absolute control over the company's managerial hierarchy. "The French managerial tradition in industry," one student of European business executives has recently observed, "is based on the Napoleonic model . . . in which all top management is concentrated in . . . the *président-directeur général*." [30] As president, Mercier ruled his corporations like an autocrat. He and his assistant, the *administrateur délégué*, were the only links between the corporations' managerial staffs and their boards. Mercier also doubled as board chairman and even helped direct some of those banks represented on the boards—including the mighty Banque de Paris et des Pays-Bas.[31] In the interwar years, as one prominent French business leader remarked, only the president and the *administrateur délégué* counted in corporation management.[32]

In practice the boards of directors were quite willing to allow Mercier's rule. Many board members did not even represent stockholders, but merely lent their reputations to the company's masthead and regarded their positions as purely honorary. Mercier himself held so many of these honorary directorships that he frequently had no time to attend board meetings. Moreover, board members were seldom company officers. They gathered a few times annually, usually confining their discussions to financial matters, and every twenty years or so selected a new president. One trenchant account of a board meeting gives a vivid picture:

> No board member, however informed about the management of the enterprise, would permit himself to express anything other than a timid opinion at the board meeting. He knows that the direction of a business is complex and delicate, and that one must refrain from having a spontaneous opinon about the subject; any experienced board member prefers to talk about politics, hunting, or travel in the meet-

[30] David Granick, *The European Executive* (Garden City, N.Y., 1962), p. 259. Granick (pp. 82–83) suggests that presidents were more subservient to their boards before 1940 than they have been since then, but this does not detract from the tradition.

[31] Although Mercier disliked his banking duties, in his prime he assisted in the direction of the Banque de Paris et des Pays-Bas, the Crédit Commercial, and the Crédit National. Only after the First World War did it become common for industrial managers like Mercier to sit on the boards of *banques d'affaires*. This exchange of managers was a result of growing ties between these banks and big business; see Baldy, p. 321.

[32] Interview with Alfred Lambert-Ribot, July 2, 1964.

ing—anything except the matter at hand which he is supposed to be managing.

The chairman of the board and the secretary read their reports, to which no one listens, perfunctorily and rapidly. Everyone nods his head and approves. When everything is going well, they congratulate the *administrateur délégué,* and when everything is going badly they offer condolences, but they would have great difficulty in giving him any advice whatsoever.[33]

The board of directors was thus not the locus of managerial power, except when financial problems pressed. Above all, the banks in the Messine group seldom interfered with the president's direction. Mercier insisted that Baron Brincard, who was the most powerful banker on the board of Lyonnaise des Eaux, never hedge on his promise to leave company policy to the president.[34]

In sum, as president, Mercier wielded nearly absolute control over his subordinate company executives and encountered little interference in the confines of the boardroom. Indeed, the extent of his autocracy, taken together with the nonconformism that he showed in public affairs, is fairly strong proof against charges that he was manipulated by his financial backers. His independence of spirit was far too strong for him to have tolerated much manipulation.

This independent spirit has earned Mercier a significant place in French entrepreneurial history, for he represents the rise of a dynamic, technocratic mentality among the business elite in the twentieth century. More and more, students of economic history have emphasized the role of the entrepreneur as a determinant of economic growth. Thus the remarkable burst of energy in France since 1952 has been largely attributed to the emergence of "new-model entrepreneurship"—managers and bureaucrats who are ardent proponents of productivity and efficiency.[35]

In retrospect, the relative stagnation of the interwar years, especially the '30's, was in part due to the dominant ultraconservative, "Malthu-

---

[33] Eugène Schueller, *La Révolution de l'économie* (Paris, 1941) , pp. 80–81. On the passivity and incompetence of most boards see R. Morin, "Conseils d'administration," *Revue de France,* Mar. 15, 1929, pp. 379–380.

[34] Untitled document written upon the death of Brincard, Mercier papers.

[35] See David S. Landes, "New-Model Entrepreneurship in France and Problems of Historical Explanation," *Explorations in Entrepreneurial History,* XV (Fall, 1963) , 56–75. Landes does not use this as a monolithic interpretation, but stresses that other structural changes have encouraged the spread of the new entrepreneurial behavior. See also Charles Kindleberger, "The Postwar Resurgence of the French Economy," in Stanley Hoffmann *et al., In Search of France* (Cambridge, Mass., 1963) , pp. 118–158.

sian" pattern of entrepreneurial behavior.[36] The rank and file of French businessmen preferred high profits, a secure market, and limited competition, to expansion and risk-taking. To them, the economic and social situation was static, the problems chronic—all to be endured, or at best, to be manipulated to their advantage. One bitter critic wrote:

> The French businessman . . . has only one preoccupation: to come to an understanding with his colleagues in order to put an end to all competition in the home market . . . then to obtain from the government a protective tariff so that he may be free of all foreign competition. After this, having abolished risk, he ceases from effort. Every opportunity of extending his business which has the least element of adventure seems to him an unnecessary risk; every effort towards technical improvement seems to threaten his security. His maxim is to produce little in order to sell dear.[37]

Since such Malthusians set the pace for French economic life, they were an important cause of the nation's slow economic growth.

There were some exceptions, however. Certainly one must not underestimate the emergence of a few atypical, enterprising business leaders like Ernest Mercier. These managers, who made a cult out of industrial productivity, were the predecessors of the "new-model entrepreneurs" of the '50's. In the '20's these men were popularly known as "neo-Saint-Simonians." [38] Mercier epitomized the neo-Saint-Simonian, not because he was a conscious disciple of the early-nineteenth-century prophet of industrialism, but because he shared the same overriding passion. He was restless, impulsive, always excited by the sense of creating, producing, and building. Once when he went against the advice of others and invested privately in a mining venture in his native Algeria, this passion for creating and building cost him three-quarters of a million dollars. When the venture collapsed, he said to his brother, "Do you see, we were not made to live in the idle security of wealth." [39] Mercier had no respect for the traditional economic pattern or for his Malthusian colleagues. And he believed that economic, social, and even political disorders were no different from

[36] For the Malthusian outlook see John E. Sawyer, "The Entrepreneur and the Social Order, France and the United States," in William Miller (ed.), *Men in Business: Essays in the History of Entrepreneurship,* (Cambridge, Mass., 1952), pp. 14–19.

[37] Francis Delaisi, *Oil: Its Influence on Politics,* trans. C. Leonard Leese (London, 1922), p. 81.

[38] See Albert Thibaudet, *Les Idées politiques de la France* (Paris, 1932), pp. 62–68.

[39] See "Les Bénéfices de 22 années de vie industrielle," Oct. 8, 1940, Mercier papers, and *Ernest Mercier,* p. 26.

the everyday problems of business: they could all be mastered with sufficient expertise and will. He was, in short, the perfect technocrat.

There was a strong minority of these neo-Saint-Simonians who held strategic posts in the economy. In the world of finance, for example, Mercier's closest friend was the dynamic director of the Banque de Paris et des Pays-Bas, Horace Finaly.[40] Louis Pineau, though a civil servant rather than a businessman, was another. André Citroën of the auto industry was still another. Mercier could always count on many supporters among the managerial class, and together these modernizers deserve much of the credit for making the '20's the most expansive period between 1914 and 1952 for the sluggish French economy. Indeed, a recent study by the French economic historian Claude Fohlen [41] attributes much of France's prosperity in the '20's to the emergence of two new industrial sectors, electricity and oil—precisely the sectors in which Mercier and the technocrats were most prominent.

One sees some continuity between the neo-Saint-Simonians and the contemporary new-model entrepreneurs. The relationship between Mercier and Pierre Massé, today one of France's leading technocrats, is an example: Massé, also a Polytechnician, directed the construction of hydroelectric plants in the '30's and for a time was associated with the Messine group. Working with Mercier, he has recalled, was "one of the great joys of my life." [42] After the Second World War Massé first directed the expansion of French electric power resources, then managed the nationalized Électricité de France, and in 1959 he became the director of the government's economic planning commission. Despite the obvious differences between private enterprise and nationalization and planning, Massé and Mercier shared a dedication to modernization, and it was this spirit, rather than the Polytechnique or an old friendship, that bridged the gap of a generation and the shift to nationalization.

In other relationships, with amazing consistency, Mercier's colleagues were all graduates of the École Polytechnique. Whatever other

[40] Mercier first met Finaly, a Jew, at the Ministry of Armaments in 1918 and later worked with him in petroleum affairs. In January, 1935, Finaly extended an invitation to join the board of the Banque de Paris et des Pays-Bas, and Mercier reluctantly accepted. Mercier said he resigned from the bank in June, 1937, "because M. Finaly had just been dismissed from his post as *directeur général* under circumstances with which I did not want to be associated" ("Notes," Mercier papers). According to Roger Mennevée (*Les Documents politiques*, September, 1937, pp. 401–419) Mercier resigned when his left-wing clique, which included Finaly and Edgar Stern, came into conflict with the bank's conservative president, Émile Moreau, and was defeated.

[41] *La France de l'entre-deux-guerres* (Paris, 1966), pp. 72–76.

[42] Interview with Pierre Massé, June 25, 1964.

causes inspired the progressive entrepreneurial spirit of today—and there have been numerous suggestions [43]—the *grandes écoles,* notably the Polytechnique, must be given due credit as the place where a large segment of France's modernizing managerial elite received their training. Mercier was, of course, an unusually outstanding graduate, and his rise to the top of the electrical industry was mainly the result of his own technical and managerial brilliance, but it was a fellow-Polytechnician who launched his career.

As head of the most important public utility syndicate, Mercier held an imposing position in the French economy. A colleague wrote that his authority was "so great within the electrical industry that nothing of importance could be accomplished in that field unless he had planned or given it his approval." [44] Because of his success, Mercier was easily one of the key figures in a vigorous minority among the French business elite. If he was too aggressive and too progressive for most French businessmen of his day, he was in harmony with an important minority of enterprising managers. Mercier embodied, and to a degree created, the important movement in modern France toward technocratic dominance.

[43] David S. Landes ("New-Model Entrepreneurship") explains the French entrepreneurial vitality of the 1950's and 1960's as a response to a number of factors ranging from the psychological effects of the defeat of 1940 to the stimulating influence of the Common Market. Henry W. Ehrmann (*Organized Business in France* [Princeton, N.J., 1957], p. 137) argues that modern entrepreneurial attitudes prevail in the dynamic sector of the economy among "the heads of large and efficient business units, whether managerial or patrimonial." Eugene W. Burgess ("Management in France," in *Management in the Industrial World,* eds. Frederick Harbison and Charles A. Myers [New York, 1959], pp. 218–219) sees "technology and sheer size" as "the two most powerful forces spearheading the need for professional management," and he also notes the progressive management practiced in nationalized industries. A different approach is taken by John E. Sawyer ("The Entrepreneur and the Social Order," p. 19), who mentions that historically it has been those groups outside the dominant social pattern—the Protestants, Freemasons, Jews, and foreigners—who have supplied France with its great entrepreneurs. The view that corporation managers are the principal modernizers was given its classic statement by James Burnham in *The Managerial Revolution* (New York, 1941). The sociologist Michel Crozier uses the case-study technique to provide fresh insight into French management in *The Bureaucratic Phenomenon* (Chicago, 1964).

[44] Boutteville, in *Ernest Mercier,* p. 71.

3

The Compagnie Française des Pétroles

A REVOLUTION IN OIL

THE First World War proved to France that the lack of but one major natural resource could jeopardize the defense of the nation and hinder industrial progress. Without large deposits of oil under its control, France was dependent on foreign suppliers for this vital raw material. During the last winter of the war, the oil shortage was so severe that the French military machine was nearly halted. After the war, when the rapidly expanding petroleum needs of French industry continued to require massive imports, the Third Republic finally launched a "national petroleum policy" aimed at securing for France greater independence from foreign suppliers.

There were two main objectives, toward which both public officials and private businessmen worked hand in hand: first, to acquire oil deposits abroad, and, second, to create a native refining industry. The results of their efforts were so spectacular that they amounted to a revolution in the petroleum industry. The collaboration was marked by frequent and bitter quarrels, but in the end a spirit of cooperation prevailed. Those who led this revolution and who were most adept at conciliating differences in order to move ahead were the "new men"—Ernest Mercier and a small cadre of managers and public officials including Louis Pineau, Louis Loucheur, Robert Cayrol, and Horace Finaly. All these men were pragmatic modernizers, neo-Saint-Simonians, who were relatively free of political dogmatism and eager to build this vital industry for France. They believed that the task could only be achieved through a combination of private initiative and state power. But as Loucheur remarked, such a viewpoint was simultaneously attacked as "étatiste" and "anti-étatiste." [1] Before analyzing Mercier's role in this revolution it is necessary to sketch the character of the French oil industry from before the First World War

[1] Chambre des députés, treizième législature, session de 1928, *Procès-verbaux de la commission d'enquête sur les pétroles* (Paris, 1928), No. 5449, p. 48 (hereafter cited as *Commission d'enquête sur les pétroles*).

to the establishment of an effective "national petroleum policy" in 1928.[2]

In the early 1900's a handful of oil companies enjoyed a *de facto* monopoly of the French market. These firms, known as the Cartel des Dix, suppressed competition by means of a market-sharing agreement and tariff protection. They controlled no important source of crude oil nor did they build a genuine refining industry. When the state tried to tax the profits of their pseudo-refineries, the Cartel closed them down and began buying refined oil products from abroad. By 1914 the members of the Cartel were simply oil importers who engaged in the distribution of finished foreign products.

Even before the war revealed the deficiencies of the oil industry, the Cartel was the object of widespread attack.[3] These privileged importers amassed enormous profits, yet made no effort to give France a native oil industry. The Cartel was almost totally dependent upon the Standard Oil Company of New Jersey, which supplied the bulk of its needs, and the American company fixed prices, set quotas, and eliminated potential competitors. Little effort was made by the Cartel to free itself from this dependence on foreign business by prospecting for oil deposits in French territories,[4] and in the mad scramble for oil in the early 1900's by American, British, and Dutch companies, the French were largely bystanders. Nor did the Cartel provide France with an independent tanker fleet, sufficient reserves, or adequate port and storage facilities.[5] In 1914 the French tanker fleet consisted of fourteen small vessels, most of which flew the British flag. "Eight of these ships were sunk during the war," wrote one critic, "and when the Cartel was asked to build new ones it refused, 'so as not to give offense' to the great trusts." [6] Indeed, it was industrialists like these oil men whom the neo-Saint-Simonians damned for their Malthusianism.[7]

[2] For an excellent critical history of the oil industry in France see Edgar Faure, *La Politique française du pétrole* (Paris, 1938) .

[3] These attacks prompted several legislative proposals to extend state control over this private monopoly and its "scandalous profits." In January, 1914, certain deputies called for the creation of a *régie intéressée* to control the refining and importation of oil, but this measure died in the Chamber. For criticism of the Cartel see Anton Mohr, *The Oil War* (London 1926) , pp. 87–93, and Pierre l'Espagnol de la Tramerye, *The World Struggle for Oil*, trans. C. Leonard Leese (New York, 1924) , pp. 201–206. The political influence of these oilmen is suggested by Jules Romains, *Les Hommes de bonne volonté: le six octobre* (Paris, 1932) , I, 146–147.

[4] One of these oilmen allegedly remarked: "The greatest disaster for us would be to discover oil deposits in France" (quoted by Faure, p. 63) .

[5] See Faure, p. 65; also Henry Bérenger, *Le Pétrole et la France* (Paris, 1920) , pp. 20–21.

[6] L'Espagnol de la Tramerye, p. 203.

[7] Francis Delaisi (*Oil: Its Influence on Politics*, p. 69) had such oilmen in mind when he wrote: "Since the death of the last follower of St. Simon, French businessmen seem to suffer from a paralysis of the will."

From the very onset of hostilities in 1914, the French government, especially the navy, was embarrassed by the dearth of oil reserves and anxious lest its supply line be severed. The government quickly signed contracts with the Cartel that established a priority for military needs and called for increased stockpiling. Though difficulties mounted, this arrangement endured until 1917. Transport was the chief difficulty because oil was contraband and its shipment was illegal even by a neutral such as the United States. Although American tankers risked the U-boat danger to supply France, deliveries became increasingly erratic, while French military needs sharply increased. The motorization of war—planes, tanks, trucks—doubled requirements between 1914 and 1917. When submarine warfare grew worse and some American shipowners withdrew their tankers from the dangerous Atlantic run, the shortage of oil reached alarming proportions.

By December, 1917, the oil shortage was so acute that it threatened to paralyze the French war effort. The crisis of that winter forced French leaders to action. In July, 1917, to meet the growing emergency, the French government had created a Comité Général du Pétrole under the presidency of Senator Henry Bérenger. Early in December the Cartel warned the government that it could no longer meet the nation's oil needs. On December 12 Bérenger presented a gloomy report to a Senate committee: reserves of oil and gasoline were so low, Bérenger stated, that the army could withstand another attack like that of Verdun for only three days. He predicted that the dwindling reserves would be depleted by March 1, 1918.[8] Additional American oil was not immediately forthcoming, and on December 15 Premier Clemenceau sent a cable to President Wilson urgently requesting extra tankers. Clemenceau's message was grave: "A failure in the supply of gasoline would cause the immediate paralysis of our armies and might compel us to make a peace unacceptable to the Allies. . . . If the Allies do not wish to lose the war, it is necessary that fighting France, now at the moment of the great German offensive, be provided with the gasoline which is as necessary as blood in the battles of tomorrow." [9]

Although the necessary supplies arrived in a week's time, the realization that France was unable to fight without the aid of foreign oil made the backward petroleum industry a national issue. The republic, seeing that its permissive policy toward private enterprise in developing the petroleum industry brought near disaster in 1917–1918, reacted to correct the situation. Once awakened, the state led the effort in finding oil deposits and building tankers and refineries for France. In March, 1918, the government intervened to ensure its needs for the re-

[8] Bérenger, p. 42.
[9] Quoted in *ibid.*, pp. 59–60.

mainder of the war. Despite the resistance of the Cartel, a petroleum consortium was organized which made the state the sole importer of petroleum and empowered it to fix prices. Shortly after the Armistice Bérenger vividly affirmed the part oil had played in winning the war: "The present victory was . . . won by the blood of the *poilus,* the Tommies, the *arditi,* and the Yanks, but it could not have been won without that other blood produced by the earth called oil." [10]

If the crisis of war had alerted France to its need for oil, the fortunes and demands of war put France into a better position to secure oil. For one thing, as a result of the confiscation of Germany's foreign petroleum holdings by the victorious Allies, France acquired rights to new sources of oil, notably in Rumania and the Middle East—the areas in which Mercier was to provide the leadership that made him one of the founders of the modern French petroleum industry. Secondly, a number of the "new men," who were to be instrumental in shaping France's postwar oil policy, were directly involved in the crisis of 1917–1918. André Tardieu, for example, as the government's commissioner, had the task of procuring oil in the United States. Similarly, Loucheur and Mercier suffered through the emergency at the Ministry of Armaments. To these men, a return to the *status quo ante bellum* in the oil industry was inconceivable.

Yet the Third Republic struggled for a decade with the problem of elaborating a "national petroleum policy." It failed in its effort to establish a permanent state monopoly over oil imports and in the early '20's retreated to a system of *liberté conditionnée,* or almost unregulated competition. This policy proved to be regressive when the great foreign companies rushed to secure a share of the newly opened French market. Abandoning their role as mere suppliers, Jersey Standard, Royal Dutch Shell, Anglo-Persian, and others moved into the retail field by buying up French companies and making them subsidiaries. Only three members of the prewar Cartel managed to maintain independence in the face of the foreign invasion.

The foreign giants, arguing that "distribution should belong to the producers," extended and modernized their retail outlets; soon the gasoline pump with its colorful advertisements seemed to decorate the front of every roadside *épicerie.* Ruthless price wars were waged to attract new customers or to eliminate smaller competitors. The prewar stability vanished almost overnight, and the competition grew wilder and wilder. In early 1927 a destructive price war was halted only after the government announced that it was revising the import system and launching an investigation of the industry. In all this, the French com-

[10] *Ibid.,* p. 176.

panies were far outstripped by the foreign competitors, who made it difficult if not impossible for them to expand their distribution facilities.

Meanwhile, the Chamber of Deputies elected in 1924 and controlled by the Cartel des Gauches showed growing interest in ending the existing anarchy by extending government controls. In 1925 the leftist majority had introduced a licensing system for wholesale oil importers. In addition a National Liquid Fuel Office (Office National des Combustibles Liquides) had been established to coordinate the nation's efforts at attaining petroleum independence. Its first director was Louis Pineau, Mercier's longtime friend. But the price war of 1926–1927 and the gains made by foreign companies—to whom France was paying two to three billion francs a year—aroused the Chamber to adopt stronger regulatory measures. In 1926 it accepted in principle the establishment of a state monopoly of oil imports, reminiscent of the wartime consortium, but this measure was never implemented. Then the parliamentary investigating commission, created in 1927 to inquire into the unstable condition of the French market, uncovered the growing power of the "trusts." [11] The price war seemed to be an attempt by foreign oil companies to extend their control over France by eliminating domestic enterprises. The committee's findings led to the adoption of a new instrument of state control in 1928, the real "constitution" for the French petroleum industry.

This legislation, adopted in March, 1928, gave final form to the "national petroleum policy," which had emerged slowly and erratically after the war, and was characterized by increased state regulation and closer collaboration between government and private enterprise. The four main objectives of the new "constitution" were to curtail the "Anglo-Saxon trusts," to build a refining industry, to bring order to the market, and to develop the French share of Mesopotamian oil.[12] Henceforth all wholesale oil importers were to be limited to strict quotas, and authorizations for importing refined products were to be narrowly restricted in order to encourage the construction of refineries on French soil. Moreover, importers were to be under the obligation of holding reserves and "the execution of contracts of national interest."

[11] See n. 1 above. This report is an extremely enlightening source for the history of the oil industry, but like some other parliamentary investigations that touched on delicate issues, its findings were suppressed and not published in the regular collection of documents in the *Journal officiel*. It can be found in the Bibliothèque Nationale under the call number 4Le 89, 26bis.

[12] For details see the excellent analysis by René Hubert, "Le Problème du pétrole devant le parlement," *Revue politique et parlementaire*, CXLIII (June 10, 1930), 376–396.

A protective tariff established new rates and closed old loopholes to promote the "rebirth" of the refining industry. Finally, a new Compagnie Française des Pétroles was to act as the center of this entire system designed to liberate France from foreign interests. It promised to develop the Mesopotamian deposits and to provide France with its own source of crude oil.

During 1916–1917 Mercier had, as we have seen, gained considerable experience in Rumanian affairs and had made friends within that nation's governing circles. After he became attached to the Ministry of Armaments, he remained in close contact with developments in Rumania,[13] and he soon became keenly interested in investing French capital in the Rumanian oil industry. While at the ministry he met Horace Finaly, the energetic director of the Banque de Paris et des Pays-Bas. This bank, the greatest *banque d'affaires* in France, promoted the formation of both the petroleum and the electrical industry, and Mercier's close friendship with its director was the basis for his career in oil.

The Banque de Paris et des Pays-Bas had attempted unsuccessfully to gain a foothold in the Rumanian oil industry prior to the war, and after the Armistice it launched a massive program to create a French petroleum industry that would supplant German economic influence in eastern Europe.[14] One of the consequences of Germany's defeat had been the confiscation of the holdings of the Deutsche Bank in the Steaua Romana, a large Rumanian oil company. The Banque de Paris et des Pays-Bas and other French financial interests seeking to purchase the German controlling interest in the Steaua Romana established a holding company, the Omnium International des Pétroles. Late in 1920 Finaly asked Mercier to assume the presidency of this new corporation.[15] Since the San Remo oil agreement of the same year provided that France and Great Britain would share equally in the spoils in Rumania and elsewhere, the Anglo-Persian Oil Company joined the Omnium. This company became the first truly international oil company when, at Mercier's urging, part of the German shares were sold to a syndicate of Rumanian banks, thus transforming the Omnium into a

[13] His intermediary at Allied headquarters in Rumania was Marcel Champin, who later became the representative of the Banque Mirabaud which invested heavily in Rumanian oil.

[14] See Robert Aron, *Une grande Banque d'affaires: la Banque de Paris et des Pays-Bas* (Paris, 1959), pp. 23–24; also Baldy, *Les Banques d'affaires en France depuis 1900*, pp. 299–300. In 1920 the Banque de Paris et des Pays-Bas became the controlling partner with Jersey Standard in establishing the Cie. Standard Franco-Américaine.

[15] "Notes," Mercier papers.

joint British-French-Rumanian enterprise. The French group in the Omnium formed the Steaua Française with Mercier as president, and at Mercier's insistence French engineers participated in the operation of the Steaua Romana. Despite such efforts, however, France received only a small fraction of its oil needs from Rumania during the interwar years. Even the Steaua Romana, according to Mercier, did not prove to be a profitable venture.[16] Yet Mercier's success in representing French interests in collaboration with foreign oil companies soon brought him to the attention of his government and appointment to the most important post in the French petroleum industry.

France's major effort to solve its petroleum problem came in the Middle East, where it sought, and finally won, a share in the Turkish Petroleum Company (TPC). From its inception in 1912 this famous company had been a source of conflict among the great powers.[17] After years of quarrels and intrigue, the various interests that had been competing for a right to oil exploration in the Ottoman Empire reached an agreement among themselves. The TPC grouped British and German interests with those of the Armenian oil magnate, Calouste Gulbenkian. In March, 1914, the British government intervened to reorganize the company, making the Anglo-Persian Oil Company owner of approximately half the total shares; the remainder was equally divided between Royal Dutch Shell and the Deutsche Bank, while 5 percent of the profits was reserved for Gulbenkian. The shareholders agreed that the TPC would enjoy a monopoly of all oil discovered in the Ottoman Empire; thus they promised not to compete with one another and to work exclusively through the TPC. The British and German ambassadors then secured a letter from the Grand Vizier which leased the oil deposits in vilayets of Baghdad and Mosul to the TPC but reserved the right of the Turkish government to define the terms of the concession at a later time. This concession, or promise of a concession, was granted on June 20, 1914, only five weeks before the be-

[16] Mercier found his Rumanian affairs "extremely interesting," but they "did not pay me for my effort" ("Notes," Mercier papers). For data on the Rumanian oil industry see Mihail Pizanty, *Petroleum in Rumania* (Bucharest, 1930).

[17] For summaries of the founding of the TPC see Stephen Longrigg, *Oil in the Middle East: Its Discovery and Development* (London, 1954), pp. 13–14, 27–32, 43–47, and Edward M. Earle, "The Turkish Petroleum Company: A Study in Oleaginous Diplomacy," *Political Science Quarterly*, XXXIX (June, 1924), 265–279. A fine, concise history of this diplomacy from the French point of view is Guillaume de Labarrière, *La Compagnie Française des Pétroles: les sociétés de pétrole à participation de l'état dans divers pays* (Brest, 1932), pp. 129–154. An important summary based on company records is by Jean Rondot: *La Compagnie Française des Pétroles: du franc-or au pétrole-franc* (Paris, 1962). A useful collection of data can be found in Mehdi Hessabi, *Le Pétrole en Irak* (Paris, 1937).

ginning of the war. The events of the next four years, of course, completely altered the situation in the Middle East.

During the war, with the struggle for oil greatly intensified, disputes arose among the Allies over control of the TPC. The British and French navies, alerted to the need for safe supplies of fuel oil, urged their governments to adopt more aggressive policies in pursuit of foreign resources. As early as 1914 the British government intervened in petroleum affairs by purchasing a controlling interest in the Anglo-Persian Oil Company.[18] This company was to act as the Admiralty's agent in procuring dependable oil supplies for the British fleet. The French navy demanded that its government render similar assistance, and this led eventually to the formation of the Compagnie Française des Pétroles. The essence of the new "oil diplomacy" ushered in by the war did not escape one acute observer who wrote:

> The war . . . proved conclusively . . . that oil was indispensable to the navy. [This] has caused the governments of all the great powers to take a much keener interest in oil than they did before the war. . . . It is this fact, if anything, which has caused the oil diplomacy of the post-war years, in which it is not, as is so often supposed, so much a case of unscrupulous oil companies using governments for their own wicked ends, as of unscrupulous governments using oil companies for their own ends.[19]

France received a boon in its drive for oil in 1916 when the Sykes–Picot agreement assigned Syria and the Mosul vilayet to its zone of influence. The Mosul region promised to be the very core of oil deposits in the Turkish lands, and Syria lay astride the shortest pipeline route to the Mediterranean. Letters of clarification between the French and British governments, however, protected British interests by confirming the validity of the TPC concession in which Anglo-Persian held the lion's share. Meanwhile Gulbenkian, the so-called Talleyrand of oil diplomacy, and Sir Henry Deterding, the director of Royal Dutch Shell, were maneuvering to bring the French into the TPC. Angered by the British government's forcible reorganization of the TPC in favor of Anglo-Persian in 1914, Gulbenkian and Deterding sought revenge by urging the French government to request the shares of the Deutsche Bank which the British had confiscated. Deterding was confident that Royal Dutch Shell could obtain control of these shares and thus achieve an equal footing with Anglo-Persian in the councils of

[18] See Winston Churchill, *The World Crisis* (New York, 1923–1929), I, 133–139.
[19] Christopher Brunner, *The Problem of Oil* (London, 1930), p. 21.

the TPC.[20] The British Foreign Office agreed to the French request, mainly because the Sykes–Picot agreement had already assigned the Mosul vilayet and the most suitable course for a pipeline (Syria) to the French.[21] Actual negotiations were slow, but on April 24, 1920, the San Remo oil agreement formally ratified the transfer of the German shares to France and also set out the main lines for Anglo-French collaboration in the exploitation of oil fields in various regions all over the world.

Even after San Remo certain ambiguities remained regarding French participation in the TPC which were to cause bitterness between the Allies and difficulty for Mercier. According to the agreement, if the British government chose to have the TPC operate as a "private company" in developing Mesopotamian oil, France would receive "a 25 percent participation." [22] This pledge, however, left undefined whether France would receive a fourth of the TPC's dividends or a fourth of its production of crude oil.

But the most critical weakness of the San Remo pact was the intentional omission of the United States.[23] American oil interests, in particular Standard Oil of New Jersey, demanded a share of the potentially rich deposits in the former Ottoman Empire. The U.S. State Department complained to the British government that it was violating the Open Door Policy, or the principle of equal opportunity, in the mandated territories by denying the United States a share in the oil resources of this region. A long and acrimonious debate ensued in 1920–1921 with Washington basing its case on the Open Door Policy and questioning the validity of the original 1914 concession. London relied on the sanctity of international contracts and argued that the United States was not entitled to equal opportunity in the mandates since it had refused to join the League of Nations. Eventually the British gave way and negotiations between the TPC and an American oil syndicate seeking admission were undertaken in 1922–1923. A provisional agreement stipulated that Anglo-Persian would divide its shares

[20] To this end Royal Dutch Shell created a French subsidiary which was to win the privilege of purchasing the former German shares from the French government. Regarding this important maneuver see Ralph Hewins, *Mr. Five Per Cent: The Biography of Calouste Gulbenkian* (London, 1957) , pp. 112–113; Labarrière, p. 136; l'Espagnol de la Tramerye, pp. 217–219.

[21] John Rowland and Basil, Second Baron Cadman, *Ambassador for Oil: The Life of John, First Baron Cadman* (London, 1960) , p. 89.

[22] Hessabi, pp. 49–50.

[23] For the American role in this diplomacy see John A. DeNovo, *American Interests and Policies in the Middle East, 1900–1939* (Minneapolis, 1963) , pp. 176–202.

with the Americans, giving the latter approximately a one-fourth interest in the TPC. However, American participation was far from defined
when Mercier arrived on the scene a year later.

Because of the chaotic political situation in the Middle East, the
frontier dispute between Turkey and Iraq over the Mosul region, and
the negotiation of a new concession, there was little progress made in
reorganizing the TPC before 1923. Eventually Iraq was awarded the
Mosul area, and in 1925 the TPC obtained a new grant from the Iraqi
government. The TPC then entered a new phase in which businessmen replaced statesmen in the positions of command. Yet one observer
wondered whether "the cosmopolitan fraternity of great oil men that
will compose the new board of the company will not quarrel about the
working of the concession as much as their governments did about obtaining it." [24]

Mercier entered the councils of the TPC only after the British government had decided to allow private enterprise a part in developing
the concession. The British informed the French government of its decision in July, 1922, and a year later requested the French to designate
a private or mixed company (mixed government and private ownership) to buy the German shares. Since Premier Poincaré and Louis Pineau, his adviser on petroleum affairs, were eager to take advantage of
this opportunity to free France from its foreign suppliers, they ignored
Deterding's bid to buy up the German shares through the newly
formed French subsidiary of Royal Dutch Shell. Poincaré was hardly
of a mind to turn over control of these new oil rights to the foreign
giant.[25] The problem was to find a French oil company powerful
enough to negotiate on an equal basis with the "Anglo-Saxon trusts"
within the TPC. Poincaré then made the crucial decision against having the state itself invest in the development of the rights it had won
by war and diplomacy. He was afraid of straining the unsteady treas-
ury with a potentially expensive, risky, and long-term obligation. Furthermore, French business strongly opposed the formation of a mixed
company, like the Anglo-Persian, in which the state would hold shares
directly.[26] As an alternative, Poincaré proposed the establishment of a
new national oil company, to be called the Compagnie Française des
Pétroles (CFP), which would combine not only all the petroleum companies in France but also the major French banks. On September 20,

[24] *Economist*, Mar. 21, 1925, p. 536.

[25] For Poincaré's position see Loucheur's testimony in the *Journal officiel de la
République française, débats parlementaires, Chambre des députés*, Mar. 24, 1931, p.
2152 (hereafter cited as *J.O. débats*). Also Rondot, pp. 11–12.

[26] See Loucheur's testimony in *J.O. débats*, March 24, 1931, p. 2153.

1923, at Pineau's suggestion,[27] Poincaré asked Mercier to organize the new company which would buy up the sequestered shares.

In his letter to Mercier, Poincaré carefully outlined the purpose of the new enterprise.[28] The CFP was to be explicitly French in character, giving France a representative similar to America's Standard Oil, or Britain's Anglo-Persian, and it was to be the "instrument" of French liberation. It was to develop the petroleum resources of France and of its colonies, as well as those obtained by diplomacy, specifically the Mesopotamian rights. Finally, Poincaré wrote, the company was to help ensure France's supply by searching for deposits in Central and South America and by purchasing Russian oil.

The choice of Mercier as president is indicative of the heterogeneous character of the CFP. To be sure, Mercier was uniquely qualified for the post; he had experience in international oil affairs, particularly in working with the Anglo-Persian in the Omnium. More important, he had remained on intimate terms with the French navy, which had a special interest in oil. In addition, as Poincaré privately confided, Mercier could act as a mediator between two of the largest competing oil groups, the Banque de Paris et des Pays-Bas and the Union Parisienne,[29] because he was associated with Horace Finaly of the former and he also enjoyed the confidence of the Union Parisienne which helped finance the Messine syndicate. Mercier well understood the difficulties of the assignment and to enhance his role as an independent mediator he chose to serve without salary.[30]

From the outset, Mercier found it necessary to use all his diplomatic skill to persuade the Malthusian French banks and oil companies to participate in the new venture. The problems were complicated, he later wrote:

> . . . none of the initial investors begged for the favor of being admitted into the CFP and several companies invited to join did not feel that they ought to accept. This was because in 1923 there was the greatest uncertainty about the ex-

[27] Interview with Mme Ernest Mercier, June 22, 1964. In fact Loucheur was Poincaré's first choice to head the CFP, but Loucheur refused the offer; see Loucheur to Poincaré, Feb. 8, 1923, Loucheur papers, Bundle XII.

[28] This letter has not been published in its entirety, but it can be pieced together from various excerpts: *Journal officiel de la République française, documents parlementaires, Chambre des députés,* 1929, pp. 1201–1202 (hereafter cited as *J.O. documents*) ; Labarrière, pp. 143–144.

[29] Notes of Loucheur on a conversation with Poincaré, Jan. 7, 1923, Loucheur papers, Bundle XII. On the distribution of French banking interests in the petroleum industry see l'Espagnol de la Tramerye, pp. 241–242.

[30] "Notes," Mercier papers.

tent and the practical value of the Mesopotamian oil fields, and also because many sensible people doubted whether it would be possible to succeed at a task that seemed so complex, so full of international difficulties, and so handicapped by the government's policy of bringing together directly competing interests.[31]

Private enterprise also feared that the establishment of the CFP was a step toward the creation of a state monopoly over the entire petroleum industry.[32] Private firms balked at organizing themselves into a single company which the state might control. The memory of the wartime consortium and the efforts by the parliamentary Left to transform the petroleum industry into another state monopoly (like matches or tobacco) predisposed oilmen against the scheme. The potential shareholders therefore opposed the formation of a mixed company or of even an ordinary joint stock company that enjoyed any monopolistic privileges. Mercier overcame such fears by winning assurances from Poincaré and was thus able to attract private investors.[33] By March, 1924, Mercier had convinced some ninety enterprises, mainly French oil companies and banks as well as some subsidiaries of foreign oil companies, to purchase shares in the CFP.[34]

Throughout the negotiations over the constitution of the CFP the Third Republic was so haphazard in its policy that the state sacrificed much of its control over Mosul oil. Poincaré in his haste to send his long overdue reply to the British government—which had been waiting for eighteen months—further jeopardized the state's rights. On January 28, 1924, he informed the British that the CFP, though still officially unorganized, was his *désignée* to purchase the German shares. In March, when Louis Loucheur became Minister of Commerce in a reshuffled Poincaré cabinet, he found that formalities had begun for transferring the shares to the CFP without any detailed agreement having been reached specifying the state's rights in the company! To make matters worse, the Poincaré government lost the May 11 election and rushed to constitute the CFP before the incoming Cartel government

[31] *Courrier des pétroles,* May 12, 1930.

[32] "As for the cause of the opposition to the company, it was based solely on the fear that the various petroleum companies had of constituting a *de facto* monopoly through their own doing" (Loucheur memorandum, Loucheur papers, Bundle XII).

[33] Poincaré accepted Mercier's request that the CFP not receive "any monopoly or immunity placing it in a privileged position," and that shareholders were not obligated to subscribe to future increases in the company's capital (Labarrière, pp. 155–156).

[34] Foreign ownership was limited to less than 18 percent in the company (*J.O. documents,* 1929, p. 1203). A list of the board of directors and the interests they represented can be found in the *Petroleum Times,* Mar. 29, 1924, p. 455. See also *ibid.,* Oct. 18, 1930, p. 629.

took office. A leftist government, it was feared, would upset the existing understanding by demanding the formation of a mixed company.

On May 17, 1924, Loucheur and François-Marsal, as the government's representatives, signed a hurried convention with Mercier that became a kind of constitution for the CFP.[35] The company was authorized to purchase the German shares of the TPC. In exchange the state received the right to name two commissioners (with rather limited powers) to the board of directors. Since the CFP was to represent France, its top managers and board members—the latter to be of French nationality—required government approval. The state would receive a share of excess profits. But the state's general option to purchase up to 80 percent of the company's oil for its needs encountered strong opposition from the board of directors, who wanted Mosul oil reserved for purposes of national defense and not for all state-controlled public services. Mercier later commented that this last-minute crisis over the state's option nearly paralyzed the company "before it took its first step." [36] In fact, the entire agreement seemed on the verge of collapse since the Poincaré government's mandate had almost expired and the company refused to sign until the option was restricted. Mercier then signed the agreement himself, despite the ambiguity of the option, and presented his board of directors with a *fait accompli*.[37] Not completely outmaneuvered, the board withheld its final approval until the option was defined.

The electoral victory of the Cartel des Gauches and the formation of a new government by Édouard Herriot in June changed the entire situation. This break in governmental continuity coupled with the ambiguity of the original convention allowed Mercier to modify the option clause to the CFP's satisfaction. Herriot, as had been expected, wanted tighter governmental control over the CFP, but he admitted that he was bound by his predecessor's contract and thus limited to "transmission and interpretation." [38] Moreover, when Mercier asked the new Ministers of Finance and Commerce for an interpretation of the option they were naturally uncertain of what the original understanding had been. Loucheur advised them that the common intention had been to meet the needs of national defense, that is, war and navy departments, plus all "public services." But Pineau, who had also been privy to the

[35] Loucheur later admitted his dissatisfaction with these negotiations in a letter to Mercier (Feb. 18, 1931, Loucheur papers, Bundle XI). See also *J.O. débats,* Mar. 24, 1931, pp. 2152–2153. The convention and the interpretive letters can be found in Rondot, pp. 165–178.

[36] *Courrier des pétroles,* May 12, 1930.

[37] Loucheur memorandum, Loucheur papers, Bundle XII.

[38] *J.O. débats,* Mar. 25, 1931, p. 2191.

negotiations, agreed with Mercier that the option was to have been restricted only to defense purposes. In June and July the Herriot government exchanged interpretive letters with Mercier which specified that the state's option ". . . will be reserved to satisfy the needs of the war and navy departments, and of those services presently managed directly by the state which are in no way commercial operations." [39] In the opinion of Loucheur and many others, the state thus sacrificed half its option, but the Herriot government considered that the state had extended its option by including those public services of a noncommercial nature. Partly by intent and partly by default, the Third Republic in the end kept its participation and control in the CFP to a minimum, although it stumbled into this policy because of its own timidity, haste, and financial weakness and because of the determined resistance of private industry to any government control.

Between 1924 and 1928 at the international conferences held in London, Mercier tried to determine the organization and operation of the TPC. He later called these years "the hardest of my life." [40] The bargaining atmosphere was heavy with mutual animosity. Mercier's opposites were Sir John Cadman (chairman of the TPC), Walter Teagle (Standard Oil of New Jersey), Sir Charles Greenway (Anglo-Persian) Sir Henry Deterding (Royal Dutch Shell), and Calouste Gulbenkian. Conflicting business interests were not the only source of disagreement. The TPC was also the touchstone of "oil diplomacy," the battleground for the conflicting aims of the victors of the Great War. Mercier wrote of the "unequal" battle he had to wage against his powerful adversaries and their governments. He in turn frequently sought support from his government, especially Pineau at the Fuel Office, and he relied heavily on Finaly at the Banque de Paris et des Pays-Bas. Finaly was associated with Jersey Standard, and he often interceded for Mercier to persuade Teagle to be "more understanding." [41] During the early stages of the negotiations, at a time when the franc was weak, the British deliberately raised the company's capital in an effort to force the French out of the TPC. It was only when Mercier in desperation turned to Finaly at the Banque de Paris et des Pays-Bas that the situation was saved.[42]

Mercier's colleague in representing the CFP at London was Robert Cayrol, the managing director of the largest independent French oil company, Desmarais Frères.[43] Cayrol, another of the "new men," was a

---

[39] Quoted in Rondot, pp. 173–174.

[40] *Ernest Mercier: une grande destinée*, p. 28.

[41] "Notes," Mercier papers.

[42] See *Commission d'enquête sur les pétroles*, p. 129.

[43] See Maurice Guierre, *Robert Cayrol, 1883–1959: de la mer au pétrole, l'unité d'une vie* (Paris, 1960).

naval technician who had joined Desmarais after the war and was turning it into a worldwide distributor. Both Mercier and Cayrol were, of course, clearly understood by the other delegations to be representing the French navy in the councils of the TPC, much as Anglo-Persian represented the British Admiralty. At the bargaining table Mercier was the conciliator, the diplomat, and Cayrol the stubborn defender of the CFP's position.

The negotiations were frequently bogged down over matters in which one or two members opposed the others. The American syndicate, represented by Teagle, insisted that the Open Door Policy required both a cancellation of the self-denying clause and a strict limitation of the scope of the TPC concession in order to open the former Turkish lands to competition from American companies. Since both Mercier and Gulbenkian were against any reduction of the TPC concession or any opening of it to competition, they together opposed attempts by Royal Dutch Shell, Anglo-Persian, and certain American companies to seek concessions on their own, in violation of the self-denying clause. In 1927 Mercier, with the strong support of the Quai d'Orsay and Pineau, initiated a civil suit against his three Anglo-American partners.[44] The suit maintained that the original engagements signed by the TPC members were binding and called on a British tribunal to uphold their validity. Fortunately for the CFP, British law protected minority interests in corporations, and a last-minute compromise averted taking the dispute to court.

Gulbenkian also provoked a quarrel by obstinately blocking his partners' plan to make the TPC a simple producer of crude oil. Gulbenkian himself lacked the facilities to refine and market crude; he wanted dividends, not crude oil, and commented, "I had risked capital in this venture with a view to obtaining profits in cash." [45] In this, Mercier and Cayrol adamantly opposed Gulbenkian. It suited their plans for France that the TPC should be limited to the production of crude oil, for France could use the crude as raw material for new refineries. If, on the other hand, the TPC enlarged its functions, the CFP would lose the opportunity to develop into an industry and would be nothing more than a financial partner collecting dividends.[46]

The discord at London was suddenly broken by a dramatic event in Iraq. On October 15, 1927, oil was struck at Baba Gurgur in the Mosul fields. The well erupted with such violence that two drillers were

---

[44] Mercier wrote that he was "abandoned by M. Poincaré, but fully supported by Philippe Berthelot and Louis Pineau" (*Ernest Mercier*, p. 28).

[45] Quoted in Hewins, *Mr. Five Per Cent*, p. 115.

[46] The American group supported Mercier's position on this point. Both the French and the Americans also preferred crude because TPC dividends were subject to a 22 percent British tax (*Commission d'enquête sur les pétroles*, p. 120).

killed and the oil flowed uncontrolled for a week. This strike profoundly altered "both the economic fortunes of Iraq and the oil-history
of the world." [47] Certain now that the TPC owned valuable oil deposits, the dissident groups were forced to reach an agreement. Further
delay was intolerable. At home, Mercier suddenly found it easy to double the capital of the CFP.

The outstanding disagreements were resolved by the Group Agreement, or Red Line Agreement, of July, 1928. Mercier and Cayrol had
their way and the TPC became a producer of crude and has operated
in this way ever since. Each member received an amount of the crude
proportionate to its financial participation. Gulbenkian was pacified
by a private arrangement with Mercier which called for the CFP to
purchase Gulbenkian's share of crude oil at the market price. The
problem of the distribution of shares was settled by giving each major
partner 23.75 percent (CFP, Anglo-Persian, Royal Dutch Shell, and
Jersey Standard), with Gulbenkian retaining his famous 5 percent.
The Americans were satisfied by a compromise that limited the TPC to
developing only a specific number of plots and allowed the remainder
of the concession to be opened eventually to outside competition. Finally, within a thick red line drawn on a map by Gulbenkian which
delineated the borders of the old Ottoman Empire, the partners
pledged not to compete with one another but to work exclusively
through the TPC. The following year the TPC changed its name to
the Iraq Petroleum Company (IPC). Mercier was proud of the agreement: "Our adversaries have compromised, giving us complete satisfaction." [48]

After the signing of the Working Agreement, Mercier noted that
"the atmosphere changed and little by little our relationship with our
powerful partners became more and more marked by mutual esteem,
cordiality, and finally friendship." [49] Only the pipeline issue required
his attendance at IPC meetings after 1929.[50] The newly discovered
wells had to be capped until the necessary installations were con-

[47] Longrigg, *Oil in the Middle East*, p. 71.

[48] Quoted in Guierre, p. 28.

[49] *Ernest Mercier*, p. 29.

[50] One other question that arose at this time has earned Mercier some indirect
criticism. In 1930 Abdul Aziz ibn Saud offered the IPC the concession to his realm of
al-Hasa in Saudi Arabia. Mercier and the British refused to pay the price for this
unpromising concession. In 1935 American companies (Aramco) purchased these
rights and discovered enormous deposits. A current director of the CFP has defended
Mercier's decision by pointing out that prudence was required in 1930 since the very
existence of the CFP was under attack by the Chamber (René de Montaigu, in
Guierre, pp. 31–33). An official historian of the CFP writes that, "if the IPC had
obtained the al-Hasa concession in 1935, it would have become the greatest producer
of oil in the Middle East" (Rondot, p. 48).

structed and a pipeline laid. Again political considerations took precedence over business prudence. Both the French and the British wanted the pipeline to traverse its mandated territory and end at a Mediterranean port under its control: Mercier argued that the line should run across Syria to the Lebanese port of Tripoli, and Cadman argued that it should run across Transjordan and Palestine to the port of Haifa. Distance, security, and topography—all these, they argued, were to be taken into account. But in the end political conciliation won out, and a double pipeline was built, with a northern or "French" branch and a southern or "British" branch. From a financial point of view the construction of two lines requiring additional pumping stations and communication systems was absurd. However, when the British line was forced to close during the Second World War, oil continued to flow through the other branch. The actual construction of the pipeline did not begin until late 1932, but despite the many difficulties of the desert terrain, the work was completed rapidly. By 1934 Iraqi oil had begun to flow, transforming the entire character of the French petroleum industry.

Mercier at last reached a solution in the Working Agreement only to find himself the center of a long public controversy over the constitution of the CFP at home. Following the initial quarrel over its inception in 1923–1924, the CFP had ceased to be a news item. Then came the spectacular gusher at Baba Gurgur and the conclusion of the Working Agreement. For the first time, as Mercier said, "the general public began to be interested in our company." [51] From 1928 to 1931 Mercier tried to reconcile the differences between the public and private interests that composed the CFP. Indeed, Mercier said he "always considered his mission" was to act as the "defender of both the state's interests and those of the company." [52]

It will be recalled that France needed both a refining industry of its own and its own oil resources to free it from dependence on foreign oil companies. The 1928 "constitution" for the oil industry was intended to encourage a native refining industry and to control the Anglo-American giants by a system of import quotas. It also sought to develop the enormous resources of crude oil that were soon to reach France from Mosul by way of the CFP. It seemed obvious to Mercier that the CFP, as a French company representing both private and public interests, should refine this crude to complete the task of "national liberation." He discovered there was powerful opposition to this assumption.

The powerful Anglo-American companies, with their French subsid-

[51] *Courrier des pétroles,* May 12, 1930.
[52] *Ibid.*

iaries, still had a monopoly over the distribution of petroleum products in France. The representatives of these foreign oil companies, who sat on the board of the CFP, bitterly resented the importation of Mosul oil and wanted to limit the function of the CFP to the supplying of crude oil—in other words, to prohibit it from engaging in refining and marketing operations. They were supported by certain independent French oil companies that feared the competition of CFP products. Faced with such strong opposition from his own board to his plan for establishing a CFP refinery, Mercier sought help from the government. In December, 1928, he wrote to Poincaré, who was once again premier, expressing his disappointment that internal disunity had paralyzed the company [53] and offering his resignation as a means of solving the difficulties. Poincaré refused the resignation and suggested that they map out a new instrument regulating relations between the state and the company and authorizing the CFP to refine its crude oil.

On March 19, 1929, Mercier and two government ministers signed a new agreement. To muster support for Mercier against the divisive interests within the board, the government reversed its earlier policy and transformed the CFP into a true mixed company by agreeing to purchase a 25 percent interest in the company and to hold one-fourth of the seats on the board of directors. The CFP was authorized to form a subsidiary refining company, the Compagnie Française de Raffinage (CFR), destined to become the nation's largest refining company; CFP was to hold 55 percent of the stock of the CFR, the state 10 percent, and the public the remainder. If the CFR succeeded, it would break the Anglo-American monopoly of refined petroleum products. The most controversial clause of the new contract was Article 12, which—following the 1928 oil "constitution"—required all petroleum importers to take up to 25 percent of their annual needs from the CFR. The "25 percent clause" allowed the CFR to have its refined products marketed without disrupting or adding to the nation's already overburdened retailing system. The new convention, designed by Mercier and the government, was not welcomed by the board of directors, who complained that the state waited until the CFP was a sure success before it invested any government funds. The board ratified the agreement, but they regarded it as their last sacrifice.[54]

The unforeseen consequence of the new convention was that it opened a Pandora's box and turned the CFP structure into an issue of popular interest. None of the preceding agreements between the government and the CFP had been submitted to parliament for ratifica-

[53] Rondot, p. 36.
[54] *Courrier des pétroles*, May 12, 1930; *Petroleum Times*, May 17, 1930, p. 885.

tion because they did not entail any state financial participation. But the new 1929 instrument did, and required parliamentary approval. The long and turbulent controversy over the CFP that erupted in the Chamber during 1930–1931 forced Mercier onto the stage of parliamentary politics.

In 1930 the Tardieu government attempted to win the Chamber's approval of the 1929 convention without consideration of prior agreements with the CFP. To the dismay of the government and Mercier this proposal was intensely criticized by parliamentary committees even before it reached the floor of the legislature.[55] Many committee members considered the state's over-all participation in the CFP and CFR shamefully inadequate. One committee resurrected the old issue of the 80 percent state priority (which was irrelevant since it pertained not to the 1929 convention but to the original 1924 convention). In addition, the newly formed independent French refineries, represented by the Marquis de Vogüé, informed the committee of their objection to the "25 percent clause." De Vogüé argued it was self-defeating for the state to encourage the establishment of French refineries and then force them to operate at 75 percent of their capacity in order to absorb the CFR's output. In the finance committee Léon Blum demanded that the 1924 constitution also be subjected to parliamentary ratification since it and not the 1929 agreement had established the guidelines for the company's structure. The Socialist leader insisted that the government could not legally transfer public property to a private company without parliamentary approval. He found wide support from deputies disturbed by Tardieu's attempt to present them with a *fait accompli* and ignore parliament's prerogatives.[56]

Faced with the possibility of renegotiating the entire edifice of the CFP with the Chamber of Deputies, Mercier defended the contract with every weapon in his arsenal. At the company's annual meeting and to the press he argued that the sanctity of all contracts would be imperiled if the state attempted to alter the existing agreements. He even questioned the authority of the Chamber over this matter:

> There is no doubt in my mind that constitutionally the right of negotiating, discussing, and drawing up contracts belongs to the executive branch. The Chamber possesses a sovereign power of control, and in cases where the executive has to submit the agreements it has concluded, the Chamber has the absolute power of accepting them or rejecting them. But in no circumstances does the Chamber itself have the power to un-

[55] *J.O. documents*, 1930, pp. 368, 492–495, 829–831, 1094–1096, 1108–1109, 1375–1377; Hubert, "Le Problème du pétrole," pp. 387–396.
[56] *Petroleum Times*, Sept. 6, 1930, p. 391.

dertake the discussion, negotiation, or drawing up of such contracts.

He made it clear that he blamed the obstructionism in parliament on his longtime opponents: "Certain private interests, not in good favor with the government, have felt it expedient to find fault with the work which we have pursued for six years and to present it in a light which I refrain from describing. These private interests obtained rather unexpected assistance by means which it will be interesting to expose at the proper time." [57]

Foreseeing defeat, the Tardieu government changed tactics. Before submitting the 1929 convention for ratification the government requested and received from the CFP some concessions in the form of an amendment (June 25, 1930). But the maneuver only further antagonized the rebellious deputies, who felt that their privileges were being bypassed. An opposition spokesman claimed that "parliamentary tradition" required legislative approval "for the smallest transference of state property." And, he added ironically, "to sell a rock whose sole value is a few migrant seagulls requires a law, but to transfer the rights of France in a global oil transaction has no such requirement!" [58]

On July 8 when the ratification of the 1929 convention was presented to the Chamber, the deputies refused even to debate the matter until the prior agreements had been discussed separately and if necessary renegotiated. The defeat distressed Mercier, since it jeopardized the delicate structure of the CFP and weakened his bargaining position in the IPC, which was then debating the pipeline question. He was also keenly disappointed by this first direct experience with parliamentary politics, which had shown that even his friend Tardieu could be unreliable under pressure. He later wrote, "I had the entire Chamber against me." [59]

The Chamber continued to postpone ratification—intensifying Mercier's convictions about the republic's inherent inefficiency. He had waited fourteen months and watched the coming and going of four cabinets. In early February, 1931, he threatened to resign if passage were not secured within a week. When debate was resumed the new Laval government acquiesced and offered each agreement for separate approval. Mercier urged the immediate ratification of the existing

---

[57] *Courrier des pétroles*, May 12, 1930. Later Mercier placed the blame on "a certain Blumenfeld who had known how to win the support of M. Léon Blum" ("Notes," Mercier papers).

[58] Charles Guernier (*J.O. débats*, July 8, 1930, p. 2967).

[59] "Notes," Mercier papers. Earlier Mercier had welcomed Tardieu's efforts on behalf of the CFP; see Mercier to Loucheur, Dec. 11, 1929, Loucheur papers, Bundle XI.

agreements, insisting that further delay undermined his position in the IPC, but the Chamber stubbornly held out for further concessions by the company. For more than a month the debate continued, with arguments from all sides.

The Left refused to accept the CFP as constituted by the agreements. The Socialists, supported by most of the Radicals, revived their campaign for the creation of a state monopoly which would control all petroleum imports. In the debates, Léon Blum himself led the attack on the CFP. The state, he contended, must not give up part of the "national patrimony" to private hands; nor had Poincaré ever intended the CFP to be an autonomous enterprise, as it had become. He had meant it to be a tool of the state, an intermediary at the negotiating table. Blum was especially critical of the reduction of the state's priority on CFP oil. He even urged the replacement of Mercier and the CFP by Pineau and the National Liquid Fuel Office. The real question, he said, was whether or not the Chamber wanted to keep or give away the rights to the Mosul oil fields: "Will you preserve for the state what belongs to it? Will you abandon [these rights] without compensation, without necessity, without justification?" [60]

The Radical Alfred Margaine and the Communist Jacques Doriot took occasion to denounce Mercier as a "straw man" of the "trusts" which, they claimed, controlled the CFP. According to Margaine, no less than seven of the sixteen directors of the CFP were "agents of the trusts"; four of them, he said, represented the Banque de Paris et des Pays-Bas–Jersey Standard combine, which meant that they had more votes than the state in the company.[61] Mosul oil should liberate France, he declared, not further enslave it to foreign interests. Doriot attacked Mercier as a *patron de combat*, one of France's greatest plutocrats who resorted to the "horsewhip" instead of treating his workers fairly, and both he and Margaine warned that Mercier would use the profits of Mosul oil to finance "reactionary" or "Fascist" political organizations. Doriot called attention to the parliamentary investigation of the petroleum industry in 1927 which, he said, had proved that oil companies were solicited for contributions by Mercier's pressure group. The Communist spokesman concluded: "After the description that I have just given of M. Ernest Mercier, ratify the convention if you so wish it. Entrust the bastardly, pseudo-monopoly of the CFP to this mortal enemy of the working class and the public interest." [62]

The extreme Right had milder objections to ratification; it focused

[60] *J.O. débats*, Mar. 25, 1931, p. 2190.
[61] *Ibid.*, Feb. 12, 1931, pp. 627–632.
[62] *Ibid.*, Mar. 20, 1931, p. 2101.

its criticism on the "25 percent clause" that obligated all refineries to distribute products for the CFR. But the Center and most of the Right consistently supported the government's request for ratification. The Moderates, represented by two parties, the Alliance Démocratique and the Gauche Radicale, were particularly vocal.[63] Loucheur, who headed the latter party and acted as the parliamentary floor leader for Mercier and the "new men," used as his main argument for the government the idea that "works of national interest" were best organized through "an association of state and industry." He warned that the government alone would not be able to supply the necessary capital or the qualified personnel to operate the CFP.[64] In support, other Moderates rose to praise Mercier's talents and to insist that the existing CFP cadres be retained. One said, for example: "In every case, M. Ernest Mercier has admirably acquitted himself in the task that the nation entrusted him. He showed himself to be a most skillful diplomat, a most discerning businessman. . . . The heads of the great trusts found in him a man of their caliber. . . . M. Ernest Mercier has carried well, if I may say so, the colors of the French team." [65] The Quai d'Orsay sent a spokesman to testify that Mercier was an able defender of French interests against the Anglo-Americans. Even Herriot said that though he and Mercier were "on opposite sides of the barricade," he must "render homage" to his work.[66] And Mercier's old friend Pineau, speaking for the Fuel Office, added his support of Mercier and urged immediate ratification. Finally, Louis Rollin, the Minister of Commerce, came to argue that it was too late to begin building another CFP. If the contract were not ratified, he said, either the shares of the CFP would be bought by the "Anglo-Saxon trusts," since the partners had first repurchase rights, or the "trusts" would exact heavy concessions to return them to the French government. In other words, France risked losing all its gains made since San Remo. It was this argument that eventually carried the day for the government.

[63] The Alliance Démocratique, a right-center party, probably deserved its reputation as a big business party. This is the thesis of Beau de Loménie, *Les Responsabilités des dynasties bourgeoises.* But there is evidence that the Gauche Radicale, a center party, played a similar role. The following members all had close ties with business: Loucheur, Étienne Clémentel, Germain-Martin, and Raynaldy (later a Radical).

[64] *J.O. débats,* Mar. 24, 1931, pp. 2154–2155. At the height of the debate Mercier quarreled with Loucheur when the deputy admitted to the Chamber that he too disapproved of the reduction of the state's oil priority. In private Mercier angrily accused his old friend of wavering in his defense of the CFP (Mercier to Loucheur, Feb. 13, 1931, Loucheur papers, Bundle XI). Mercier's anxiety over ratification drove him to attack his own patron for flinching in debate.

[65] Fernand Engerand (*J.O. débats,* Mar. 25, 1931, p. 2182).

[66] *Ibid.,* p. 2191.

Even with this support, the Laval government had to make last-minute alterations to pacify the opposition and obtain ratification. On March 4, 1931, it negotiated a final amendment with the CFP, which Mercier reluctantly accepted.[67] The amendment revised the "25 percent clause" to override the objections of the independent refineries represented by the extreme Right. Specifically, the CFR relinquished the "forced clientele" that was obligated to market its products, but in return it received authorization to refine 25 percent of the nation's needs. To mollify the sharpest objections of the Left, the government increased the state's shares to 35 percent and the state's votes to 40 percent, raised the state's portion of excess profits, and restored the state's absolute 80 percent priority. Thus parliament's insistence on a modification of the CFP's original constitution resulted in a considerable expansion of the state's controls and benefits in the company. Eight years of negotiation between business and government had ended in a compromise that satisfied the minimum demands of nearly everyone except the Left, which included most of the Radicals. The vote on March 27, 1931, ratified the constitution of the CFP and the CFR by a margin of 299 to 230.

Mercier and the CFP, along with their supporters in parliament and the government, were satisfied that they had won the struggle to avoid a state monopoly and had maintained the company as a combination of both public and private interests. Mercier wrote jubilantly to Loucheur on the day after the final vote:

> It was a good fight; you led it, and you won it!
> For the independent French petroleum industry this is a real occasion—I hope that the future will prove us worthy . . . the future that you have made possible.[68]

By way of a postscript to Mercier's letter—"the future" was a bright one for the CFP and the French effort to gain oil independence. On the night of August 16, 1934, the tanker *Henri-Desprez* docked at Le Havre with the first cargo of Mosul or "French" crude. The subsequent arrival of substantial quantities of Mosul oil and the effective operation of the protectionist legislation resulted in a transformation of the French petroleum industry. As expected, the imports of finished petroleum products from Anglo-American refineries dropped steadily,[69] and petroleum refining, which had been almost nonexistent

[67] *J.O. documents*, 1931, p. 587.

[68] Mar. 28, 1931, Loucheur papers, Bundle XI.

[69] See the graph in Rondot, p. 34. In 1935 Mercier was again confronted with intense pressure from the oil distributors to curtail the marketing of CFP oil. Another threatened resignation quieted this final revolt (Mercier to Pineau, June 8 and July 2, 1935, Mercier papers) .

in France before 1928, became a major industry.[70] On the eve of the Second World War, largely because of the CFP, the French refining industry ranked first in western Europe (excluding Great Britain) and fourth among the world powers.[71] By 1936 more than 42 percent of French crude oil imports came through the IPC, and the CFR's two modern refineries provided 20 percent of the nation's needs.[72] Furthermore, the CFP's shipping subsidiary, which was also headed by Mercier, had either acquired or had under construction four modern tankers, one of which was the largest afloat.[73]

[70] In 1928 there were only three small refineries operating in France; ten years later fifteen plants were producing 88 percent of the nation's needs. See Faure, *La Politique française du pétrole,* pp. 88, 137–138; Étienne Dalemont, *L'Économie pétrolière,* ed. P. H. Frankel (Paris, 1948), p. 218.

[71] INSEE, *Études et conjoncture: L'Industrie française* (1953), pp. 146–147. Actually the capacity of the refineries in France was greater than that of those in Britain, but up to the Second World War the British tended to build their refineries where the oil was extracted rather than at home.

[72] Georges de Gasquet, *L'Industrie française de raffinage du pétrole* (Aix-en-Provence, 1957), p. 57. For the activities of the CFP since the '30's see Rondot, pp. 67 ff.; Étienne Dalemont, *Le Pétrole* (Paris, 1963), pp. 91 ff.

[73] In 1920 the total capacity of the French oil fleet was less than 30,000 tons, but by the end of 1933 it exceeded 400,000 tons; see Robert Cahill, *Economic Conditions in France* (London, 1934), p. 155.

4

The Formation and Program of the
Redressement Français, 1925–1927

A WAVE OF ANXIETY and insecurity swept through the French business community during the mid-1920's. René Duchemin, president of the general employers' association, the Confédération Générale de la Production Française (CGPF), said in his annual speech that 1925 should be marked with "a black gravestone," for it was "a year of material and moral disequilibrium, a year of recession, and in spite of the activity of our industries, a year of ruin." [1] The critical problem facing business was the fall of the franc. Although France experienced growing inflation during and after the war, the situation worsened following the election of the Cartel des Gauches in 1924. The Cartel was unable to stop the collapse of the franc and governments came and went in 1925 and 1926 with a rapidity spectacular even for the Third Republic.

Businessmen on the whole favored some depreciation of the franc to "undervalue" it and give French exports an advantage, but they realized that excessive inflation undermined monetary stability and might precipitate a financial disaster like that of Germany in 1923. Mercier's electric power industry, which depended heavily on capital loans, became concerned when inflation, which made its payment of debts seem easier, also forced banks to raise their mean interest rate from 5 percent in 1918 to more than 10 percent in 1926. Also in 1926, as a result of tightening credit, requests for hydroelectric concessions reached their postwar nadir.[2] This financial instability also seriously hampered Mercier's efforts to raise capital for the embryonic CFP.

Many French producers, including Mercier, looked beyond the fall of the franc and saw the danger of a growing foreign competition, especially from mass-produced American and German goods. They realized that the backwardness of France's creaking industrial plant would be

[1] René-P. Duchemin, *Organisation syndicale patronale en France* (Paris, 1940), p. 17.

[2] Jacques Doreau, *Rapports entre l'état et les sociétés de production–transport–distribution de l'énergie électrique* (Paris, 1928), pp. 30–34. Also see William F. Ogburn and William Jaffé, *The Economic Development of Post-war France: A Survey of Production* (New York, 1929), pp. 161, 260.

exposed once inflation ended. In late 1924 and the first half of 1925 a brief but ominous recession brought a fall in industrial production, a contraction of credit, and a decline in exports.[3]

There was also growing social unrest. In 1926 there were more strikes than there had been even in the turbulent years just after the war.[4] And communism, though it was in fact losing its momentum, seemed to many businessmen to be spreading throughout the French working class. Simultaneously, a number of antiparliamentarian movements sprang into activity. Right-wing extremist groups like the Jeunesses Patriotes, the Faisceau, and an early prototype of the Poujadists, the Fédération des Contribuables, were formed, and the Action Française reached the peak of its postwar popularity.

Mercier, the man of action, could hardly accept this situation passively. His accomplishments in organizing and directing men in business, along with his pride in being a Polytechnician, gave him a confidence which went beyond his own technical field. Like most of his "camarades," he was very conscious of the supposed intellectual and moral superiority of the graduates of "X." Polytechnicians have always taken great pride in belonging to a ruling caste which has a special obligation of social leadership,[5] and Mercier had none of the typical French businessman's inhibitions about entering public life. He believed it was his calling to help rescue his country from its postwar troubles.

In part, this attitude was inspired by Mercier's fellow-Saint-Simonian on the rue de Messine, Albert Petsche. Petsche believed that all politicians were in some way prisoners, either of material self-interest or of sterile ideology, and therefore unfit for the exercise of power.[6] He convinced Mercier that only an apolitical, technical elite could provide the republic with sound and vigorous government.

Another important influence on Mercier at this time was Marshal Lyautey, whose article on the social duties of an officer,[7] a classic of its kind, and career as a colonial administrator in Morocco had made him

---

[3] Ogburn and Jaffé, pp. 91, 99, 112.

[4] Pierre Laroque, *Les Rapports entre patrons et ouvriers* (Paris, 1938), p. 340.

[5] Auguste Detoeuf, *Propos de O. L. Barenton, confiseur, ancien élève de l'École Polytechnique* (Paris, 1960), pp. 193–201, cleverly scoffs at this attitude in an imaginary letter from a patronizing Polytechnician to a colleague from the École Centrale. See also Marcel Prévost, "Polytechnique: idées et souvenirs," *Revue de France*, Jan. 1, 1931, pp. 64–68. A recent study of the social background of graduates of the *grandes écoles* is Alain Girard, *La Réussite sociale en France, ses caractères–ses lois–ses effets*, Institut national d'études démographiques, Cahier No. 38 (Paris, 1961), pp. 165–230.

[6] Mercier, *Albert Petsche*, pp. 48–49.

[7] "Du Rôle social de l'officier," *Revue des deux mondes*, Mar. 15, 1891, pp. 443–459.

an influential figure in certain right-wing circles. After Lyautey retired in 1925, there developed a kind of "Lyautey school," having as its principal ideals those of an "elite" conscious of its "social role," and a reconciliation of social classes through "team spirit." Many prominent businessmen were attracted by these ideals, as well as by certain other aspects of the school, like the emphasis on creativity.[8] One of Lyautey's maxims was, "The soul's joy lies in doing." Mercier had met Lyautey before the war when the Messine group built a utilities subsidiary in Morocco at Lyautey's request, and after 1925 the two men dined frequently together.[9] Mercier thought the venerable Marshal shared some of his Saint-Simonian convictions: "he feels himself driven by a limitless ambition. Not the ordinary ambition of getting ahead which leaves man imprisoned in his personality, but the ambition of accomplishment which projects the individual outside of himself into the act itself."[10] Later Lyautey was to accept Mercier's request to support the latter's reform movement.

The deepening domestic crisis, and a trip to the United States in 1925 transformed Mercier's elitist and activist inclinations into crusading zeal. Late that year he and Petsche traveled to the United States as guests of General Electric. They were much impressed with American production methods and the power and prestige of American businessmen, and they returned convinced that the future of France depended on imitating the American economic model. They decided to initiate a movement for general reform among the "directing classes" of the nation.[11] The younger and more energetic Mercier took charge of the crusade.

Mercier believed the crisis required action by the elite of France to give a new direction to national life. The salient fact in contemporary society, as he saw it, was the rise of the masses, who, driven by emotionalism and materialism, made their power effective though collective action.[12] This kind of power was dangerous to France because the masses

[8] For Lyautey's influence among business leaders, see *Lyautey, Maréchal de France, par les anciens de son équipe,* Cahiers Charles de Foucauld (Vichy, 1954), pp. 191–206; André Maurois, *Marshal Lyautey,* trans. H. Miles (London, 1931), pp. 40–41. One business manager even adapted the ideas of Lyautey's essay for the modern engineer; see Georges Lamirand, *Le Rôle social de l'ingénieur* (Paris, 1937). See also Guillaume de Tarde, *Lyautey, le chef en action* (3rd ed.; Paris, 1959), p. 154.

[9] Mercier's youngest brother, Louis, had served as a diplomatic aide for Lyautey in Morocco and was also a member of the Marshal's circle.

[10] "Lyautey," Mercier papers.

[11] Mercier, *Petsche,* p. 47.

[12] Ernest Mercier, "Réflexions sur l'élite," *Revue des deux mondes,* Feb. 15, 1928, pp. 882–895.

were not prepared for the responsibilities of leadership—they had neither technical nor intellectual training, nor even the proper moral
background. In France, Mercier believed, the phenomenon was aggravated by several special factors: the passionate and dogmatic nature of
popular demands, a relatively backward social situation, fawning politicians, and an ineffectual elite. The French elite, despite its superior
quantity and quality, was impotent when contrasted to its American
counterpart, because it lacked solidarity and purpose, and it shunned
public life as being beneath its dignity. But now, Mercier insisted, it
must proclaim a goal higher than personal satisfaction and must guide
the awakening masses.

The "elite," as he defined it, possessed "dedication without reserve
to the public welfare, to the collectivity, and to the nation"; this gave
it supreme moral authority.[13] One could find the elite in nearly all social categories—among a good many the feeling of dedication had existed since 1914—but Mercier counted most on the business community. Other potential elites had abdicated leadership: the political elite
had submitted to the demagoguery of universal suffrage; the intellectual elite either ignored national affairs or entangled itself in party
politics. There remained only "private business leaders" who retained
the capacity to act creatively and thus held the "levers of command." [14]

The concept was essentially managerial. The true elite of modern
France consisted of "producers" or "creators" who had risen not by
way of "birth or fortune" but by their own "intelligence and talent,"
their "enterprising and audacious spirit." The elite was a "product of
natural selection." [15] Because of their superiority, the business managers had a duty to enter public affairs: "In a society founded on economic liberalism, if the directors of economic life strictly contain
themselves in their professional role, they fail to accomplish their essential duty of moral leadership which rests on the elite of every regime." [16] Moreover, the business elite was, to use Mercier's favorite
word, the only "disinterested" force in French society. Mercier asserted
that most Frenchmen were dominated by political loyalties or material
self-interest, whereas businessmen dealt with all kinds of men, "distin-
guishing them only by their actions and not by their beliefs." [17] Businessmen possessed "the necessary . . . education, technical knowledge,

---

13 *Ibid.*, p. 892.

14 Ernest Mercier, *La Crise et l'élite* (Paris, 1933) , pp. 10–13.

15 Mercier, "Réflexions sur l'élite," p. 892; also Redressement Français, *Compte
rendu de l'assemblée générale du 14 décembre 1927* (Paris, 1927) , p. 11 (hereafter
cited as *Assemblée générale 1927*) .

16 Mercier, *Petsche*, p. 47.

17 Mercier, *Crise et l'élite*, p. 14.

and culture . . . , the indispensable moral training," to be impartial leaders.[18] Armed with technical ability, and free of both petty materialism and political fanaticism, the business elite could provide practical solutions to national problems—and if it did not know the answers, it could find the experts who did. Mercier seemed to think there were simple solutions to all the problems of the nation, which the politicians could never find because they spent too much time quarreling among themselves. He thus ascribed the highest ideals of the Polytechnique to the business elite and thereby probably exaggerated both its competence and its altruism.

Mercier began to think it was the "holy mission" of the business elite to spread the gospel of *rapprochement* among Frenchmen. It would be a new solidarity based on production rather than on politics—as in America, where, he thought, one saw the proof that a modern society could rest on "a community of effort." [19] In the shop or factory Americans learned that the general welfare depended on strengthening collaboration, which increased production and led to a higher standard of living for all. Rising productivity gave the masses the opportunity to acquire property and education, taught the virtues of order and mutual assistance, and above all, brought general prosperity.

In December, 1925, Mercier set about forming a movement to "gather the elite and educate the masses." [20] It was to be called the Redressement Français. First, he enlisted a small number of influential leaders to form a temporary but appropriately named "board of directors." He wanted the support of individuals ("men of good will") who would work actively, rather than of organizations. At times, indeed, his appeals to friends and colleagues were so vigorous that he lost potential backers. The original board of directors, seventeen in all, consisted mainly of business managers, but there were also several editors and academicians. With one exception, all the business leaders represented the electrical industry; almost all were Polytechnicians associated with the management of the Messine group.[21] Among the editors there were two spokesmen for the business community—Émile Mireaux and Jacques Bardoux, directors of the Société d'Études et d'Informations

[18] *Assemblée générale 1927*, p. 11.

[19] *Ibid.*, pp. 10–11.

[20] From a brochure reprinted by Mennevée, *Les Documents politiques*, November, 1926, p. 475.

[21] These managers were: Jacques Level, a close friend of Mercier's, who was later president of the great chemical and metallurgical company Péchiney, and a director of Lyonnaise des Eaux; Arthur Bommelaer, a manager of the Sté. Alsacienne; Paul Eschwege, who represented the Rothschilds in the electrical industry; and Eugène Geoffroy, Paul Nivard, and Jean Siegler, all Messine managers. The only one not connected with the Messine group was the financial expert Jacques Lebel.

Économiques, which was the organ of the steel industry's trade association, the Comité des Forges—and two conservative publishers—the Comte de Fels, owner-director of the staid *Revue de Paris,* and Max Leclerc, the financier-editor (Armand Colin). The academicians were distinguished in several fields: Professors Émile Bourgeois (history), J-L. Faure (medicine), Louis Germain-Martin (economics), and Achille Mestre (law). Raphaël Alibert, who completed the board, had formerly been associated with the Action Française and was a member of the republic's top administrative agency, the Conseil d'État.

During 1926 this vanguard tried to rally the elite to the cause, partly by the distribution of brochures,[22] partly by personal contact. It directed its appeal to important businessmen, ranking civil servants, academicians, writers, and leaders of military and veterans' organizations.

The main task of the new organization was to draw up a detailed and comprehensive program of reform. To do this, Mercier and the board of directors took a simple and technocratic course: they asked experts in business and other fields to tell them what they thought was wrong with the nation and what they thought should be done. The experts responded enthusiastically to this flattering appeal for advice. Some 223 technicians, organized in study committees, labored four months and prepared 127 reports, covering a wide range of problems.

The reports of the committees were edited, and published in 1927 in thirty-five volumes under the title *Cahiers du Redressement Français.* The series, which was presented to the public as a "citizen's library," was printed in an edition of 40,000 copies, half of which were sold or otherwise distributed within the year.[23] Given the wide variety of opinion among the two hundred experts, one would hardly expect harmonious reports from the committees. Mercier had tried to create a spirit of national rapprochement by assembling a heterogeneous group of notables—including such men as his old friend from the navy, Admiral Lacaze, the executive Edmond Giscard d'Estaing (whose son Valéry became Minister of Finance in the Fifth Republic), and the left-wing economist Francis Delaisi. Thus there were, almost inevitably, unresolved disagreements within certain committees—such as those studying education, trade, and parliamentary reform. These differences foreshadowed later divisions within the Redressement. Mercier himself did not fully endorse all the recommendations contained in the cahiers,

---

[22] The Redressement's early brochures were reproduced by Mennevée in *Les Documents politiques,* November, 1926, pp. 468–476.

[23] *Assemblée générale 1927,* p. 2. See the Bibliography for a list of the cahiers and the contributors.

since he was responsible for only a small part of the series. Nor was there any attempt to work out a consistent program that unified the various cahiers. At best, each report was internally consistent. As a total program, they contain obvious contradictions. For example, though the aim of the program generally was to reduce the role of the state and lower its budget, the proposed reforms for agriculture, national defense, social assistance, and colonial development called for an increase in the state's activities, with a corresponding increase in budgetary allotment. The Redressement pragmatists, apparently unaware of the implications of their proposals, recommended hundreds of changes, including constitutional tinkering and economic revolution.

The only real unity to this unwieldy array of rather unimaginative suggestions lay in a special reforming spirit, a kind of technocratic zeal which undertook to modernize the government and the economy by introducing efficiency, productivity, and rationality—not, indeed, far different from the sort of technocratic streamlining that we have witnessed in France in recent decades.[24]

One Redressement handbook explained why the organization based its program on *rationalisation*—the modernization of production, which could lead to a modernization of the entire economy. The status of a nation in the twentieth century, it said, depended upon its industrial might: "The slightest slowing-down in the nation's industrial effort manifests itself in losses or suffering at home as well as in advantages gratuitously conceded abroad." In the intensely competitive modern world, the standing of a nation was no longer judged by "the eloquence of its representatives, the gentleness of its manners, or the nobility of its traditions," but by what the people did "to increase their power, their well-being, and the vitality and efficiency of their collective labor." In this universal competition, France was a "backward nation" in danger of dropping to the rank of "a second-rate people." [25] The cause lay, according to the handbook, in the last half-century when the leaders of France turned from the real problems of modern life to a preoccupation with purely political issues. And only by reorganizing the economy would France bring itself back to its proper standing as a great power.

As Mercier himself wrote in one of the cahiers: "One law brings all

---

[24] For a study of the problems raised by technocracy in France since the Second World War, see the two volumes by Jean Meynaud: *Technocratie et politique,* Études de science politique, No. 2 (Lausanne, 1960) , and *La Technocratie, mythe ou réalité?* (Paris, 1964) .

[25] See Lucien Romier, *Le Redressement Français: idées très simples pour les Français* (Paris, 1928) , pp. 8–11, 59. This handbook is a popularized summary of the Redressement program.

nations under its discipline, the law of production." America was evidence of the good that would come from industrial modernization; there one saw almost an "ideal industrial organization" in which mass production reduced costs and enabled producers to lower prices and pay higher wages.[26] Henry Ford had realized that by taking advantage of cheap, growing production, one could raise wages without limit and create one's own market, giving the workers the opportunity to have domestic comforts, to own the cars they themselves produced, and even to invest in the company. But Ford insisted, of course, that consumers accept a uniform product—the black Model T. It was the mass production of standardized products that permitted business concentration, and enabled centralized plants like General Electric to establish impressive industrial research centers. As a result, Mercier observed, in the near future America would utilize its low prices to develop its exports—in the face of which France must itself do something to reorganize its economy.

Germany, too, Mercier pointed out, was making great strides toward modernization.[27] Big business had exploited the 1923 inflation, and German banks, with limited available credit, had forced further cartelization, a process in which the state had assisted by lowering commercial taxes. The working class, seemingly docile, had accepted a "Prussian type" of industrial concentration which brought temporary mass unemployment—for the trend toward cartelization meant not only a reduction in operating capital and costs but also a reduction in personnel. The result, Mercier predicted, would be "an economic aggression of unexpected proportions" from across the Rhine.

Clearly, a backward French economy could hardly compete with such industrial rivals; it must modernize. The trouble with the French was that they were too undisciplined and individualistic. They operated too many small enterprises, which meant higher production and research costs, a wasteful diversity of products, and large cash reserves. There was too much mutual distrust and business secrecy, too little cooperation and innovation. France had an inactive internal market, an obsolete commercial organization, mediocre research facilities, and investment habits which ignored business. Moreover, "state shackles" restricted certain areas of the economy, and politics in labor unions and trade associations divided those who should collaborate.

[26] Ernest Mercier, "La Production, le travail et les échanges," in *La Production et le travail*, Cahiers du Redressement Français, Series I, No. 14, pp. 9, 11.

[27] The Redressement showed keen interest in Germany's industrial modernization and eagerly listened to the address of the German economic expert Julius Hirsch: *La Rationalisation de la production* (Paris, 1927). For an excellent study of this economic change see: Robert A. Brady, *The Rationalization Movement in German Industry* (Berkeley, 1933).

Mercier's solution was: industrial concentration, standardization of products, and higher productivity. He proposed that industrial reorganization in France be "flexible"—he wanted no slavish imitation of America that would transform France into "a republic of termites"—but the methods of mass production and plant concentration could be put to use in almost all areas of French industry. Even the manufacturers of luxury goods needed some streamlining, such as pooling of research facilities, and such industries as automobile manufacturing, metallurgy, chemicals, textiles, leather, and clothing required thorough reorganization.[28] The ideal way to reform was to merge the multiple producers within a single industry into one economic unit. (Mercier was undoubtedly thinking here of the success of the Union d'Électricité.) But since this step was not always possible, or even desirable, he recommended "intermediate steps" like "simple commercial selling agreements" or "selling cartels."[29] And since he had an overwhelming confidence in the mystique of production and the good will of businessmen, he foresaw no evil results from this suppression of competition. Indeed, the new American type of producer-consumer community made it impossible: "Mass production necessitates active consumption—increasingly active consumption—which can only be obtained by the reduction of prices and the improvement of the quality of products: it is this which creates between producers and consumers a positive community of interests that would automatically prevent production from abusing the practical absence of effective competition" (ibid., p. 20). For a "modern producer," increasing production rather than competition was an adequate economic regulator.

A Redressement handbook stated: "Individualism is very nice; it's very pleasant. But it's obsolete."[30] Small French producers with inadequate credit could not possibly compete with monolithic foreign concerns which had their own banks and research centers and could buy and sell on the world market. Economic freedom was, of course, Mercier knew, dear to the small- and medium-sized employers, but he thought that their sentiments could be altered by propaganda among this "unquestionably intelligent" group.[31] If that failed, the intransigent ones were certain to be eliminated by competition. The marketing system, too, suffered from the inefficiencies of individualism, and here again stubborn independent merchants would be overwhelmed by large producers selling through large retailers. The small shopkeeper

[28] Ibid., pp. 42–46.
[29] Ernest Mercier, "Les Conséquences sociales de la rationalisation en France," in L'Aspect social de la rationalisation, Cahiers du Redressement Français, Series I, No. 10, p. 4.
[30] Romier, Idées très simples, p. 62.
[31] Mercier, L'Aspect social, p. 21.

would either participate in the streamlined marketing system, that is, become a branch distributor for the new retailers, or he would disappear.

Mercier, seemingly insensitive to the magnitude of the changes he urged, was confident that the new wealth that would be produced would amply compensate for the loss of a way of life for France's multitude of small producers and merchants. Like many engineers, he justified his dedication to efficiency by consecrating it as a moral principle: "*Rationalisation* . . . must always be accompanied by a rise in general morality. Nothing conforms more to the moral law than the elimination of waste, the economizing of human labor . . . making it easier, more productive. It pays the finest homage to human dignity." [32]

Clearly, the Redressement was a big business movement, which, under the guise of a directing elite, intended to develop the big at the expense of the little. The Redressement claimed that industrial concentration would actually promote a "renaissance" of the rural family workshop because mass production required these artisans to finish the "elementary pieces of production." The real competitor of the artisan, medium-sized industry, would disappear in the course of modernization.[33] "To win the industrial battle, let us renounce our individualism" [34] was a progressive slogan, but it also sanctioned a drive to power by the managerial elite.

Mercier wrote glowingly of the good social effects of economic modernization.[35] He was certain that the working class, with its increased purchasing power and improved living conditions, would be the chief beneficiary of his plan. Workers would receive expanded government assistance in the form of public housing and social insurance, which would be paid for by increased government revenue from a growing economy. Although the plan for industrial reorganization was supposedly apolitical, Mercier pointed out that it would help to battle the growing influence of communism in the poor suburbs which had been especially hard hit by postwar living conditions. Of course, modernization required the cooperation of labor in order to succeed, but the rise of the corporation would make such cooperation easier. The old class struggle would disappear in this modern form of industrial organization, for here the employer was a salaried manager, and the worker became an owner by purchasing shares. Mercier's dream depended upon

[32] *Ibid.*, p. 40.

[33] See Auguste Detoeuf, *La Réorganisation industrielle,* Cahiers du Redressement Français, Series I, No. 7, pp. 20–21, 32–34.

[34] Romier, *Idées très simples,* p. 57.

[35] This next section is based on Mercier, *L'Aspect social,* pp. 22–37; also Romier, *Idées très simples,* pp. 15–36, 71–77.

the realization of economic solidarity in which workers raised output and employers passed on reduced costs in the form of higher wages.

When Mercier began meeting strong opposition from both French business and labor, he was ready with answers. To those who said the assembly line destroyed worker initiative and intelligence, Mercier replied that only a few, "the weakest physically and the least gifted intellectually," did routine jobs.[36] The others organized the tasks, cared for the machines, and checked for precision. Furthermore, the assembly-line worker suffered less fatigue and had more energy for pleasure and education than the ordinary worker. Under the new system, industry would help workers to use their leisure more profitably by giving them sporting and cultural organizations; and in the plant it would encourage them to think creatively about their jobs (the suggestion box, for example). The "assembly-line mentality" would be only temporary, according to his plan, because mechanization would soon transform the worker from "a cog in a machine" to a controller of the machine. Nor would unemployment be a problem, for, at worst, it would be temporary. France, indeed, had little to fear, owing to its manpower shortage caused by the war and its comparatively feeble industrial productivity. If unemployment did occur, alien workers could be sent to the colonies, or the excess labor could be used to help "recolonize" the depopulated rural interior. Here, too, Mercier seemed unconcerned with the human suffering that would result from his production scheme, by even temporary unemployment or the mass relocation of labor.

The Redressement's vast program of modernization was tantamount to economic revolution, the leaders of which would be the managerial elite. Only they could bridge the gap between the dynamic and static sectors of the economy. Small producers could be frightened into modernizing by being told of the perils of foreign competition and mass production, and persuasion of a similar sort could also be used to alter "the traditional ideas of patriarchal industry" and to convince these old-fashioned employers to pay higher wages and production bonuses.[37] Convincing workers that raising output would not lower wages was, perhaps, a "more delicate" problem. But the real task of modernization rested with big business itself, for it alone could initiate the movement by establishing producers' agreements or cartels as "preludes" to actual mergers. Eventually, the state might assist the managers in this revolutionary effort by creating a ministry of national economy to coordinate their efforts, and by endorsing industrial concentration.

Mercier himself was never less than confident about the appeals of

---

[36] Mercier, *L'Aspect social*, p. 22.
[37] Mercier, *Production et travail*, p. 58.

his program—much less of its value. But even one of his Redressement colleagues expressed certain misgivings:

> There is no country . . . where it is more difficult to sell the same thing to two clients. No country, consequently, where it is harder to achieve organization or *rationalisation*. . . . Prudence and parsimony, horror of uniformity on the part of the client, excessive desire for originality by the manufacturer —all these characteristics could be altered. One might consider them faults, but they have really been our genius. They have made France's fortune and must be preserved. Thus it is not a question of destroying them, but only of limiting the excesses which up to now have not appeared dangerous.[38]

The Redressement's plan for economic modernization had, of course, an overwhelming industrial bias, but it also sought agricultural reform. The cahier edited by the farm expert Michel Augé-Laribé condemned "the anti-agricultural policy" that had been followed since the 1914–1918 war and proposed to stop the rural exodus by improving rural working and living conditions.[39] In addition, the report suggested that agricultural production could be increased by introducing scientific farming methods and stimulating competition—the latter in part by removing certain export prohibitions and even lowering some protective tariffs which had long kept agricultural prices outside the natural workings of supply and demand. Augé-Laribé saw rural France supplying industry with a growing internal market. There was, certainly, an implied contradiction between the Redressement's agricultural and industrial programs: Augé-Laribé tried to stem the rural exodus, at the same time that Mercier aggravated it by calling for higher industrial wages that would draw the farmers to the big cities.

The proposals for the reform of international trade stressed European economic interdependence, favored international producers' agreements, and firmly opposed protectionism. Francis Delaisi, who edited the cahier on international commerce, urged Europeans to restore the free trade areas that they enjoyed before 1914. Industrial concentration on a national scale, Delaisi also recommended, would make protectionist policies unnecessary and allow the gradual reduction and perhaps the elimination of tariffs.[40] Another adviser, Arthur Bommelaer, a manager of the Sté. Alsacienne, advocated international producers' agreements as the solution to the disorganization of European

[38] Detoeuf, *Réorganisation industrielle*, pp. 11–13.

[39] Michel Augé-Laribé, "Organisation rationnelle de l'industrie agricole," in *Agriculture*, Cahiers du Redressement Français, Series I, No. 5, p. 51.

[40] Francis Delaisi, "Les Entraves au commerce," in *Échanges commerciaux*, Cahiers du Redressement Français, Series I, No. 13, pp. 25–36.

trade. Such business arrangements, he suggested, harmed no one; production would be equitably distributed, prices would be stabilized, and the dumping of goods on the market curtailed. Although these agreements were to be drafted by private businessmen, they could be extended under the aegis of the League of Nations.[41]

Colonial economic problems occupied other Redressement experts, who recommended closer integration of the economies of metropolitan and colonial France. In this plan—scarcely in accord with the principles of free trade—metropolitan France would provide technical and social assistance to the colonies, which in turn would reserve most of their products for the French market. The program of colonial development would be preferably a joint private and government effort.[42]

On the important subject of political modernization the Redressement advocated applying the principles of technocracy to the structure of the Third Republic. The typical technocrat, as one authority has written, views the state not as an expression of the popular will or the class struggle, but as an affair to be managed, or as a service to be operated efficiently. The nation is no longer considered a human, geographic, or historical entity, but an economic resource that should yield optimum productivity.[43] To this end the Redressement technocrats designed reforms to free government from party politics and to give the experts a role in determining policy. This technocratic point of view was awkwardly joined to an obsolete nineteenth-century Liberal concept of government: "The state has no value in itself. The state exists only in order to fulfill a practical function . . . to guarantee the maintenance and progress of the national collectivity . . . and to favor the free and peaceful development of individual activity. . . . There is only one means of strengthening the state, which is, to limit its function." [44] The Redressement envisioned a strictly limited state, pruned of many of its economic functions, more independent of political parties, and assisted by technicians drawn from the civil service and private life.

Raphaël Alibert (who was later to become Pétain's adviser on constitutional matters at Vichy), headed the Redressement committee on

[41] Arthur Bommelaer, "Ententes internationales," *ibid.*, pp. 136–142.

[42] Édouard Payen *et al.*, *La Mise en valeur de notre domaine colonial*, Cahiers du Redressement Français, Series I, No. 32, p. 131. During the '20's the Redressement actively aided the campaign for the development of the colonies. The elegant periodical *Monde colonial illustré*, partly owned by the Redressement, publicized this program.

[43] Jacques Ellul, *The Technological Society*, trans. John Wilkinson (New York, 1964), pp. 264–265.

[44] Romier, *Idées très simples*, pp. 124–126.

political reform. On the whole, his report expressed Mercier's views, but it departed from Mercier's thinking by deploring the state's excessive role in the economy. The state acted, the report said, as industrialist and merchant by operating the tobacco monopoly, and served as banker by making its post office clerks into bank tellers. Furthermore, all state-run enterprises were badly managed, hence unprofitable. "The state does not know how to choose managers, and if it finds them, it pays them badly," and as a result, "private industry attracts worthwhile men by its greater advantages." [45] Worst of all, state monopolies created a force of poorly paid civil servants who introduced politics into the fabric of the administration. The remedy was to have the state transfer to private control many of its economic services, including supervision of the distribution of electricity and the gathering of economic statistics. Alibert's proposal to strip government of its economic functions, though quite representative of business thinking,[46] was on the whole the most reactionary aspect of the entire Redressement program, and it was quite unpalatable to Mercier.

Alibert's committee claimed further that the republic's administrative agencies suffered from political manipulation and from a general lack of independence. They were victims of the overwhelming power of parliament, which made administrative directors the political pawns of changing cabinets. The Redressement technocrats proposed a system of permanent undersecretaries of state who would provide the administration with technical advice and stability: "The nomination of the undersecretary of state should be clearly free of all politics: a technician is necessary for this position. The law will thus exclude from this post men who have only political qualifications; it will allow only high civil servants, members of the Conseil d'État, or men taken from outside public service because of their competence." [47] In general, the Redressement had great respect for civil servants of the higher ranks and advocated higher salaries and greater power for them in government.

A special cahier, also prepared under Alibert's direction, dealt with parliament. The crux of the Third Republic's difficulties, according to the Redressement political experts, was the Chamber of Deputies—it was at once too powerful and too dependent on the electorate. The legislative branch dominated the other branches of government as well as

---

[45] *La Réforme administrative, organisation politique et administrative,* Cahiers du Redressement Français, Series I, No. 27, pp. 16, 67.

[46] See Marguerite Perrot, *La Monnaie et l'opinion publique en France et en Angleterre de 1924 à 1936,* Cahiers de la Fondation nationale des sciences politiques, No. 65 (Paris, 1955), pp. 181–186.

[47] *Réforme administrative,* p. 77. For a comparison, see Walter Sharp, *The French Civil Service: Bureaucracy in Transition* (New York, 1931), pp. 532–534.

the administration, and in this way could consider as part of its domain all aspects of political life from minute local quarrels to national issues, and could have a say even in legal and administrative problems. But instead of recognizing the responsibilities of their power, the deputies responded to every whim of the electorate; thus they forfeited their independence and upset the smooth functioning of the governmental process. Inevitably, also, with so much power and so much pressure, there was corruption.

The cahier on parliamentary reform proposed to place severe limitations on the power of the Chamber and to free the deputy from the voter. This it proposed to do by reducing the number of deputies and extending the term of office to six years, with half the Chamber being elected every three years.[48] To meet the increasingly numerous and complex demands on government, especially in the economic field, deputies were to be given the benefit of technical advice—by experts who would sit in on parliamentary committees. These experts would provide general background on legislative proposals and would also draft and defend the proposals in public. Given a deliberative and not merely an advisory role, they could intervene in committee disputes. Such a system, "the collaboration of national forces with parliament," [49] would vastly improve the quality of parliamentary work, making it speedier and clearer and less superficial. Other reforms concerning interpellation and budget procedure would curtail parliamentary deliberation and further reduce the Chamber's power.

Alibert's political experts did not, however, propose to alter parliament's structure by including representatives of economic organizations. The Redressement committee rejected reforms of the "corporative" type that granted employers' associations or labor unions legal authority, or made membership in them obligatory, or introduced them into parliament through some means of "professional representation." These experts foresaw two disturbing possibilities if such organizations were granted political power: either they would disrupt government by bringing "narrow interest oligarchies" into it, or else political parties would absorb and pervert them.

Here again, the Redressement's reforms centered not on trade associations or labor unions but on "representative professional leaders." It urged the appointment of members of the economic elite to the Con-

---

[48] *La Réforme parlementaire,* Cahiers du Redressement Français, Series I, No. 25, pp. 47–68. This report also criticized the 1919 electoral law for promoting artificial electoral alliances which hindered the development of strong political parties, but the issue of electoral reform was one instance of irreconcilable disagreement among the experts.

[49] *Ibid.,* pp. 84–85.

seil d'État, to parliamentary committees, even to parliament itself: "It would be . . . extremely useful and utterly just to introduce into parliament, certain persons of note who have neither the leisure nor the inclination to plunge into the electoral fray. Their presence would enhance the prestige of parliamentary proceedings; especially since these men would not owe their position to an electoral victory too often purchased at the price of degrading concessions, thus preserving intact their personal prestige and independence." [50] Political power evidently could corrupt economic interest groups but not "persons of note." The implication is that these business reformers, not wanting to jeopardize their existing influence in government, shied away from such radical ideas as giving official recognition to organized economic interests.

Finally, to strengthen the executive, the Redressement's advisers urged the consolidation of certain ministries and an expansion of the premier's power. They made no attempt, however, to alter the position of the president of the republic and rejected as "dangerous" the idea of a popularly elected president. This view may have reflected the business elite's fear of the masses rather than its declared fear of authoritarian rule.

When asked if any politicians were members of his organization, Mercier replied, "No. . . . We are outside and above parties. As good, hard-working Frenchmen, we will propose our reforms to anyone who wants to support them and we will defend anyone who will support them." [51] Nevertheless, though it declared itself aloof from party politics, the Redressement embarked upon a program of political action. An early brochure stated that the group "has no politicians in its midst, so that its members would be liberated from any personal political aim. But it maintains close contact with all politicians determined to follow it. It will exercise great care to choose, for the next renewal of the Chamber of Deputies . . . candidates who seem to merit its confidence." [52]

From its inception, the Redressement professed a keen interest in the approaching 1928 elections. But to those who might be suspicious of its motives, it protested that it was not an "ephemeral, hypocritical or occult organization, for it acted in the open." The Redressement's early brochures vaguely mentioned that the "principal aim" of the organization was "the establishment of a large party . . . guaranteeing governmental stability," and "the disappearance of the old parties,

[50] *Réforme administrative*, p. 35.
[51] *Monde colonial illustré*, April, 1927, p. 75.
[52] *Les Documents politiques*, November, 1926, p. 470.

which are only unnatural cadres imposed on political life by irresponsible electoral committees." [53] Throughout its existence, the Redressement operated with this fundamental contradiction—an avowed independence from and contempt for party politics, along with the goal of political action.

Given the political nature of France, where a multiplicity of parties on the Center and Right hinders effective government, the technocratic approach of the Redressement's program must be granted a certain merit—despite the inconsistencies with which it was first presented. Where government often falls into the hands of badly divided coalition ministries, apolitical experts can provide the authority. Moreover, the Redressement's program was far from being reactionary or unattractive. It accurately assessed France's needs in the '20's by urging economic modernization, social reform, constitutional reform, and a more international point of view.

At the same time, however, the program showed a one-sided concern with the economic interests of big business, and a certain callousness toward French tradition and human feelings. It also overestimated the appeal of Henry Ford to Frenchmen. The Redressement's spirit was definitely elitist and antidemocratic—since it is a characteristic of the technocratic doctrine that it doubts the competence of the people to govern themselves. The talented or the trained, the competent elite, are the proper directors of the nation; neither the masses nor their representatives in parliament can provide strong and enlightened leadership.

The depreciation of the franc, which had been the main stimulus for the creation of the Redressement, reached such dangerous proportions in 1926 that the new group felt compelled to set aside preparing its program and take action. It launched a campaign at the height of the crisis in July for immediate de facto stabilization. It issued a pamphlet entitled "The Battle of the Franc," in which it charged that incompetent governments had provoked the financial panic by their postwar fiscal encroachments on capital and savings; the Left in particular was to blame for threatening to "make the rich pay." [54] Simply put, the monetary instability, so the pamphlet said, resulted from a budgetary deficit which in turn was caused by excessive government spending and an oppressive fiscal system.

[53] *Ibid.*, pp. 470–472.
[54] L. Charles-Bellet, *La Bataille du franc, réflexions d'un producteur* (2nd ed.; Paris, 1928), pp. 4–18. Cf. Comte de Fels, "Le Redressement Français," *Revue de Paris,* May 1, 1926, pp. 5–19, and July 15, 1926, pp. 241–257. Since Mercier immediately repudiated these articles for their blatant attack on "state socialism," they should not be considered as accurate reflections of the Redressement's program.

Since parliament could not meet the problem, the Redressement suggested a technocratic remedy—the creation of a special council composed of private individuals chosen by the president of the republic and the Conseil d'État. It would work with the government and the Bank of France to "impose not propose" stabilization by means of economic decrees.[55] The Redressement also advocated reduced spending, administrative reorganization, and tax reform—the last being especially important in order to correct allegedly abusive taxes which subverted "wealth in formation" by destroying capital or driving it abroad.

Mercier went beyond mere pamphleteering, however, in his efforts to bring about the formation of a Poincaré government in July 1926. Working with Deputy Maurice Petsche, Albert Petsche's son, the Redressement apparently helped to organize more than two hundred members of the Chamber to petition President Doumergue in favor of Poincaré.[56] Mercier later wrote that "the movement was strong enough within the parliamentary milieu to help bring about the advent of the Poincaré government." [57] Actually, the Redressement's influence, though real enough, was only a small factor in the recall of Poincaré. But the confidence generated by Poincaré's return to power in late July stopped the inflationary spiral, and by November he had achieved de facto stabilization.

According to Mercier, the Redressement was greeted with growing enthusiasm during its first months. Once the Poincaré government had ended the financial panic, however, the organization grew more slowly. Its peak of popular interest had been reached and passed in 1926. The early organizational period culminated in a gathering of notables at the Redressement's "National Congress of Metropolitan and Colonial Organization" held in April, 1927, where the experts' reports were reviewed and approved. The climax came at the formal closing session held in the amphitheater of the Sorbonne. On the last evening, hundreds of spectators assembled to hear the closing speeches and to see the celebrated sponsors of the movement. Among those who publicly endorsed the new organization were: from the military, Marshal Lyautey and Admiral Lacaze; from business, René Duchemin, president of the CGPF, and Henri de Peyerimhoff, president of the coal industry's trade association, the Comité des Houillères; from agriculture, the Marquis de Vogüé, president of the Société des Agriculteurs de France; plus numerous academicians, religious leaders, ambas-

55 Charles-Bellet, p. 26.
56 Beau de Loménie, *Les Responsabilités des dynasties bourgeoises,* IV, 237.
57 "Vita," Mercier papers. See also *Cahiers de l'impartial Français,* Feb. 7, 1928.

sadors, and high-ranking civil servants.[58] Although Mercier had called his movement strictly apolitical, the Poincaré government sent a minister and the darling of the technocrats, André Tardieu, to demonstrate its support. The honorary president of the Redressement was a Polytechnician who had become a national hero—Marshal Foch, who was one of the movement's most devoted and powerful patrons.[59] Foch declared in the closing speech: "It is not sufficient to conceive and formulate intentions. It is necessary to realize them." [60] Unfortunately for Mercier, his movement was unable to live up to Foch's admonition.

[58] "Comité de patronage," Mercier papers.

[59] See *Redressement Français: Bulletin mensuel*, April, 1929. (Hereafter cited as *Bulletin*).

[60] *Ibid.*, May, 1927, p. 31.

5

The Frustrations of the
Redressement Français, 1927–1932

To be powerful, a movement must unite the elites and attract the masses; thus it must respond to popular aspirations."[1] After the Redressement's first national assembly in April, 1927, it prepared to disseminate its program on a mass basis. To symbolize a rapprochement of national elites, the original board of directors had included industrialists, academicians, publishers, and a government administrator. This board gradually changed composition as the Redressement grew, adding a few officials from farm and artisan associations, but the new faces usually resembled the old. Business managers, mostly Polytechnicians from the electrical, chemical, petroleum, and metallurgical industries, predominated. Later a factory foreman, a bank employee, and a coppersmith were added to a greatly enlarged board, but none of the three had any importance in organized labor and their presence indicated no more than a perfunctory representation of labor. Moreover, this board, which met monthly, only nominally directed the organization.

The real power lay in a small Comité de Direction, which, Mercier said, was so "disinterested" that it was "the wall" which protected the organization from possible charges of venality.[2] As this committee evolved, it included the key members of the original board of directors; other business managers like Marcel Champin (who succeeded Mercier as president in 1932) ; Mercier's wife and his brother Gustave; plus two members of the staff, the political editor Henri Cacaud and the general secretary Paul Duléry. But the member of this executive committee who gave the movement intellectual stature and enjoyed authority second only to Mercier was Lucien Romier. He was the Redressement's chief spokesman and most prominent personality. Romier joined the movement late in 1927 after leaving his position as editor-in-chief of *Le Figaro*. This talented historian and journalist also wrote what has been called "the breviary of generations of students of politi-

---

[1] Quoted in *Les Documents politiques,* November, 1926, p. 473.
[2] *Assemblée générale 1927,* p. 8.

cal science"—a volume of essays entitled *Explication de notre temps*.[3] He was a former editor of the business daily, the *Journée industrielle,* and a contributor to *Le Temps,* and he commanded great respect in the highest political circles.

Around this nucleus, "this team," as Mercier described the executive committee and the board of directors, a national organization was built. The focus of activity where Mercier's own interests lay was the metropolitan area surrounding Paris. The Redressement established committees, composed of local notables, in most of the communes of the department of the Seine. These groups studied problems such as housing, education, and recreation. In addition, special rural meetings, the *Loisirs au village,* were held in the countryside around Paris. To serve this critical area, the Redressement published a small weekly paper called *La Région parisienne.* Roving teams of lecturers equipped with movie projectors and phonographs toured these communes and villages showing films and discussing the Redressement's program. Beyond the Paris region, an effort was made to construct autonomous provincial centers. These groups were locally financed and had little contact with the central organization except that their officers met in Paris twice annually for national assemblies. As an organization, the Redressement's strength was clearly located in Paris, the suburbs, and the surrounding communities. By the end of 1927 it possessed 10,000 dues-paying members and 53 committees in the Paris region, plus 82 provincial centers.[4]

In 1926 the movement began publishing an official monthly *Bulletin* which analyzed current events and presented organizational news.[5] The cover of the magazine depicted—as a symbol of national regeneration—a wounded Gaul rising from the ground to rejoin the battle. This periodical was distributed without charge to the nation's elite, and excerpts were regularly published in some two hundred newspapers throughout France.

In addition to a national organization and two official publications, the Redressement used other means to enlist popular support. The cahiers were either given to distinguished national leaders or sold publicly. Study committees met periodically and produced reports which were published in a second series of cahiers. The Redressement also acquired the services of "men of action": journalists, lecturers, and officials of various pressure groups. Among the most prominent were

[3] Robert Aron, *Histoire de Vichy, 1940–1944* (Paris, 1954) , p. 379.

[4] *Assemblée générale 1927,* pp. 2–4. See also *Journée industrielle,* Dec. 16, 1927.

[5] According to its own estimates, there were usually about 25,000 to 30,000 copies of the *Bulletin,* and 30,000 to 40,000 copies of the *Région parisienne* published.

the writers Pierre Dominique, José Germain, and René Hubert; the syndicalist theoretician Hubert Lagardelle; the veterans' leader Jean Goy; and the founder of the Catholic employers' federation, Joseph Zamanski.

The Redressement also subsidized various periodicals through its agency, the Société Anonyme de Propagande et d'Éditions (SAPE).[6] One of SAPE's publications was the distinguished business monthly, the *Revue industrielle,* which after 1926 carried a political editorial by Henri Cacaud. About the same time, the ladies' magazine *Minerva* appeared; it mixed Redressement ideas with fashion news and theater criticism. *Nos Plaisirs,* also published by SAPE, was a family and veterans' magazine which campaigned to make ex-servicemen more active politically. The Redressement was also half-owner of the aristocratic *Monde colonial illustré.*[7]

Obviously, this extensive publishing program was expensive, but at least initially the Redressement was immensely wealthy. Its assets were estimated at 40 million francs (or well over a million dollars) in 1926.[8] Since the membership fees were fairly modest, they clearly did not support the activities. Rather, various private companies and business organizations contributed large annual subsidies—sometimes in excess of 50,000 francs.[9] Who actually financed the Redressement cannot be determined accurately, but probably the principal contributors were electrical, metallurgical, steel, and petroleum interests, as well as certain investment banks. As money was needed, Mercier simply asked individual firms and trade associations for it; this method netted a good deal at first, but it became less remunerative when repeated, especially after the movement lost its initial impetus.

The Redressement was distinctive among big business organizations because of its strong appeal for ex-servicemen. Its president was a

[6] See Henri Cacaud, "Histoire du Redressement Français," Mercier papers. This brief history, which was prepared in 1955 for Mme Mercier's memorial volume for her husband, was never published. (Hereafter cited as Cacaud, "Histoire.")

[7] Mercier's reputation for subsidizing the press almost involved him in the *Quotidien* scandal of 1926. According to the *Grand Guignol* (No. 36, 1927, pp. 74–78), Mercier was approached by the director of *Le Quotidien* for financial aid, and refused, since he expected the imminent collapse of the paper.

[8] *Les Documents politiques,* November, 1926, p. 467.

[9] Interviews with former Redressement leaders. The organization's finances were publicly exposed during the government investigation of the petroleum industry in 1927. Robert Cayrol admitted that Marcel Champin had asked the Chambre Syndicale des Pétroles, of which he was president, for money to support the Redressement. Cayrol testified that the petroleum association eventually refused to give the subsidy on the grounds that trade associations should not mix in politics—although he said he himself believed that such contributions by private companies were legitimate; see *Commission d'enquête sur les pétroles,* p. 145.

much decorated war hero, and the name "Redressement Français" or "French Renovation" expressed both a modernizing and a patriotic spirit. The most typical supporters were fifty-year-old industrialists who had fought as officers in the Great War. At meetings members wore tricolor armbands, and the speakers were frequently prominent military leaders.

With such a broad appeal, the Redressement naturally had a certain looseness. It was not a monolithic organization in which all members or supporters agreed with the views expressed in the official publications. Decisions were made by an executive committee dominated by Mercier and Romier, and official Redressement policy clearly reflected the attitudes of big business, on which the group depended for both leadership and financial support. One director later described the organization as "a group of industrialists who gathered around them men of good will of all types." [10] The Redressement was, in other words, a propaganda arm of the progressive industrial elite, which hoped to sell its ideas to the nation. Therein lay its fundamental problem, for to become an effective national movement, it somehow had to escape this narrow oligarchical character.

Mercier's movement never in fact achieved the first step toward becoming a mass movement, because it was unsuccessful even in extending its influence throughout the business community. From the beginning it made almost no attempt to enlist the support of small- and medium-sized producers, but concentrated its attention on the industrial elite. It is important in this regard to consider, first, the appeal of the Redressement as an organization, and then its program of economic modernization, since the latter proved more attractive to French captains of industry than the former.

True, the movement had got off to a brilliant start, attracting men and money from big business, but Poincaré's success in halting inflation and re-establishing political stability quickly dampened the reforming ardor of many businessmen, who were, after all, far more interested in profits than in rewriting the constitution. Some businessmen refused to help the movement because they feared that Mercier might attempt to manipulate them for his own political ends, or would, at least, lead them beyond the safe limits of political activity. Mercier enjoyed the respect but not the confidence of a great many business leaders, who thought him overambitious and abnormally successful. The zealous economic and social program of his group alarmed them—and for good reason, since Mercier hoped to change the habits

[10] *Bulletin,* November–December, 1935, p. 14.

of French business. As he bluntly commented in private, he intended to "tear away a good part of the bourgeoisie from their absurd social conservatism." [11] But the businessmen, for the most part, were happy enough with the status quo. As one former Redressement leader remarked, most businessmen in those days were "napping" and were too shortsighted to pursue fundamental reform.

Nor did the movement attract substantial support from most employers' associations. The quasi-official national employers' confederation, the CGFP, did not cooperate, either officially or privately, with the Redressement, and its organ, the *Journée industrielle*, merely reported Redressement news from time to time. [12] The CGFP, indeed, carefully avoided politics and devoted itself to defending the existing economic order and encouraging the organization of employers. On all these points the CGPF and the Redressement were in conflict. Nor was there any official connection between Mercier's movement and the powerful Comité des Forges, although heads of certain metallurgical companies did provide him with assistance. [13] For his part, Mercier was concerned with mobilizing the "modern elite" and "men of good will" rather than promoting employers' organizations, and he was not active in the CGPF or in any other trade association. [14] The ambitious reforms, the indifference to employers' organizations, and the political interests of the Redressement simply precluded its cooperation with most trade associations.

Although the Redressement as a movement failed to draw the participation or the interest of most of the business elite, its chief idea, that of economic reorganization, did gain an important following. "Fordism" became increasingly popular among French businessmen, until by 1929 it was quite the vogue. [15] The CGFP organized study committees

[11] Mercier to Loucheur, Feb. 26, 1926, Loucheur papers, Bundle XI.

[12] Interview with Claude-J. Gignoux, May 9, 1961. Gignoux edited the *Journée industrielle* until 1936 when he became president of the federation. The only figure from the CGPF in the Redressement was Étienne Fougère, who served on the board from 1927 to 1928. Romier, of course, was a former editor of the *Journée industrielle*, but he had not been an officer in the federation.

[13] A former leader of the Comité des Forges, Alfred Lambert-Ribot, provided this information (letter to the author December 2, 1966). Some cooperation may also have arisen from the presence of MM. Bardoux and Mireaux, who were editors of the steel association's *Bulletin quotidien,* on the board of directors of the Redressement.

[14] Interviews with Roger Boutteville, May 19, 1961, and Claude-J. Gignoux, May 9, 1961. Apparently Henry Ehrmann (*Organized Business in France,* p. 65) is inaccurate in his description of Mercier's role in the CGPF.

[15] P. Bourgoin, "La Rationalisation," *Revue de France,* Nov. 15, 1929, pp. 269–294. A spokesman for French business described in detail the popularization of American manufacturing and commercial techniques in the late '20's and pleaded for a further expansion of this "Saint-Simonian policy"; see Pierre Bonnet, *La Commercialisation de la vie française du premier empire à nos jours* (Paris, 1929), pp. 327–336, 411. For

on the topic, and the engineering industry trade association endorsed *rationalisation* as the massive application of French Cartesianism to industry.[16] Pierre-Étienne Flandin, a leader of the Alliance Démocratique, a party associated with big business, advocated increased production or *surcapitalisme américain* as the answer to France's social problems.[17] And to the joy of the Redressement, in 1929 Premier André Tardieu introduced "a prosperity policy" with a plan for "national retooling." Nevertheless, the captains of industry remained divided between the enthusiastic promoters and the cautious advocates of reorganization. And after the collapse of the American model in 1929, the skeptics of course were quick to remind the others of their earlier doubts.

All along, the most ardent proponents were the "neo-capitalists" or "neo-Saint-Simonians." One observer described neo-Saint-Simonianism as a "philosophy" of the '20's which attempted to embellish capitalism with an ideology. It was a kind of "enlightened industrialism" which used production as a weapon against social injustice.[18] Indeed, the great hope of modernization was that it would bring the victory of "Ford over Marx." [19] The neo-capitalists were unlike the pre-1914 economic liberals in a number of ways—above all in their advocacy of a policy of high wages and in their support of collective action by employers and employees. They sought to elevate the worker's position in capitalist enterprise beyond that of a simple wage earner through such schemes as profit sharing, and they contemplated a more positive economic role for the state—though on both these latter issues there were wide differences of opinion among them.[20] A distinction must be made, however, between the avowed devotees of Saint-Simon who revived the

an estimate of the actual progress of *rationalisation* in industry and commerce, see Cahill, *Economic Conditions* (1934), pp. 664–669. A general discussion of the French reaction to America in the '20's is Paul Gagnon, "French Views of the Second American Revolution," *French Historical Studies*, II (Fall, 1962), 430–449.

[16] *Journée industrielle*, Jan. 26, 1928. See also *Production nationale*, April, 1927, pp. 783–789. Even the paternalistic spokesman for the textile industry, Eugène Mathon, endorsed it; see Henri-Louis Dubly, *Vers un ordre économique et social, Eugène Mathon, 1860–1935* (Paris, 1946), p. 335.

[17] "Le Problème social," *Revue de Paris*, Feb. 1, 1928, p. 503.

[18] Albert Thibaudet, *Les Idées politiques de la France*, pp. 62–68. For an example of this effort by big business to ameliorate the social problem by increasing labor's stake in the capitalist system, see Edmond Giscard d'Estaing, "Le Néocapitalisme," *Revue des deux mondes*, Aug. 1, 1928, pp. 673–688.

[19] For an extreme statement of this view, see the business paper *Pax* (May 4 and 11, 1928), which argued that reorganization would create semirural, industrial "burgs." These communities, built around small specialized plants, would reduce labor concentration and make workers part-time farmers.

[20] See Gaëtan Pirou, *Les Doctrines économiques en France depuis 1870* (Paris, 1934), pp. 153–157.

long-extinct periodical *Le Producteur* in the early '20's,[21] and certain others who, like M. Jourdain in *Le Bourgeois gentilhomme,* spoke prose without knowing it. Mercier was one of these, also Loucheur, Finaly, and so on, as well as André François-Poncet, a Comité des Forges official; the executive, Edmond Giscard d'Estaing; Étienne Clémentel, a wartime Minister of Commerce; and Henri de Peyerimhoff, president of the coal association. These were the vanguard of the "new men" who led the struggle to modernize France. Though they were essentially in tune with the spirit of neo-Saint-Simonianism, they were not in any way associated with the real devotees.

Peyerimhoff, like Mercier, extended the implications of neo-Saint-Simonianism to include constitutional change. He predicted "a new Götterdämmerung, a kind of twilight of parliaments," because politicians could no longer cope with modern economic problems.[22] He advised, for example, remodeling the Senate into an assembly representing economic groups. Pierre Mendès-France, who was a left-wing Radical who also diplayed distinct technocratic inclinations in the interwar years, recently proposed a similar reform for the Senate of the Fifth Republic though his intentions are more genuinely democratic than were Peyerimhoff's.[23] Indeed, Mendès-France represents a continuing democratic tendency in the French technocratic tradition.

In the late '20's there were also a number of young technocratic reformers, or "neo-syndicalists," who believed, as the neo-Saint-Simonians did, that a modern industrial economy required "a modern state." [24]

[21] The best study of these twentieth-century disciples of Saint-Simon is Marc Bourbonnais, *Le Néo Saint-Simonisme et la vie sociale d'aujourd'hui* (Paris, 1923). Included in this group were the director Gabriel Darquet, Ferdinand Gros, Henri Clouard, and M. Tournier, and enthusiasts like Francis Delaisi. The *Producteur* differed from the Redressement in its syndicalist orientation and in its aim of destroying the "financial plutocracy." It was also more revolutionary in seeking the abolition of the right of inheritance and proposing an economy directed by "technical bureaus" composed of producers and technicians. This caused the *Journée industrielle* to ask if the *Producteur* was for or against the existing capitalist system (Bourbonnais, pp. 114–115). An excellent summary of Saint-Simonian economic thought has been written by E. S. Mason: "Saint-Simonism and the Rationalization of Industry," *Quarterly Journal of Economics,* XLV (August, 1931), 640–683. See also C. Bouglé, "Le Bilan du Saint-Simonisme," *Annales de l'Université de Paris,* September–October, 1931, pp. 446–463, and November–December 1931, pp. 540–556.

[22] "Les Formules modernes d'organisation économique," *Revue des deux mondes,* Mar. 15, 1929, p. 452.

[23] *A Modern French Republic,* trans. Anne Carter (New York, 1963), pp. 73–86.

[24] The best analysis of this movement is by René Pinon, "Les nouvelles Conceptions de l'état," *Revue économique internationale,* October, 1929, pp. 7–30. See the summary in Jean Touchard *et al., Histoire des idées politiques* (Paris, 1959), II, 831. Some of the movement's principal works are Maxime Leroy, *Les Techniques nouvelles du syndicalisme* (Paris, 1921); Charles Albert, *L'État moderne: ses principes et ses institutions* (Paris, 1929); Georges Valois, *L'État syndicale et la représen-*

Georges Valois, Pierre Dominique, and Charles Albert were among those who argued that an economy based on mass production needed a government fortified by technicians and devoted to the development of productivity. These neo-syndicalists regarded a vocational association or *syndicat* as the building block of this new technical state. Extremists like Valois proposed the election of a parliamentary assembly by *syndicats* and an executive composed of a bureau of technicians. Albert, less radical, suggested special technical bodies to propose legislation to parliament. Certain Redressement collaborators, notably Pierre Dominique and José Germain, outlined a "New Republic" which would foster social reform and rising productivity and would give greater power to workers' and employers' organizations. These neo-syndicalists commended neo-capitalists like Mercier, Peyerimhoff, and Tardieu for their "modern spirit" which substituted skyscrapers and high wages for small shops and *rentes*. Valois went further and wrote that tomorrow's rulers would be neither the bourgeoisie nor the proletariat but the technicians and managers who had the skills to direct a complex industrial economy.

The neo-syndicalists sought Mercier's collaboration in organizing a unified technocratic movement, but the two groups were hardly in agreement on fundamentals. Mercier, like the neo-syndicalists, wanted a state which would turn over economic policy to the technicians, but he was against vocational organization. Valois made numerous attempts in 1929 and 1930 to enlist the Redressement's aid, but eventually the Redressement decided to reject his overtures and published a report to that effect in the June 1930 *Bulletin*.[25] In the report, Romier accused all workers' and employers' associations of being glorified interest groups useful only for materialistic self-defense. He predicted that if they were given legal recognition or a place in the already weak French government, all public authority would be torn to shreds by their quarrels. As it was, he warned, government was paralyzed by fear of displeasing one interest group or another. In addition, the Redressement characterized most existing vocational associations as nonrepresentative bodies which aligned themselves with various political par-

---

tation corporative (Paris, 1927) and *Un nouvel Age de l'humanité* (Paris, 1929). The reformers' views also appeared in various periodicals: Albert in *Volonté*; Georges Hoog in *Jeune république*; Charles Gallet in *Le Rappel*; Pierre Dominique and José Germain in *Paris-Phare*; and Valois in *Nouveau Siècle* and *Cahiers bleus*.

[25] See Valois' articles in *Cahiers bleus*: Dec. 7, 1929, pp. 28–29; Mar. 15, 1930, pp. 25–26; July 5, 1930, pp. 17–18. Valois later became one of the most hostile critics of the Redressement. For the interesting discussions among the various neo-syndicalists see the articles collected in *L'Avenir de la république* (Paris, 1927). The Redressement officially rejected the movement in an assembly devoted to "La Question du syndicalisme"; see *Bulletin*, June, 1930, pp. 9–23.

ties; thus it officially rejected any attempt to organize the state along vocational lines.

Mercier himself was more skeptical about the merits of vocational organization than many of his colleagues.[26] He thought such *syndicats* represented materialistic private interests and were unconcerned with the moral and intellectual dimensions of the individual. And he considered any notion of compulsory vocational organization repulsive: " 'Syndical' organizations . . . whatever their political views, function by the methodical elimination of the exceptional, by the elimination of men of superior intelligence or entrepreneurial spirit, or intrinsic qualities above the average. It is, consequently, a leveling organization. . . . It is the Soviet method. I insist on this point emphatically: the uncritical adoration of collective discipline represented by 'syndicalism' leads to the Soviet formula. It's logical, it's automatic." [27] Yet many of his friends disagreed with his dismissal of the value of trade associations. Mercier grudgingly acknowledged in public that Redressement members were joining such groups. Still unconvinced, he told a Redressement general assembly in 1930 that all their accomplishments to date, either privately or through the Redressement, had been achieved as individual representatives of the elite, as "men of good will," and without the assistance of trade associations.

An important but often ignored aspect of this movement for modernization in the '20's was its broad international approach to economic problems. In the era of "good feeling" after Locarno, Mercier and the neo-Saint-Simonians led French business toward European economic integration. Mercier and Peyerimhoff, for example, headed the French side of the Comité Franco-Allemand d'Information et de Documentation which in the late '20's tried to effect a rapprochement between French and German industry and reduce the tensions arising from the occupation of the Ruhr.[28] Another cause Mercier championed was the negotiation of European-wide producers' agreements. He even fondly hoped one day to bring about a broad international agreement which would allocate the supply of certain raw materials. It is no coincidence that the most ardent proponents of such agreements were leaders like Mercier, Loucheur, Tardieu, and Clémentel, who had all

[26] See his comments in *Bulletin,* June, 1930, pp. 21–23. Zamanski, for example, was himself an employers' association official and his views were to stray far from Mercier's; see *Forces nouvelles* (Paris, 1933) .

[27] *Bulletin,* June, 1930, p. 21.

[28] Wladimir d'Ormesson to Mme Ernest Mercier, Jan. 24, 1959, Mercier papers. On this so-called Mayrisch committee see Otto Abetz, *Histoire d'une politique franco-allemande, 1930–1950* (Paris, 1953) , pp. 59–60; Carlton J. H. Hayes, *France, A Nation of Patriots* (New York, 1930) , pp. 335–336.

shared in the task of provisioning Allied armed forces during the war and had discovered the benefits of international cooperation. The proposals of all these men involved international economic cooperation, and were not mere schemes to further the interests of big business. When the League of Nations held an international economic conference in 1927—largely through Loucheur's efforts—the French businessmen who most enthusiastically supported it were the modernizers.[29] Mercier himself attended the conference as an adviser, and the trade studies prepared by the Redressement were intended to assist the French delegation at Geneva.

Pan-Europe was yet another effort made to advance European economic integration which directly involved Mercier. After the First World War Count Coudenhove-Kalergi, a European nobleman of international ancestry and wide interests, led a crusade for Pan-Europe. He won many followers in France, including for a time Premier Briand, but met strong opposition among French businessmen, who feared making concessions to German industry. In 1927 Briand appointed Loucheur as president of the French Pan-Europe committee, hoping he could win over the businessmen,[30] and after Loucheur's death in 1931, Mercier succeeded him in that office. He took up the crusade energetically, but since Briand had just vetoed the proposed Austro-German customs union, the Pan-Europe movement was doomed. Coudenhove-Kalergi had much praise for Mercier's efforts, however; he wrote in 1956: "Among the precursors of a united Europe in France, Ernest Mercier merits a very special homage. He devoted a quarter of a century to this idea, with exemplary zeal. . . . At present everyone is more or less European. This was not the case at the time when Ernest Mercier rushed into this venture. He remained faithful to this ideal until his death." [31]

But the strength of the traditional French economic pattern made many members of the business elite loath to accept modernization and

[29] See the newspaper *Pax* which was founded in 1926 and eagerly promoted the Geneva conference. It was directed by business leaders like Jacques Seydoux of the Banque de Paris et des Pays-Bas, Charles Laurent, Peyerimhoff, the economist David Serruys (*Les Documents politiques*, July, 1927, pp. 272–276). The financial interests behind *Pax* also invested in other European papers, partly to win support for the League. See the interesting letters relating to this promotion effort in the Loucheur papers, Bundle XII.

[30] See *Louis Loucheur: Carnets secrets, 1908–1932*, pp. 163–166; Richard N. Coudenhove-Kalergi's *Crusade for Pan-Europe: Autobiography of a Man and a Movement* (New York, 1943), pp. 96–99, 117–124, 209. Coudenhove makes an interesting point when he observes (p. 123): "As a matter of fact, I found that the heads of the electrical industry all over Europe were generally more broad-minded than most of their colleagues in other production branches."

[31] Letter to Mme Ernest Mercier, Feb. 11, 1956, Mercier papers.

its political, social, and international implications. Indeed, the debate over *rationalisation* reflected a fundamental dilemma for French industry in the '20's. Although manufacturers often wanted and needed mass-production techniques, they were reluctant to sacrifice traditional practices. As one observer put it, "In one word, should our industry aim for quality or quantity?" [32] One of the most outspoken modernizers, François-Poncet, was perhaps overcritical when he wrote in 1927: "The organization of production has made little progress. The 'rationalizers' have, up to now, preached in a void. The movement has not gone beyond theory. It has not found its pioneers or its enthusiasts. Workers and employers have considered the idea with distrust and they both have kept aloof." [33] At the peak of its vogue, the president of the Paris Chamber of Commerce rejected it as a panacea and warned that it could not be applied to an economy whose distinctive character was that of producing luxury products.[34] More surprising, however, Duchemin, the president of the CGPF, expressed misgivings about the prevalent "mystique of modernization," which he feared would lead to overproduction and to the growth of international industrial conflicts. He stressed employers' organization rather than modernization as the means of ordering the economy.[35] Duchemin was one of many French businessmen who said I told you so when the New York stock market crashed in October, 1929. Had the depression not intervened, some of these businessmen might perhaps have come round; in any event, it is clear that the movement was only gaining momentum in 1929.

Besides failing to gain substantial support within the business community, the Redressement also earned the hostility of the extreme Right. There had been an ultraconservative wing in the leadership of the organization from the outset, and squabbles rather quickly brought complete alienation. The dispute began in the spring of 1926 when the Comte de Fels, a member of the original board of directors, was asked to write a publicity piece for the new movement. Before publishing the article, de Fels asked for Mercier's comments. Mercier criticized the defiant tone of the article and suggested "some slight, purely stylistic, alterations. . . . The tone of these modifications is inspired only by a certain feeling of reserve. . . . This reserve should dis-

[32] G. Welter, *La France d'aujourd'hui, agriculture–industrie–commerce* (Paris, 1927) , p. 99.

[33] *Capital*, Nov. 18, 1927.

[34] *Journée industrielle*, Jan. 19, 1928. For the indifference of the business community to modernization, also see A. Verdurand, "L'Homme d'affaires et la France," *Revue hebdomadaire*, December, 1927, pp. 339–341.

[35] See his 1928 address in Duchemin, *Organisation syndicale patronale en France*, pp. 39–42.

appear progressively to the degree that our power increases." [36] De Fels made a few minor changes in the article and published it in his *Revue de Paris* in May; he said later that most of the Redressement received it so enthusiastically that he wrote a sequel for the July 15 issue.[37] But Mercier strongly disapproved of the reactionary convictions of these articles, especially their attack on the state's economic and social activities, and two days later publicly disassociated the Redressement from them.[38] He was also angered by de Fels's agitation in favor of aligning the Redressement with reactionary political parties. The next month Mercier expelled de Fels and a second founder, Germain-Martin, for an "inadmissable deviation." [39]

The next development in this schism occurred in the summer of 1927 when Mercier published an important Redressement manifesto in *Le Temps*.[40] He called for the government to introduce "a minimum social program" consisting of low-cost housing, social insurance, and improved educational facilities—financed, however, by rising productivity and not by increased taxes. He also declared his intention to "establish regular relations" with all political parties, "except revolutionary or dictatorial parties," in order to "permit it [the Redressement] to intervene in electoral proceedings for the purpose of imposing necessary discipline and thus assuring the triumph of its program." This progressive manifesto was inspired by Mercier's search for a broad electoral appeal and by his awareness of social problems, but it was not welcomed by those Redressement members who were sympathetic to de Fels's position.

The dissension within the Redressement's ranks was finally exposed by a vendetta against Mercier by François Coty, the reactionary owner of *Le Figaro*. In the fall of 1927, Mercier lured Romier, who was Coty's editor, to the staff of the Redressement. Coty sought revenge by publicizing the schism within Mercier's movement. In lead editorials in *Le Figaro*, Coty declared that Mercier had purged de Fels and Germain-Martin because he had fallen under the sinister influence of certain new leftist elements in his organization. Coty accused "pure Herriotists" like Cacaud and Romier of sowing discord within the Redresse-

[36] Letter from Mercier to the Comte de Fels, Apr. 13, 1926, reprinted in *Le Figaro*, Nov. 23, 1927.

[37] "Le Redressement Français," *Revue de Paris*, May 1, 1926, pp. 5–19, and July 15, 1926, pp. 241–257. Beau de Loménie (*Les Responsabilités des dynasties bourgeoises*, IV, 192–194) completely misinterprets the Redressement by arguing that these articles represented its program. This book contains numerous such inaccuracies and innuendoes which mark it as an extremely unreliable source.

[38] *Le Temps*, July 17, 1926.

[39] Cacaud, "Histoire," Mercier papers.

[40] July 1, 1927.

ment and maneuvering it into the camp of the Cartel des Gauches. He alleged that Mercier had continued to drift further left until his "statist" manifesto overturned the Redressement's original program. Certain members, declared Coty, were dissatisfied with this manifesto which asserted that increasing productivity could finance an expensive social program. He also believed that Mercier wrongly reproached French employers for their backwardness: "Thanks to private initiative, our country is in the first rank in the area of social progress without the help of legislation, and in spite of the blunders of lawmakers." [41] As for the cahiers: "Who has read them? Who will read them? Do they [the Redressement] think they will save France by a debauchery of economic and social literature?" [42]

Mercier wrote an open letter to Coty denying that the de Fels articles represented the Redressement's position and repudiating the charge that his group had drifted to the left. The progressive manifesto, he explained somewhat lamely, was intended mainly for "electoral purposes." [43] De Fels thereupon challenged Mercier to deny that the *Revue de Paris* articles were approved by the movement's rank and file. Soon other ultraconservatives, including *Le Gaulois*, joined the argument on Coty's side.[44] Charles Maurras' *Action française*, which had so far been critical but not hostile to the Redressement, accused it of wasting "valuable energy" and "material resources." [45]

In an attempt to quiet the internal discord exposed and possibly aggravated by Coty and his friends, Mercier solemnly assured a Redressement general assembly in December, 1927, that there had been almost no resignations from the organization. But, he added, the members must choose: either Coty was correct in his accusations or else he lied. If anyone doubted the Redressement's intentions, declared Mercier, he might challenge him on the spot. No one in the audience stirred. Mercier struck the table and announced that the matter was closed.[46] Yet there is little doubt that *Le Figaro*'s campaign disclosed the lack of unity within the organization: two founders had resigned, and there

[41] *Le Figaro,* Nov. 8, 1927. For Coty's other editorials see the following issues: Nov. 7, 17, 18, 21, 23, 30, and Dec. 1, 1927.

[42] *Ibid.,* Nov. 18, 1927.

[43] *Ibid.*

[44] See the issue of Nov. 9, 1927. This paper had earlier approved of the Redressement.

[45] Nov. 19, 1927. This paper, the organ of Maurras' nationalist league, had first analyzed the Redressement's program as a mixture of good and bad, criticizing its position on industrial relations and international trade; Francis Delaisi, it said, did not even "think in French." The doctrinaire *Action française* also thought Mercier's movement lacked a "directing idea"; see the issue of Apr. 10, 1927.

[46] *Assemblée générale 1927,* p. 12.

was considerable uneasiness about the progressive tone of the manifesto.[47] No doubt the public feud also harmed the Redressement by
frightening hesitant conservatives away from what seemed to be a controversial and possibly left-wing movement. More fundamentally, the
right-wing assault demonstrates how certain Frenchmen wanted to
identify the Redressement as either fish or fowl, Right or Left, and
would not tolerate a group trying to stand in the Center. In fact, Mercier's group was to face continual political crossfire because neither extreme accepted its uncommitted posture.

While vainly attempting to mobilize conservative opinion, Mercier
also launched a vigorous campaign during 1927 and 1928 to rally the
Left. The earnestness of this effort made the working class view the Redressement as the principal spokesman for the movement for economic
modernization. Mercier, for example, personally explained the social
benefits of mass production to labor leaders.[48] For the "Red suburbs"
of Paris, the Redressement published its informative weekly *La Région
parisienne*—its motto, "work and cooperation." In addition, the Redressement subsidized (though did not publish) Gustave Gautherot's
somewhat flamboyant anti-Communist review, the *Vague rouge*.[49] As a
candidate from a "Red suburb" in the 1928 elections, Gautherot campaigned openly as a Redressement adherent but failed to oust the in-
cumbent Communist deputy. The most naïve, and certainly rather
amusing, propaganda publication was the expensive sports weekly, *Le
Muscle*. This periodical, aimed at a "workers' elite," mixed commen-
tary on social solidarity, modernization, and the Redressement with
sporting news. Sports, it suggested, taught the value of team spirit, a
spirit that labor and management had not yet achieved. *Le Muscle*
contended that if workers accepted "the employer as the team captain," all could work together for a common victory. Stories of the
Horatio Alger type related how enterprising workers became wealthy
employers. And one article entitled, "The Liaisons Between Elites,"

---

[47] A former member of the executive committee recalled that there were "fundamental divergencies within the group from the quadruple point of view of organization, ideas, purpose, and goals" (letter to author from Raphaël Alibert, Feb. 6,
1962).

[48] In 1927 he addressed a mixed business and labor group, the Association Française
pour le Progrès Social, which included officers of the most important French trade
union federations and the International Bureau of Labor; see *L'Aspect social de la
rationalisation*, Cahiers du Redressement Français, Series I, No. 10, pp. 41 ff.,
103–106.

[49] Cacaud, "Histoire," Mercier papers. Gautherot was an active Redressement
member and even shared offices with the organization's staff. The *Vague rouge*,
formerly the *Revue antibolchevique*, specialized in exposing the "true character" of
world communism: anarchy, rape, and starvation.

spoke of employers helping dedicated employees to rise to managerial status.[50]

Mercier's own workers considered him an enlightened employer. The Union d'Électricité extended a variety of social benefits to its employees, including interest-free loans for home construction and substantial family allowances; it also provided dispensaries and recreation facilities. The company paid high wages and Mercier promised further increases if labor cooperated in cutting costs. On the whole the company's employees were content, except for an occasional quarrel between management and the local Communist trade union; even during the labor disturbances of the Popular Front period in 1936, Mercier's plants were tranquil.

Within the ranks of the Confédération Générale du Travail (CGT), the national trade union federation, and the Socialist party, the Redressement as a movement found only faint support, although modernization met with cautious approval—particularly the prospect of higher wages. In 1928 the CGT officially endorsed *rationalisation*—if it were accompanied by increased wages, specific worker controls, and collective bargaining agreements.[51] The CGT agreed with those who said that the assembly line transformed workers into "trained gorillas," but it insisted that it was "pure nonsense" to try to prevent the inevitable.[52]

The civil servants' union, which was the backbone of the CGT, became sufficiently concerned about Redressement influence to warn its members against neo-capitalist solicitations.[53] Robert Lacoste, speaking for the union, argued that the Redressement's administrative streamlining would not bring higher wages, but would only turn the economic functions of the state over to the "financial oligarchy"—since, he pointed out, Mercier's group stood opposed to any state intervention that would help the consumer or control cartels. Thus the Redressement was caught in a crossfire from Left and Right: the CGT on the one hand opposed it as the enemy of socialism, and de Fels and Coty on the other charged that it was heading precisely in that direction.[54]

[50] See the issue of Jan. 9, 1927, pp. 3, 8–9.

[51] *Tribune des fonctionnaires,* Apr. 7, 1928. A critical insight into the French workers' view of "Fordism" is provided by Hyacinthe Dubreuil, *Standards: le travail américain vu par un ouvrier français* (Paris, 1929) .

[52] *Tribune des fonctionnaires,* Aug. 4, 1928.

[53] For the CGT's view of the Redressement, see *ibid.,* Jan. 7, Feb. 4, 18, 25, Mar. 10, 17, and Apr. 14, 1928. For its initial, noncommittal reactions see *Le Peuple,* Apr. 3–10, 1927.

[54] De Fels in his *Revue de Paris* (Feb. 15, 1928, p. 726) attacked "a category of neo-industrialists, almost all suppliers of the state" who were "imitating Russian

Yet as one left-wing periodical said, even some Socialists were "charmed by the new song" composed by Henry Ford and popularized by the Redressement.[55] The leadership of the Socialist party openly disagreed on the proper attitude to adopt toward reorganization. Léon Blum doubted that capitalism could ever eliminate waste and disorder. He thought that France, with its limited internal market, its stationary population, and its "greedy" employers, was incapable of extensive modernization. Blum warned that industrial concentration strengthened the "economic oligarchy" and allowed it to increase its interference in politics: "Will *rationalisation* not lead us to a kind of industrial Bonapartism?"[56] Another Socialist leader who was a Polytechnician, Jules Moch, disagreed with Blum and insisted that modernization would bring benefits to all society. Moch reiterated the CGT's position that the working class must facilitate this inevitable economic change. Yet both Moch and Blum distinguished between a "good" and "bad" type of modernization depending on how it was introduced. Both men were also suspicious of the Redressement: Moch thought it was unfortunate that Mercier talked vaguely of "social peace" rather than about "his will to collaborate with trade unions on an equal basis."[57] To abandon the initiative to the Redressement, Moch believed, would be a mistake, for it might make a travesty of an advantageous economic change.

These cautious but promising reactions from the CGT and the Socialists were offset by bitter attacks by the Communists, certain syndicalists, and other leftists. The Communists resented Mercier's efforts to weaken their hold over Parisian electrical workers. *L'Humanité* charged that it was easy for Mercier to offer higher wages because consumers ultimately paid for them through higher electric bills.[58] Perhaps by intention, just after the Redressement's national assembly met in April, 1927, the Communist union at the Citroën plant struck against the "Fordists" who were trying to "dehumanize" labor.

Nepmen in order to carve out an advantageous place for themselves in the new order."

[55] *La Lumière,* Mar. 10, 1928, p. 2. This periodical itself admired some aspects of the Redressement: "There is, to be sure, a neo-capitalism in our country. A fraction of the employers have tried to infuse new blood into traditional capitalism, and to furnish it with an improved social and political program. The Redressement Français is, in a sense, nothing more than a condemnation of the old methods of the capitalist autocracy." See also Valois, *L'Homme contre l'argent,* p. 359; Jacques Chastenet, *Histoire de la troisième république* (Paris, 1952–1963), V, 226.

[56] In Jules Moch, *Socialisme et rationalisation* (Brussels, 1927), pp. vii, 15–16. See also *Le Populaire,* Apr. 23 and May 10, 1927.

[57] Moch, *Socialisme,* p. 124.

[58] June 13 and 14, 1928.

Some syndicalists foresaw absolutely no gains from the Redressement's modernization program. The *Révolution prolétarienne,* an independent review voicing the "pure" revolutionary syndicalist position, argued that modernization would not even bring economic progress. The standardization of products, it said, would discourage research and innovation, and breed economic stagnation. Industrial concentration would suppress competition and benefit the "technically uninventive" large firms. It also doubted that employers could be trusted to pass on to labor any of the profits from increased productivity, and it thought it likely that the unemployed would be used to keep wages low. It urged workers to "go slow" and do everything possible to disrupt modernization.[59]

All in all, the Redressement was hardly successful in its effort to win the Left. Modernization had some appeal, but the organization itself gained at most only a tiny foothold.[60] Certainly its publications were not well received.[61] The final blow came when the American idol toppled and the depression struck France in the early '30's. With business struggling to survive, it could hardly keep promising higher wages, and thus the whole Redressement theory of improving labor relations through collaboration and production collapsed.

From the outset, the Redressement had been preparing for the elections of 1928, and its attempt to become a mass movement was part of a general effort to acquire political influence. It was disgusted with "the national vice of France . . . , political instability," which, it believed, was caused by a proliferation of parties and was maintained by artificial quarrels.[62] The most harmful myth in French political life, the Redressement insisted, was the theoretical barrier between Right and Left, between the Bloc National and the Cartel des Gauches. Neither bloc would acknowledge the other's right to hold office and the bloc out of power obstructed government on principle. Being practical men, Mercier and his business elite envisioned a stable, durable government of "republican concentration"—that is, a government based

[59] "A bas la rationalisation," *La Révolution prolétarienne,* Oct. 15, 1928, pp. 275–281.

[60] Mercier persistently claimed the organization had 10,000 working-class sympathizers, mainly from the Paris suburbs (*Bulletin,* July, 1933, p. 15). But *La Lumière* (Mar. 24, 1928, p. 4) described labor's reaction as one of "general skepticism," and ridiculed Mercier's claims of support as "a tactic" or "an illusion."

[61] Some of its periodicals were failures from the very beginning (*Les Documents politiques,* November, 1927, p. 437). *Nos Plaisirs* (1926–1927) and *Le Muscle* (1927–1928) each survived only one year, and *Minerva* found new financial support around 1928. The *Vague rouge* continued until 1931 with new help. Only *La Région parisienne,* which maintained a circulation of 30,000 till 1935, could be called a success.

[62] Romier, *Le Redressement Français: idées très simples pour les Français,* p. 106.

on the numerous parties which composed the Center and Right-Center of the Chamber. Specifically, the Redressement sought a Union Nationale government which would include most of the parties of the Bloc National and the most moderate elements of the Cartel. According to Cacaud, the Union Nationale would consist mainly of Moderates and right-wing Radicals, and it would exclude "the extremists," that is the Socialists, Communists, and "social reactionaries." [63]

Paradoxically, however, the Redressement was not prepared to act openly as a political party to achieve this union, and it never really shifted from its posture as a pressure group outside the party system trying to bring about a rapprochement of existing parties. This reluctance to participate fully in the struggle for political power was due, it seems, to these industrialists' fear of "being soiled" in the electoral fray,[64] and to their self-conception of moral superiority which placed them above the political arena. A friendly critic, the journalist Émile Buré, warned the Redressement that it was making itself politically impotent by not offering its own list of candidates. Cacaud's reply was that the Redressement could be of influence only by remaining disinterested; the last thing the republic needed, he commented, was another center party.[65] In theory, Cacaud's defense sounded attractive, but in practice the Redressement stood in danger of negating the potential power of its money, its propaganda machine, its organization, and its distinguished leadership. Without a loyal voting bloc, however small, it could never really hope to achieve any of its aims.

In 1927 the Redressement began issuing publicity urging the reelection of deputies who supported the Union Nationale. Special election propaganda, partly inspired by Poincaré himself,[66] proclaimed the necessity of maintaining political and monetary stability, and added that there was a need to fortify government with "the technically competent." The Redressement assumed that the Moderates, among whom it had considerable influence,[67] solidly supported a continuation of the

---

[63] *Assemblée générale 1927*, pp. 5–6.

[64] Letter to the author from José Germain, Jan. 24, 1962.

[65] See the discussion between Buré and Cacaud in *L'Avenir*, July 1, 8 and 17, 1927. At one point, the Redressement did contemplate helping to elect twenty "loyal deputies" who would guide and coordinate the efforts of other sympathetic members of parliament but would not act as an independent body themselves; *Bulletin*, April, 1929, pp. 5–6.

[66] Poincaré, through the governor of the Bank of France, asked Romier to write articles on the theme of a "party truce"; see Émile Moreau, *Souvenirs d'un gouverneur de la Banque de France, histoire de la stabilisation du franc, 1926–1928* (Paris, 1954), pp. 433–435, 437–439, 443–444.

[67] For example, Tardieu, who was considered the leader of the Moderates, had very close ties with the group (Cacaud, "Histoire," Mercier papers). Émile Mireaux, one of the Redressement directors, was a leader of the Alliance Démocratique, and Loucheur led the Gauche Radicale party.

Union Nationale. It believed, however, that the undecided and divided votes of the Left-Center, particularly the Radicals, required close attention. Thus its principal aims were to win some Radicals to the Union Nationale, and to defeat all "Marxist parties," since they "refused to participate in the parliamentary system." [68] Certain Radical papers carried Redressement appeals which called for social reform, a pragmatic approach to political problems, and a renunciation of old quarrels. [69] Romier aptly summarized the businesslike tone of the movement's electoral strategy by recalling a remark on French politics made to him by an American: "You Frenchmen, you always seem to lose sight of the fact that the important thing for a car is not whether you paint it grey or green, but to get it on the road and get it running." [70]

The campaign to reconcile the Radicals and the Moderates met with a bitter reaction from certain left-wing elements which opposed the Union Nationale. One journalist who specialized in exposés of the "economic oligarchy" attacked the Redressement as "pro-Fascist" and rebuked those "republicans and Freemasons" who had subscribed to it. [71] Another left-wing periodical described the Redressement's campaign as a Machiavellian attempt by capitalism to enlist the Left's support for Poincaré and "reaction." It also called Mercier's group "an anti-Socialist war machine," and accused it of being a camouflaged political party. [72]

But the Left's principal point of attack was to identify the Redressement with the reactionary Union des Intérêts Économiques (UIE), a business pressure group headed by Senator Ernest Billiet which distributed funds for electoral campaigns. [73] Since the Redressement had been founded not long after the UIE had been publicly disgraced for interfering with the 1924 elections, critics accused Mercier of acting as Billiet's successor. The *Canard enchaîné* quipped that the Redressement

---

[68] Romier, *Idées très simples,* p. 113. See also *Assemblée générale 1927,* p. 5; André Géraud, "The Coming French Elections," *Foreign Affairs,* VI (January, 1928) , 229.

[69] For a list of these papers, which included the *Dépêche de Toulouse, Le Rappel,* and *La Lanterne,* see *La Lumière,* Mar. 17, 1928, p. 6. Romier enjoyed some favor with the Left, and in 1926 had even been asked by Herriot to become his Minister of Finance.

[70] Romier, *Idées très simples,* p. 108.

[71] *Les Documents politiques,* December, 1927, p. 490.

[72] *La Lumière,* Mar. 31, 1928, p. 2.

[73] On the UIE see Chambre des députés, treizième législature, session extraordinaire de 1925, *Procès-verbaux de la commission d'enquête sur les conditions dans lesquelles le comité de l'Union des Intérêts Économiques est intervenu dans la derniére campagne électorale* (Paris, [1925]) , No. 2098 (hereafter cited as *Commission d'enquête sur l'UIE*) , and its organ, *Le Réveil économique;* see also Richard Lewinsohn, *L'Argent dans la politique* (Paris, 1931) , pp. 229–232; James K. Pollock, *Money and Politics Abroad* (New York, 1932) , pp. 305–316.

made the UIE look like a sedan chair beside Lindbergh's airplane.[74] It was even proved that the Redressement privately solicited funds for the UIE.[75] Mercier, however, rejected this identification with the UIE. "The two organizations," he insisted, "are completely independent in their composition, goals, and means of action. . . . The UIE is a professional employers' organization. The Redressement Français is an association open to all men of good will regardless of their origin or inclinations."[76] The truth seems to have been that Mercier organized individuals while Billiet brought together various commercial and industrial associations—for the most part, small proprietors and merchants as opposed to the business and intellectual elite who were sought by the Redressement.[77] A further difference was that the purpose of the Redressement was national renovation inspired by the example and propaganda of a dedicated elite, whereas the UIE confined itself to a rather crude sniping at state monopolies and specialized in dispensing campaign funds for the defense of economic interests. Thus on the issue of social reform Billiet was much more cautious than Mercier.[78] It cannot be denied, however, that there was some cooperation between these two groups whose political strategies for the 1928 elections had so much in common.

The Redressement, much like the UIE, did not confine its electioneering to popular propaganda. It instructed voters on how to select qualified candidates. It also helped to organize a national "arbitration committee" to promote electoral discipline on the second ballot among all parties supporting the Union Nationale, and it established "individual contacts" with parliamentary leaders.[79] To secure individual pledges of loyalty to the Union Nationale, the Redressement set up a number of local arbitration committees, which met at Redressement centers, and announced its pledge of financial support to candidates under certain conditions. An official bulletin read: "In order to be

[74] Dec. 21, 1927.

[75] Marcel Champin canvassed the petroleum industry for funds for both organizations; this was revealed by a government investigation of the industry (see n. 9 above). Certain observers believed the two groups worked together: Pollock, p. 305; Georges Bourgin et al., Manuel des partis politiques en France (Paris, 1928), p. 131.

[76] Reprinted in the Tribune des fonctionnaires, Mar. 10, 1928.

[77] Although big business did help subsidize the UIE, much of its support came from groups like the railway bondholders' association rather than from corporations like those in the Union des Syndicats de l'Électricité. See Commission d'enquête sur l'UIE, pp. 60, 165–170, 207–216; Beau de Loménie, Dynasties bourgeoises, III, 360–361; Lewinsohn, pp. 229–232.

[78] For example, the UIE had reservations about the Loucheur housing bill—which the Redressement wholeheartedly supported—fearing it would weigh too heavily on the budget; see Le Réveil économique, July 4, 1928.

[79] Assemblée générale 1927, p. 6.

materially aided by the Redressement Français, each candidate must sign, first of all, a formal pledge to submit to the final decision of the Comité Supérieur d'Arbitrage concerning the maintenance or the withdrawal of his candidature on the second turn: in default of this pledge, he may be obliged to reimburse the expenses contracted by him for his electoral campaign." [80]

Indeed, the electoral discipline, which the Redressement helped foster, contributed strongly to the victory of the Union Nationale in April, 1928.[81] Mercier was pleased with what his movement had done, and he thought that it had been strengthened by playing an "important role" in the elections—a role which he described as mainly "psychological" or "strategic" rather than "statistical." [82] An American observer studying the importance of money in French politics reported that the Redressement had used its funds "to the best political advantage" for the benefit of Moderates and Radicals, but that "the influence of money in elections is in no sense great or overpowering." [83] In fact, about one hundred deputies were elected with financial aid from Mercier's organization.[84] Loucheur wrote to Mercier and congratulated him for introducing "discipline" among the parties without being "crushed" by them,[85] but the Left completely ignored the Redressement's part in the election and described Billiet as the "great elector of the Union Nationale." [86] Certainly the Redressement received little credit for the victory, and some members believed, despite Mercier's assertions, that the organization emerged from the election with tarnished prestige.[87]

From 1928 to 1930 the Redressement adopted a confident pose that belied its failure to expand and its relative ineffectiveness as a political force. Though they accomplished little in these years, the drift of the times encouraged the technocrats. In November, 1928, Romier commented that, although France had set the precedent with Vauban and Napoleon, "the most powerful people on earth, the American people, have elected an engineer as their leader." Even the impending Missis-

---

[80] Reprinted in *La Lumière*, Mar. 17, 1928, p. 6.

[81] René Rémond gives credit for this discipline to the propaganda of Henri de Kerillis and to the arbitration committee organized by the Moderates and presided over by André Maginot. Since the Redressement assisted in this committee it deserves some share in the victory; see *La Vie politique en France de 1870 à 1940*, Institut d'études politiques, 1959–1960 (Paris, [1960], III, 414.

[82] *Bulletin*, November, 1929, p. 3; see also *ibid.*, May, 1928, p. 1, and July, 1928, p. 5.

[83] Pollock, pp. 305, 319.

[84] Cacaud, "Histoire," Mercier papers.

[85] *Ibid.*

[86] *L'Humanité*, Apr. 28 and May 30, 1928; *La Lumière*, Apr. 21, 1928.

[87] Letter to author from José Germain, Jan. 24, 1962.

sippi floods, he added, were no longer feared because "Hoover has arrived in Washington, Hoover the engineer is there to command." [88]

But France, in the Redressement's view, surpassed America during 1929 and 1930 under the leadership of André Tardieu. A champion of the Moderates and a critic of the parliamentary system, Tardieu officially proposed a general plan for economic modernization, social reform, and technocratic streamlining of the republic.[89] When the new premier addressed the Chamber, citing facts and figures, some deputies thought he even spoke like a businessman. Mercier greeted Tardieu enthusiastically as the first premier who had broken with tradition and attempted really to govern the country. Tardieu had always been a special friend of the Redressement, and Mercier considered him the pick of the generation which had fought in the war: the Tardieu government, Mercier observed, was welcomed by most Frenchmen because they were "sick and tired of politics and verbal quarrels." [90] Later Mercier admitted that he had been tempted to make Tardieu the official leader of the Redressement but had refrained because it would have destroyed the group's independence to tie it to a particular deputy.[91] For a brief moment in early 1930 Mercier was admitted to the inner councils of the Third Republic. He was in "constant contact" with Tardieu during the formation of his second ministry.[92] Mercier advised Tardieu to include the Radicals in his government and avoid dependence on the extreme Right. Tardieu even addressed the Redressement on the virtues of a "concentration" type of government, and Mercier called for every member in factory and office to speak out for Tardieu. But the premier was unable to persuade the Radicals to join him and returned to alignment with the Right. According to Mercier, Tardieu soon found his close association with the "leftist" Redressement embarrassing and broke off the association.

The Redressement also assumed the task of studying all social and economic measures considered by the legislature in order to advise both its members and the lawmakers. It maintained close contact with a small number of party leaders who sympathized with its views.[93] The

[88] *Bulletin*, November, 1928, p. 1.

[89] See two excellent studies: J.-J. Chevallier, *Histoire des institutions politiques de la France moderne, 1789–1945* (Paris, 1958), pp. 564–571; and René Capitant, "La Crise et la réforme du parlementarisme en France," *Jahrbuch des Öffentlichen Rechts der Gegenwart*, XXIII (1936), 1–71.

[90] *Bulletin*, November, 1929, p. 4.

[91] *Ibid.*, February, 1931, p. 10.

[92] Cacaud, "Histoire," Mercier papers.

[93] Included in the parliamentary groups of the 1928 legislature were the following deputies (marked by *) or party officials: Joseph Zamanski (Démocrate Populaire);

most important pieces of legislation of the late '20's were the social insurance law of March 14, 1928, and the Loucheur housing bill of July 7, 1928.

It was to be expected that even this modest social insurance measure would draw the wrath of many interests in French society—especially businessmen.[94] The Redressement also had certain reservations about the measure, but accepted it in principle.[95] Once the legislation was adopted the *Bulletin* advised all members to participate in organizing the program to ensure that management and labor shared equally in its administration.

The Redressement also praised certain legislation of the late '20's concerning finance and urban affairs for conforming to its program, but the one law it was proud to call its own was the Loucheur housing act—"the pure and simple application of [our] ideas." [96] The Redressement had long maintained that housing was the principal problem of the working class in Paris, many of whom, as Romier observed, still lived in miserable "wartime" temporary shacks and were thus ripe for Communist propaganda. Loucheur's housing bill provided public aid for the construction of 200,000 low-priced and 60,000 medium-priced dwellings, and he readily obtained the assistance of the Redressement in urging its passage.[97]

Despite the Redressement's show of optimism following the 1928 elections, which kept it hard at work in support of the housing bill and other measures, it was painfully clear that the movement had lost its dynamism and that its program would not be adopted. The cherished Union Nationale disintegrated during 1928 and 1929. Furthermore, the plan to have government endorse a modernization program collapsed when Tardieu proved unable to maintain a parliamentary ma-

---

Jacques Bardoux and Charles-Bellet (Union Républicaine Démocratique) ; P.-E. Flandin* and André Tardieu* (Républicains de Gauche) ; Jean Goy* (Gauche Sociale et Radicale) ; and Louis Loucheur* (Gauche Radicale) .

[94] For hostile business reaction see C.-J. Gignoux in the *Journée industrielle*, June 24, 1927; *Les Documents politiques*, February, 1930, pp. 114–130; Eugène Schneider, "A propos des Assurances sociales," *Revue des deux mondes*, May 15, 1933, pp. 427–440.

[95] A cahier (Paul Frantzen, *Les Assurances sociales*, Cahiers du Redressement Français, Series I, No. 22, p. 65) stated that this project had "the fundamental vice" of destroying tried institutions like the employer-sponsored family allowances and the mutual insurance funds.

[96] *Bulletin*, February, 1933, p. 3.

[97] *Ibid.*, June 19, 1928. Alexander Werth in *Which Way France?* (New York, 1937) , p. 29, thought the bill perhaps did more bad than good, since it "started an unprecedented building boom all over France, and transformed much of the country round Paris into a mass—an incoherent mass—of ugly red-roofed suburban houses and villas."

jority. The final disenchantment occurred when Tardieu, the neo-Saint-Simonians' hero, repudiated further assistance from Mercier's organization.

The Redressement was openly pessimistic about the 1932 election. Even though Tardieu led an extraordinarily active campaign for the Moderates, the *Bulletin* foresaw a resurrected Cartel destroying all hope for a coalition "of all republican parties from the heart of the Republican Federation to the heart of the Radical-Socialists." [98] The Redressement, on the verge of dissolution, and unable to muster strong financial support, was also much less active than it had been in the 1928 elections. Business was not interested in a movement that did not produce results, and it was unimpressed by the movement's dues-paying membership of only 15,000 after seven years. Not only were the electoral coordinating committees an impossibility for this election, but several of the Redressement's publications were either operating without their usual subsidies or had been discontinued.[99] After 1932, Mercier later admitted, it was nearly impossible to keep the organization in operation.[100] With the victory of the Cartel des Gauches in the 1932 elections, the Redressement could only lament the renewed division of Right and Left. The crushing blow had, of course, already come from Wall Street. The Redressement's social and economic program was buried by the collapse of the American industrial utopia, and the ensuing depression in France simply obliterated the renaissance of Saint-Simon.

Considering the inept means the Redressement chose to exert its influence, and the fact that the organization never transcended its oligarchical character, one cannot really be surprised at how little it ever achieved. Mercier naïvely hoped that the technocrats could shape governmental decisions without holding positions of authority within the government. Technocrats have been effective functioning as high administrative officials or as special advisers, but the Redressement directors believed they could assist in the formulation of policy merely by offering unsolicited advice—to be followed, they vainly hoped, by an invitation from the republic to assume a role in the decision-making process. And since they both feared and ridiculed the political arena, they were unwilling to organize themselves into a political party or to align themselves with one. Given this position outside the governmen-

---

[98] *Bulletin,* January, 1932, pp. 19–20.

[99] In 1929, for example, Gautherot began soliciting funds for the *Vague rouge* because the anonymous group that had covered "its expenses very generously up to now" was no longer able to continue; see *Les Documents politiques,* December, 1929, p. 737.

[100] *Bulletin,* November–December, 1935, p. 11.

tal system, there was little reason for the technocrats to expect the leaders of the republic to welcome, much less adopt, their reforms.

On the other hand, if the Redressement had become a mass movement, it might have been able to overcome this awkward political posture and exert real influence on government. But here Mercier's hopes fell short. It failed to become a national movement and never represented more than a fairly small segment of the business elite. In 1932 Mercier admitted this failing, but he sourly attributed it to the masses' insensitivity to "wisdom, moderation, prudence, and disinterestedness." [101] Albert Thibaudet gave a more accurate explanation when he wrote that neo-Saint-Simonianism was too strongly associated with the defense of economic interests to speak with authority as a broad ideological movement.[102] The Redressement was hostile to the Marxist Left, and unable to overcome labor's doubts about the benefits of a modern economy based on expanding productivity. It was also rejected by the reactionary Right, and proved unable to rally the divided Center to the banner of modernization; even its fellow captains of industry were skeptical. The Redressement was simply unable to attract a wide following once the financial crisis of 1925–1926 passed, and it was reluctant to enter fully into the struggle for political power. Thus it was doomed to a limited role of discussion and propaganda, and was never able to fulfill Foch's admonition to implement its program.

[101] *Ibid.*, July, 1932, p. 11.

[102] *Les Idées politiques*, pp. 66–68. Claude-J. Gignoux dismissed the neo-Saint-Simonians as mere opportunists who lacked a true doctrine; see *L'Économie française entre les deux guerres, 1919–1939* (Paris, [1942]) , pp. 336–337.

6

"For the Nation, Around the Veterans"
February 6, 1934

B Y 1932 Ernest Mercier was at the peak of his career. He was about to inherit the presidency of the Messine group after spending years as Albert Petsche's second. The final touches had been placed on the organization of the CFP which under his direction would soon become the foremost petroleum enterprise in France. And, despite the decay of the Redressement, he still commanded the respect of the rulers of the Third Republic. Even Édouard Herriot admitted that Mercier was "a politician who plays a very important role in the life of our country." [1]

Mercier was then in his early fifties, his light hair now turned white. A thin moustache, meticulous grooming, and quiet self-confidence gave him the air of a distinguished statesman rather than an industrialist. His features were sharp, almost aristocratic. But it was his calm blue eyes and arching brows that made his expression so incisive. In conversation he was attentive, persuasive, charming. Most people were struck by the clarity of his mind, the cool logic of his ideas—the hallmark of the Polytechnician. Yet his deep sense of purpose also made him seem overserious and at times almost humorless.

He had remarried in 1927 to the widowed Mme Adolphe Reinach. She was born Marguerite Dreyfus, the daughter of Mathieu Dreyfus, and the niece of Captain Alfred Dreyfus. The drama of the Dreyfus case had dominated her childhood and initiated her lifelong interest in public affairs. Both her first husband and her brother were killed in the service of France during the First World War. After the war, although the young widow had to care for three children, she still found time for social work. This interest brought Mme Reinach into contact with the Redressement Français. She met Ernest Mercier at an early meeting of the organization and they were married months later. She became his closest confidante and constant companion, accompanying him on all his travels.

At the time of his second marriage the youngest of Mercier's four

---

[1] *J.O. débats,* Mar. 25, 1931, p. 2191.

children was already in her teens. His two daughters were to marry two talented brothers, Richard and Wilfred Baumgartner. Richard, who was also a Polytechnician, followed directly in his father-in-law's footsteps and became a top manager in the electrical manufacturing and petroleum industries. Wilfred was to become head of the Bank of France and Minister of Finance in the Fifth Republic.

In private life Mercier was neither a narrow engineer nor a tiresome businessmen, but a cultivated gentleman. He confined his work to his office and in the evenings relaxed, read, and attended concerts—though this last form of entertainment became increasingly difficult to enjoy as he gradually grew hard of hearing. His travels, which often mixed business and pleasure, took him from one end of Europe to the other, from London to Moscow. He never lost his love for the sea and usually vacationed in Brittany or on the Mediterranean.

Among his acquaintances were many of the most illustrious personages of the Third Republic ranging from the Socialist Léon Blum to the Catholic conservative Marshal Lyautey. But his circle of intimate friends was drawn almost exclusively from the famous "H.S.P." (haute société protestante). Protestant business managers like Jacques Level were closest to him. Those within the "H.S.P." tend to belittle its importance, but to outsiders, who often see it more accurately, it is a relatively close-knit social group which enjoys enormous influence in French national life. Mercier was correctly viewed by high Parisian society as a leader of the "H.S.P." A wife of one prominent Catholic business executive even suggested that Mercier "looked like a Protestant!"

As is often the case with human personality, Mercier's greatest virtue was also his major fault. His Saint-Simonian passion to build, create, and reform made him an extraordinary industrialist. Yet this same passion led him to undertake tasks far beyond his power, such as almost single-handedly directing the French elite toward modernization. In all this, he was certain that he was selflessly dedicating his life to public service, and he detested anyone who dared question his altruism. He was, indeed, on occasion so self-righteous that he imputed malicious motives to those who disagreed with him. As a result he often misrepresented his political opponents as self-seeking villains devoid of concern for the national interest.

The Redressement was in full decline by 1932, yet it was still important for Mercier because it remained his principal vehicle of expression. Though it stood no chance of realizing its original aims, it was at any rate a forum where Mercier and his colleagues could express their views on the new troubles of the early '30's.

Beginning in 1930, Mercier and his Redressement directors were forced to turn their attention from modernization to new and alarming problems with international implications. As the world economy languished, the Redressement was more and more hard put to defend its position—though it was ready enough to criticize the government for not halting the depression. Many French businessmen reconsidered the neo-Saint-Simonians' message and decided overproduction was at fault. Duchemin charged that "the mystique of high wages" had deluded Americans and had led them to economic catastrophe.[2] The industrialist Eugène Mathon said, "The hymn to restraint has succeeded the hymn to production."[3]

As a spokesman for the Redressement, Romier tried to defend the neo-Saint-Simonians by offering an analysis of the world depression which minimized the responsibility of modernization.[4] Economic streamlining had indeed, he said, cut costs, but most industrialists, failing to understand that the modern economy had to be based on increasing production, had maintained high prices instead of passing on the savings to the consumer. However, he said, industry was not completely at fault since it had not been totally free. Everywhere governments forced it to pay for the care of urban masses and uprooted farmers, war indemnities, wasteful bureaucracies, and various interest groups which lived off the state. Modernization, in fact, had not gone far enough; the real bottleneck, distribution, still remained. And as mechanization systematically reduced production costs, more and more semiparasitic merchants entered the business world, thereby increasing the cost to the consumer and, when the consumer resisted, creating universal economic glut.

"Speculative capitalism" was the "sorcerer's apprentice" of the depression, Romier said.[5] Industrial plants, already enlarged by the war, were unwisely expanded during the unstable postwar years by profit-seeking financiers, particularly certain Anglo-American banks; and manufacturers had been forced to maintain prices at an unnaturally high level in order to repay their loans. Thus the inevitable slump in production and prices had been delayed. By this reasoning, Romier made overproduction an effect rather than a cause, putting most of the blame on eager financiers, unproductive middlemen, selfish interest groups, and inflated governments, all of whom had in a way taken advantage of the backward manufacturers. The trouble was not in the capitalist system; it was only misused.

[2] Duchemin, *Organisation syndicale patronale en France*, p. 84.
[3] Quoted in Dubly, *Vers un Ordre économique et social, Eugène Mathon*, p. 308.
[4] For Romier's interpretation see *Bulletin*, January, 1932, pp. 8–15; and *Si le Capitalisme disparaissait* (Paris, 1933) .
[5] *Si le Capitalisme*, p. 60.

On a philosophical level Romier conceded that capitalism had suffered "a moral decline"—that materialism had replaced dedication to the general welfare which was the ideal of Saint-Simonian tradition. But he blamed teachers, intellectuals, and the elite in general for not establishing proper values: "The trial of capitalism is the trial of contemporary world educators." [6] Romier apparently failed to see that the system itself might also have been responsible for the moral failure— that capitalism might have bred materialism which neither education nor example could counter. In any event he ignored the possibility that the avarice of "speculative capital" and the selfishness of interest groups were more than aberrations—were, indeed, predictable consequences of an economic system founded on personal profit.

Explaining the depression, however, did not cure it. And there was little to be cheerful about in those industries most dear to the Redressement managers. In the course of 1930–1931 some petroleum prices fell 40 percent. A leader of the electrical manufacturing industry gloomily announced that sales in 1933 were down 75 percent from 1930.[7] The expansion of the electric power industry also slowed markedly at this time. The Redressement, like the rest of the business community,[8] advanced deflation as the best means to stimulate the economy. According to Romier, the basic economic problem was "price chaos." [9] French prices were too high for the international market; thus there was a drop in exports and an increase in import costs, along with a serious decline in the tourist trade. The predicament of the internal market was more complex. Here the problem was the gap between wholesale and retail prices. Wholesale prices had fallen much more rapidly than retail prices, and this meant that producers were discouraged; and the high retail prices kept the consumers from buying. Romier argued that deflation would drive down the costs of production and marketing, thus giving producers greater profit and enabling merchants to drop retail prices and stimulate demand.

The key to the Redressement's deflationary program lay in reducing the fixed expenses which inflated both wholesale and retail prices. Specifically, these were business taxes, insurance, paid vacations, and interest charges. It asked the government to reduce "the monstrous fiscal charges which weigh on production and distribution"; [10] this would in turn require a cut in government expenditures in order to keep the

---

[6] *Ibid.*, p. 159.

[7] Henry Davezac in the *Revue générale de l'électricité,* Aug. 17, 1935, p. 82v.

[8] See Perrot, *La Monnaie et l'opinion publique en France et en Angleterre de 1924 à 1936,* pp. 209–220.

[9] *Bulletin,* April, 1934, pp. 15–16.

[10] *Ibid.*, p. 15.

budget balanced. Although an alleviation of the oppressive tax burden was necessary, according to the Redressement, it must not be achieved through a budgetary deficit. For a deficit not only endangered the franc but also increased government borrowing and shrank available credit, and thus raised interest rates on loans for business. Moreover, the government by cutting its expenditures would set an example for private business. The Redressement pointed out that although government expenses had remained at the high 1930 level, the economy had fallen sharply and could no longer support so grand a budget. Only a general trimming back would reduce French prices to meet international competition and slack demand at home.

There were other important reasons, stemming from traditional economic ideas and practices, which convinced the Redressement that deflation was the solution to the depression. First, as Romier maintained, Poincaré had used this method to save the franc in 1926. Obviously this argument from precedent ignored the fact that Poincaré had also raised some taxes and that his problem was primarily monetary rather than a general production slowdown. Second, Romier feared any imitation of Roosevelt's New Deal as an unwise extension of government interference in economic life. He criticized Roosevelt for using government credit to inflate wages and prices because this policy only prolonged the crisis by supporting inefficient production and by killing "natural credit." Worst of all, government borrowing raised the temptation of devaluation. To Romier and Mercier, and perhaps to most Frenchmen after Poincaré's devaluation, another depreciation of the currency seemed tantamount to robbery—the loss of savings, pensions, and other investments. Romier believed that devaluation brought no benefits, only disorder; it reduced purchasing power by shrinking the value of the franc, and did not assist exports. He even argued that devaluation led to antidemocratic governments and offered as "proof" that "when the mark fell to zero" the Nazi party was founded (1923 [sic]), when the pound sterling lost value the British Labor government was turned out of office (1931), and when the dollar collapsed "Roosevelt's dictatorship" began (1933).[11]

Unfortunately, the partial deflationary measures which were introduced during the early '30's did not alleviate the depression in France. Only when deflation was rigorously applied in 1935 did it bring some results. Raymond Aron has accused deflation of "sacrificing the economy to the currency," and has pointed to the period 1930–1945 as a "disastrous phase" in French economic development when the nation

[11] *Ibid.,* February, 1934, p. 3.

fell behind the rest of the Western world in industrial progress.[12] An American authority contends that deflation prolonged the depression in France and perhaps even aggravated it.[13] Most Frenchmen, seem to have been quite willing to sacrifice economic progress in order to preserve their income and savings. The Redressement industrialists foresaw no such sacrifice from radical deflation and went on to help inspire the climax of this policy under Pierre Laval in 1935.[14]

Throughout the interwar years there was a continual effort by the vanguard of both business and labor to check the disorder of French capitalism. The First World War had displayed the inadequacies of the nation's economy as compared with those of Germany and the United States, and thus during the '20's the Redressement and other reformers such as the neo-syndicalists initiated movements for economic organization. Not surprisingly, this effort to curb the anarchy and inefficiency of capitalism gained momentum during the depression, as seen in the spread of corporative theories and the elaboration of economic plans.

The Redressement's original program had in fact already deviated from the principles of classical economic liberalism. As true heirs of Saint-Simon these reformers had departed from the laissez-faire tradition by advocating a society of producers who ordered the economy not by giving free play to self-interest but by developing a business ethic based on the primacy of the public interest.[15] Other means of regulating excessive competition, according to these modernizers, were industrial concentration and producers' agreements.[16] Mercier, for example, exhorted others to imitate the electric power industry in pooling capital and sharing markets. The Redressement had also proposed the introduction of representatives of the business elite into government to provide more economic expertise. Moreover, it had advocated the for-

[12] *Immuable et changeante: de la IVᵉ à la Vᵉ république* (Paris, 1959) , pp. 97, 101.

[13] Martin Wolfe, *The French Franc Between the Wars, 1919–1939* (New York, 1951) , pp. 135–136.

[14] *Bulletin,* July, 1935, p. 1; *Le Populaire* and *L'Humanité,* Aug. 8, 1935.

[15] See E. S. Mason, "Saint-Simonism and the Rationalization of Industry," pp. 640–683.

[16] J. Tchernoff, *Ententes économiques et financières* (Paris, 1933) , shows how producers' ententes were a means of implementing modernization, and Elizabeth Dussauze, *L'État et les ententes industrielles* (Paris, 1938) discusses how these agreements continued to flourish in the '30's. But Gaston Lecordier, "Le Mouvement patronal," *Chronique sociale de France,* LCIII (January–February, 1949) , 71, argues that these ententes did not introduce any "collective discipline" to the economy because they were signed by individual entrepreneurs and not by producers' organizations. And Charles Bettelheim, a Marxist critic, sees no distinction between the modernizers' ententes and old-fashioned monopolies; see *Bilan de l'économie française, 1919–1946* (Paris, 1947) , p. 150.

mation of mixed plant committees and arbitration boards to bring order to industrial relations.[17] In short, during the '20's the Redressement technocrats believed that regular consultation between public officials and business leaders, a Saint-Simonian type of self-government among producers, plus a dash of social reform would end the disorder of free enterprise.

Once the depression struck, more extreme measures seemed necessary to discipline capitalism. Certain business leaders advocated the principle of *organisation professionelle* or "vocational organization"—that is, the strengthening of old and the creation of new employers' organs.[18] But more controversial reforms, especially corporatism, were being widely debated in business circles.[19] Corporatism, which tended to expand the view of the neo-syndicalists and the proponents of "vocational organization," proposed to reorganize the various branches of economic life, for example, the transportation industry, into official bodies or corporations. The corporation, in which membership would be obligatory, would not only guide general economic policy but would also have legal authority to enforce its decisions within its particular domain. It was no surprise that the Redressement officially rejected corporatism, though other big business groups like the Comité des Forges did so with more vehemence.[20]

A special Redressement report issued in 1934 concluded that corporative theory was based on three impractical, if not foolish, ideas.[21] First, to force labor and management to deliberate together was unworkable because the former still believed in the class struggle, and because all previous attempts to bring them together on a voluntary basis had failed. Second, it was unwise to confer legal authority on new, un-

[17] The plant committees, according to this scheme, had only limited authority and the employers' role was predominant. For details see *L'Aspect social de rationalisation*, Cahiers du Redressement Français, Series I, No. 10, pp. 43–79.

[18] Among its advocates were the Nouveaux Cahiers group, the Comité Central de l'Organisation Professionnelle, and the Jeune Patron group. See Ehrmann, *Organized Business in France*.

[19] On corporatism during the interwar period see Maurice Bouvier-Ajam, *La Doctrine corporative* (4th ed.; Paris, 1943); Paul Vignaux, *Traditionalisme et syndicalisme: essai d'histoire sociale, 1884–1941* (New York, 1943); Ehrmann, *Organized Business*, pp. 50–51 et passim; Matthew H. Elbow, *French Corporative Theory, 1789–1948: A Chapter in the History of Ideas* (New York, 1953), pp. 122–167. For the reaction of business see Gaëtan Pirou, *Essais sur le corporatisme* (Paris, [1938]), pp. 65, 95–105.

[20] See the *Supplément économique* of *Le Temps*, June 18, 1935. Pirou (*Essais*, pp. 99–101) criticized the Comité des Forges for rejecting any reform tinged with corporatism—even the Flandin–Marchandeau law of 1935—while at the same time advocating competition and enjoying the uncompetitive benefits of producers' agreements, tariffs, and quotas.

[21] *Bulletin*, June, 1934, pp. 2–17.

tried, artificial organizations. Third, the authority given the corporations would in fact only extend government interference and lead to "the economic dictatorship of the state." On this last point the Redressement offered the "corporative regimes" in Italy and Portugal as evidence. In Fascist Italy the corporative assembly, which replaced parliament, was "only a direct emanation of the dominant political party." The few efforts made to establish a true corporative regime in Italy only demonstrated the theory's absurdity—witness the artificial corporative classification which combined civil servants, lawyers, and actors in the "Corporation of Liberal Professions." Portugal was no different, and the Redressement concluded that in both countries "the corporative regime is only one aspect of the economic monarchy of the state." Sensitive to economic interference by government, these French industrialists assessed corporatism in practice with some accuracy.

Yet between 1933 and 1935 the Redressement shifted ground and made important concessions to the corporative vogue. Joseph Zamanski, the president of the Catholic employers' association and a Redressement stalwart, suggested strengthening existing professional bodies, like the Chambers of Commerce and the National Economic Council, rather than creating an entirely new corporative structure.[22] The Redressement also recommended the establishment of two new advisory councils, similar to the National Economic Council.[23] One, the Conseil Supérieur de la Production, would group representatives of production to advise parliament on economic legislation and to police the economy. The other, the Conseil Supérieur Économique, would gather representatives from the new production council, from the old Conseil Supérieur du Travail, and from consumer associations to collaborate with the bureaucracy in drafting legislation—thus supplanting the "incompetent" and overtaxed parliamentary committees. In 1935 Cacaud accepted yet another corporative encroachment on economic liberalism. He admitted that during such "an economic storm" government must help "discipline the productive forces of the nation." [24] Accordingly, he supported the proposed Flandin–Marchandeau law which would enable the state to enforce industry-wide producers' agreements.[25]

[22] *Ibid.*, October, 1933, pp. 14–16.

[23] *Ibid.*, June, 1934, pp. 6–8.

[24] *Ibid.*, January, 1935, p. 4.

[25] Government intervention was limited to extremely serious situations in which two-thirds of the producers responsible for two-thirds of the transactions in a branch of industry willingly formed an agreement. In this case, after approval of an arbitration committee, the agreement could be made obligatory by government decree for the entire industry. The Senate eventually interred this law in committee. Business was divided in its reaction to this measure. The CGPF had its reservations, according to Odette de Magondeaux, *Les Ententes industrielles obligatoires et le*

Officially the Redressement directors had always opposed obligatory or legal corporatism, which they thought smacked of surreptitious government interference and the further crystallization of society around interest groups. But though they were unwilling to embrace openly this economic "radicalism" of the '30's, in practice they modified their beliefs. They adopted the movement to fortify existing trade associations; they agreed to extend producers' agreements under government auspices; and they argued for more extensive collaboration between government officials and the business elite. This collaboration could be best achieved by establishing extraparliamentary bodies staffed voluntarily by the elite. Zamanski summarized the Redressement's position: "A directed economy? By the state? Never. By producers' cartels? The danger is obvious. What is needed is collaboration between the producers' freedom and the state's authority. Should the final goal not be to bring them together by calling the competent to be authorities for the state. At this price the state will be saved from anarchy and bankrupt parliamentarianism." [26] In fact, these managerial technocrats moved toward embracing the kind of joint economic planning by government and business that prevailed in France during the Second World War.

Within a broad historical context, the drive for economic organization in France has persisted since the First World War, led primarily by Mercier and the technocrats. Industrial concentration, producers' self-government, and consultation between public officials and the business elite as proposed by the Redressement was only an early stage of this development. In the '30's the neo-syndicalists' interest in vocational organization was revived by certain employers and was greatly expanded by the corporatists. Indeed, there was a growing sense of the importance of economic forces, and during the depression schemes for controlling capitalism ranged from the CGT's plan, which included nationalization of key industries, to corporative theories tinged with fascism.[27] The Redressement managers avoided anything so radical as

---

corporatisme en France (Paris, 1937) , p. 68. The Paris Chamber of Commerce and the Comité d'Action et de Douanière opposed the project for violating economic freedom, impeding competition, and aiding economic nationalism (Magondeaux, pp. 86–91) . Dussauze (pp. 76–87) discusses the general reaction to the law, and states that the CGT approved it with reservations (p. 115) .

[26] *Bulletin,* October, 1933, p. 16.

[27] A study group called X-Crise, which was organized by a few progressive Polytechnicians, provided a forum for discussion of economic problems during the depression. Here some of the most enlightened proposals for economic reform were debated. For a careful analysis of these discussions see Guy Desaunay, "X-Crise, Contribution à l'étude des idéologies économiques d'un groupe de polytechniciens durant la grande crise économique, 1931–1939," unpublished thesis, Université de Paris, 1965.

these, though ultimately, under the Vichy regime, they were to accept a certain amount of corporatism, which tended to merge the interests of private industry and government.

Added to the worry of the depression, the international situation was becoming increasingly ominous. Mercier had never been particularly interested in diplomatic affairs, although he had actively participated in the movement for European economic unity and as a leading figure in the world of international business, with interests stretching from the United States to Russia and the Middle East, he was extremely sensitive to developments outside France. As the optimism of the Locarno era gave way to renewed tension in Europe, he became preoccupied with the French diplomatic situation.

French thinking on foreign policy appeared dominated by hesitation and equivocation. Mercier's message in contrast was clear and simple: France was a great power and must actively defend itself against a mighty Germany bent on aggression. Early in 1932, under the auspices of the Redressement, a group of prominent experts gathered to study the international situation.[28] Among the participants were Marshals Pétain and Franchet d'Esperey, General Debeney, Alfred Lambert-Ribot, Wladimir d'Ormesson, and André Siegfried. Pétain regularly attended Redressement meetings on problems of national defense and international relations, and he later appointed many Redressement members to positions in the Vichy government.

This study committee concluded that the Weimar Republic sought "the disarmament of others in order to obtain freedom to arm itself in its own way," and that "an equitable adjustment of certain territorial clauses, supposing it were possible, could only bring additional and increasingly imperious demands by Germany."[29] A direct Franco-German agreement "appeared impossible" considering the issues dividing the two nations and Germany's intention to interpret such an agreement as a sign of French weakness. But there was a way: "in order to reach Berlin, it is necessary to take a detour: the road to Berlin goes through London. To make an entente possible with Germany, it is necessary to revive the old *entente cordiale*."[30]

Hesitant about reviving British memories of the last war, Mercier's committee suggested that France should not seek a formal alliance or a

[28] See *Politique extérieure*, Cahiers du Redressement Français, Series II, No. 1. The committee's reports were summarized in the *Bulletin*, February, 1932, pp. 2–4. For a list of titles in this second series of cahiers, of which sixteen of eighteen volumes were devoted to international relations between 1932 and 1935, see the Bibliography.

[29] *Bulletin*, February, 1932, pp. 2–3.

[30] *Ibid.*, p. 4.

military pact with Britain, but rather should rely upon the rapid intervention of His Majesty's air force. The necessary complement to a new *entente cordiale* was a Franco-Italian agreement. The study committee urged that "sentiment" be excluded from relations with Italy, and that a calculated "deal" be made with Mussolini. Once Britain and Italy were at its side, France, instead of vainly soliciting an agreement with Germany, could expect the Weimar government to approach it hat in hand.

But the primary task of France, according to the experts, was to remain strong: modernize the army, maintain financial stability, defend the League, and preserve its alliances in eastern Europe. Mercier added his views on the Soviet Union to the report; these are significant considering the radical change they were to undergo in a few years. He argued that the Soviet regime was incompatible with Western civilization since it did not play by the rules of the game in either international politics or trade. Mercier pictured the Soviet Union as an immensely powerful country guarding its mystery, and holding certain economic advantages through its state monopolies.

This foreign policy conference was scarcely concluded when Mercier observed an ominous development in Germany. The cancellation of reparations in July, 1932, by the Lausanne conference, he believed, left Germany with the most modern industrial plant, the largest population, and the lightest tax load; that is, without war debts the German taxpayer had a smaller burden than any American, Englishman, or Frenchman. He pointed out that reparations had often been misinterpreted as purely a financial problem, whereas their real importance was in giving the victors of 1918 control over the German economy. He warned that Germany, since it was in a better economic position than the nations that had defeated it, needed only foreign credit to enable it to begin its economic advance on Europe. The fear of German economic power, which was evident among certain French businessmen in the '20's, was thus intensified by the depression.

The Nazi seizure of power aroused Mercier to tell a Redressement assembly in the summer of 1934 that the question of Franco-German relations overshadowed all domestic and foreign problems. Henceforth, the German problem seemed to monopolize his attention. He warned the proponents of disarmament, specifically the Socialists, not to forget certain German national characteristics. The German genius, Mercier contended, was for "deceit" and "the armed conquest of other countries." [31] He thought the German people accepted "a regime which would revolt any other civilized nation—an arbitrary military

[31] *Ibid.*, July, 1934, p. 2.

dictatorship," because they viewed it as "a kind of redemption for their misery" leading them "toward Germany's destiny of universal domination." [32]

He felt a certain optimism because Nazi religious and armament policies were antagonizing other nations,[33] and he also observed fissures in the Nazi foundation which he thought would soon topple Hitler's edifice. Certainly, he argued, an economy in which the state purchased 80 percent of all national production for rearmament could not last since it violated natural economic laws. The Nazis would soon face the choice of revolution or war: either the regime would collapse when it abandoned overproduction and unemployment returned, or else, when it completed its rearmament about mid-1935, it would attack. In his opinion, the German people would quickly tire of parades and "swaggering," and current tension would abate. Mercier's hopes were, of course, unfounded. Within a year, for example, Great Britain demonstrated its willingness to work with Nazi Germany by concluding the Anglo-German naval agreement.

As for Italy, with whom France seemed compelled to cooperate, its "transformation" under fascism struck Mercier as notable, but he considered Mussolini's foreign policy, "a succession of errors." [34] Italy's rearmament gave Germany the claim to equal rights, and Mussolini showed Hitler what could be accomplished by bravado. Il Duce, Mercier argued, desired an expansive foreign policy, yet he was confronted with Germany as a rival in central Europe; therefore, he would bargain secretly with France to restrain Hitler, although publicly he would support the German right to rearm.

During 1934 Mercier praised Barthou's policy of encircling Germany and later claimed that the Redressement had prepared public opinion for its acceptance. Apparently some members were critical of the weakness of France's eastern allies, but Mercier stressed the need for at least keeping these nations neutral. It was in this same year that Mercier also began to re-examine his concept of the Soviet Union. In the '20's he had subsidized an anti-Bolshevik review which demanded the diplomatic isolation of the Soviets, but now he argued that France must reconsider its policy in order to prevent a Russo-German alliance. He observed that even if Polish neutrality prevented the intervention of the Red army the Soviet air force could strike Berlin directly. There were also important economic considerations since the Soviets appeared as a

---

[32] *Ibid.*, December, 1934, p. 3.
[33] For his views on the Nazi regime see *ibid.*, July, 1934, pp. 4–6, and December, 1934, pp. 3–4.
[34] *Ibid.*, December, 1934, p. 7.

likely possibility for a profitable trade agreement with France. These rather tentative observations were soon to blossom into a new and rather remarkable view of Soviet relations which was to take Mercier to Moscow.

Mercier's distrust of Germany was rather more complicated than an ordinary Frenchman's. Ever since his wartime service at the Ministry of Armaments and his experience in the occupation of the Rhineland in 1921, Mercier had been acutely conscious—even afraid—of German industrial superiority, and though he had for a time been hopeful of a Franco-German reconciliation, which would have served as a measure of control over the Germans, such hopes faded as Germany recovered its economic might and political independence. Mercier was, of course, quite as dedicated a patriot as any other veteran of the Great War, and he stubbornly refused to concede European hegemony to France's traditional enemy. The Redressement was an expression of this spirit, a practical attempt to bring about a renaissance of *la patrie*. It is evident, however, that, more than anything else, Mercier distrusted the Germans as atavistic warriors bent on military aggression.[35] In this, perhaps, he merely echoed the sentiments of a great many other Frenchmen—but with the difference that he well knew the economic and technical strength of the German colossus then readying itself for war.

For the moment, however, no effective means of stopping Germany seemed possible; events were moving beyond Mercier's control. But a part of his concern with foreign policy was reflected in a concern for parliamentary reform—and in this field several events occurred that seemed encouraging to him.

For years, Mercier and the Redressement had attacked the existing political system, especially the power monopoly of the deputies, and had campaigned for "a modern parliamentary regime"—a restoration of executive authority and administrative independence, along with technocratic streamlining. When the 1932 legislature was unable to act decisively to relieve the depression, the Redressement sharpened its attacks. In January, 1933, Mercier condemned political parties for paralyzing government with their pointless obstructionism. "Political hypocrisy," he warned, rendered every cabinet "impotent," and would

---

[35] Mercier's stereotype of the Germans was probably reinforced by his contact with an emigree teacher, Professor Friedrich W. Foerster, whose denunciations of German militarism aroused such antagonism that he was forced to flee his homeland for Paris in 1926. It is not clear when Foerster and Mercier met, but Mercier helped to subsidize the publication of a French edition of at least one of Foerster's books: *L'Europe et la question allemande* (Paris, 1937).

precipitate the fall of the regime." [36] Cacaud believed the situation was desperate because no deputy would vote real deflationary cuts for fear of alienating some of his electors. Late that same year Mercier gravely predicted that if a strong cabinet did not take power soon, there would be "violent disturbances and street riots," and Marcel Champin added that the youth of the postwar generation was "boiling with discontent" and might initiate "upheavals that we would all regret." [37]

If their inability to halt the depression had made the deputies seem inept, the Stavisky scandal, which exploded in January, 1934, made them look like criminals to boot. Certainly the Radical government headed by Camille Chautemps was not entirely blameless, and the right-wing *Action française* led the hue and cry against Albert Dalimier, Minister of Colonies, who seemed clearly implicated in the fraudulent bond affair. As other newspapers took up the story, demanding a thorough investigation of Stavisky's suicide and its ramifications, the Action Française put its youth group, the Camelots du Roi, on the streets to demonstrate. The annual general assembly of the Redressement was called in session on January 24 as these demonstrations began spreading from the Boulevard Saint-Germain to the Right Bank. Some of the delegates took heart: one staff official observed that the public was so exasperated that the Redressement stood "on the eve of attaining its goals." [38] Speech after speech criticized the corruption of the Chautemps government and predicted violence. Cacaud spoke of the bankruptcy of universal suffrage and asked not for "personal rule," but for "the re-establishment of the unity of command." [39] He saw society fragmenting into interest groups, each of which filled its pockets by purposely electing politicians who could be corrupted. Mercier believed the scandal was "very serious" when the high administration and the judiciary were implicated, but "intolerable" when political camaraderie hid the affair. Obviously, he observed, reforms were necessary: "Because of the electoral system, politics interferes in everything, introduces incompetence and irresponsibility everywhere, and leads to perpetual scandal. Without the necessary reforms we are liable to see our society—our entire civilization—sink into an ocean of scandal." But the reforms would have to be imposed: "There is no deliberative assembly which has reformed itself. This reform can only come from an authority which will impose it by virtue of the popular will. There is no other solution to emerge from this disorder than that which we

[36] *Bulletin,* January, 1933, p. 2.
[37] *Ibid.,* December, 1933, pp. 16, 19.
[38] *Ibid.,* January, 1934, p. 3.
[39] *Ibid.,* p. 7.

have proclaimed, and circumstances will soon impose: that of a government of authority supported by an irresistible popular moral force." Finally, he said, "If parliament does not delegate its authority to a government with broad support, not a government of parties, but a national government . . . then one day it will feel the effects of popular wrath." [40]

The Redressement technocrats were not alone in their attacks on parliament as the crisis raced toward a climax. Much of the business and right-wing press also contributed to the rising antiparliamentary fever.[41] The demonstrations continued and grew noisier. On January 27 Chautemps resigned, and was replaced by Daladier. Finally, on the very day when violence was unleashed, Romier wrote in the staid *Le Temps* (February 6, 1934) : "the worn-out décor of our electoral and parliamentary theater risks being destroyed one day by a sudden awakening of the nation. . . . Once their good nature is shaken, our people are recognized as one of the most violent."

During the evening of February 6 the very existence of the Third Republic was in jeopardy as rioters, howling "Down with the thieves," battled police near the Palais Bourbon. The Daladier government resigned and the next day Gaston Doumergue came out of retirement to form a Union Nationale government and attempt to save France from civil chaos. As an organization the Redressement did not participate in the fighting, but on the seventh it distributed posters declaring that the victims of the riots had not died in vain since "a government of national reconciliation" was being formed.[42] It called for all Frenchmen regardless of party to support this government and to avoid further disorder. But the violence continued and on the twelfth the Left attempted to launch a general strike. The Redressement replied with a second poster: "The uprising of February 6 was not the work of a party. It was not an attack against the republic. It was an explosion of resentment by all the Parisian populace." The poster described the sixth as a demonstration against "party politics" and "the disorder of public institutions and public morality." [43] It also asserted that the Left's strike had failed because Parisians did not want to associate with

[40] *Ibid.*, pp. 10–11, 14.

[41] See Williard, *Quelques Aspects du fascisme en France avant le 6 février 1934,* pp. 221–222; and Chambre des députés, quinzième législature, session de 1934, *Rapport général fait au nom de la commission d'enquête chargée de rechercher les causes et les origines des événements du 6 février et les jours suivants, ainsi que toutes les responsabilités encourues,* 4 vols. (Paris, 1934), IV, 59–60 (hereafter cited as *Commission d'enquête du 6 février*) .

[42] Reprinted in Georges Michon, *Les Puissances d'argent et l'émeute du 6 février* (Paris, 1934) , p. 20.

[43] *Ibid.*, pp. 22–23.

those who attempted to distort the sixth into a struggle between Right and Left.

In the *Bulletin* Mercier described February 6 as the victory of "the spirit of the Front" over "those who have organized the methodical exploitation of the republic for the appetites of their clientele"; that is, the veterans had reasserted their moral authority against a parliament dominated by material self-interest. It was the glorious moment that Mercier and others had waited for since 1918 when the "spirit of the trenches" returned to supplant egoism and party politics. He indignantly flayed those who might turn this noble sacrifice into another partisan issue, and concluded that Frenchmen must rally: "For the nation, around the veterans." [44] Although Mercier oversimplified the nature of February 6 by ignoring the role of the political leagues like the Action Française, he correctly stressed the leadership of the veterans.

The Redressement became an enthusiastic supporter of Doumergue and pleaded that he hurry with his measures for constitutional reform—that is, revive the premier's right to dissolve parliament, limit the Chamber's budgetary initiative, and place stricter controls on civil servants. It urged extremists to stop agitating and asked veterans "to assume their duties." No cabinet since Tardieu's included more friends of the Redressement or was held in higher esteem by the organization. And when Doumergue resigned in November, 1934, before implementing his reforms, the Redressement sadly watched its last hope vanish.[45] (It was a sort of portent that the staunch Romier left the organization in mid-1934 to return to *Le Figaro*.)

The role of the Redressement and Mercier in particular in this, the most serious interwar crisis of the republic, was not, however, limited to exciting public opinion against parliament or to appealing for calm once the Doumergue government assumed power. It is very significant that Mercier, and to some degree his followers, privately encouraged the two groups of rioters which supplied the bulk of the demonstrators on February 6: the right-wing veterans of the Croix de Feu and the Union Nationale des Combattants (UNC).[46] The UNC led the bloody

---

[44] February, 1934, pp. 1–2.

[45] Other business leaders also expressed their dismay at Doumergue's fall. C.-J. Gignoux wrote in the influential *Journée industrielle* (Nov. 9, 1934): "Today it is indispensable that we assure President Doumergue that the heart of France does not lie at the Palais Bourbon."

[46] René Rémond, *La Droite en France de 1815 à nos jours* (Paris, 1954), p. 208, estimates the number of participants as follows: UNC, between 10,000 and 20,000; Croix de Feu, about 7,000; Jeunesses Patriotes, between 4,000 and 10,000. Other less numerous groups which demonstrated were the Camelots du Roi (Action Française), the Communist Association Républicaine des Anciens Combattants (ARAC), the Front Universitaire, and the Solidarité Française. On the character of the riots

attack against the Chamber from the Place de la Concorde. The Croix de Feu, though less violent, gained such notoriety from the riots that it was soon regarded as the spearhead of the alleged Fascist threat. To be sure, the participants in the February 6 riot were a heterogeneous mob, and some of the political leagues that took part displayed sympathy for fascism or entertained revolutionary principles. However, a major share of the responsibility for the violence lies not with such extremists but with conservatives like the right-wing veterans and their business allies. There was a loose coalition of patriotic conservatives sparked by ex-servicemen and backed by dissatisfied businessmen, which provided much of the impetus for this major crisis of the Third Republic.

Before examining the specific relationship between Mercier and the Croix de Feu and the UNC, it is necessary to understand the historical forces that linked him and the Redressement both intellectually and emotionally with these veterans' organizations. One of the most important effects of the First World War was its enormous psychological impact on Front-line troops. Many soldiers were deeply moved by the "spirit of the Front" which dissolved social differences. Wartime camaraderie convinced many combatants not only that most class divisions were artificial, but that they could be erased if men devoted themselves unselfishly to the nation. It was this spirit born in battle which inspired many Redressement industrialists and united them with the right-wing veterans. They all believed that political parties and social classes were fictions which falsely divided Frenchmen and endangered the nation. For example, the spirit of the Croix de Feu was described as "the idea of *patriotic and social reconciliation*—among men, parties and classes." [47] Colonel François de La Rocque, the leader of the Croix de Feu, once remarked that an elaborate program was unnecessary because "without the animating mystique, a program remains sterile and withers like a plant deprived of air." [48] This mystique of the trenches carried with it a sense of moral superiority growing out of wartime sacrifices and a belief in selfless dedication to France.

During the depression, the need for fraternity appeared to be more acute than at any time since the war. The economic crisis seemed to fragment society into petty interest groups, each grasping to preserve

---

and the participants, see René Rémond, "Explications du 6 février," *Politique*, July–December, 1959, pp. 218–230; Max Beloff, "The Sixth of February," in James Joll (ed.), *The Decline of the Third Republic*, St. Antony's Papers, No. 5 (London, 1959), pp. 9–35.

[47] François Veuillot, *La Rocque et son parti comme je les ai vus* (Paris, 1938), p. 55.

[48] Quoted in *ibid.*, p. 63.

its material well-being. One scholar considers 1933 the apex of inter-est-group intervention in parliamentary deliberations, leading to the climax of extra-parliamentary activity in the February riots.[49] The nov-elty of the Redressement during the '20's had been its attempt to over-come personal and group interests and to reconcile Frenchmen through patriotism and progress. In the '30's certain veterans, espe-cially those of the Croix de Feu and the UNC, disregarded benefits and pensions and also devoted themselves to national reform, or to "public service" as La Rocque liked to say. Apparently much of the appeal of these movements sprang from a need for spiritual solidarity; whether or not there was in fact greater social fragmentation is perhaps irrele-vant, since the important thing was that many Frenchmen believed this to be the situation and welcomed efforts to halt further disintegra-tion.

The Redressement always tried to foster the "spirit of the Front" among veterans and to transform this energy into a movement for po-litical reform. In many ways Mercier's group itself was a patriotic veteran's organization. It was led by a war hero and its membership consisted largely of ex-servicemen; furthermore, its initial appeal was specifically directed toward veterans. "The spirit of the Redressement Français," according to its own propaganda, "is that of the generation that fought in the war." [50] *Nos Plaisirs,* its veterans' magazine, in-structed ex-servicemens' organizations to become politically active. Those armed with the spirit of fraternity, sacrifice, and disinteres-tedness forged under fire, should, it said, "chase the moneylenders [politicians] from the temple." [51] It urged veterans to engage in a pro-gram of national renovation and to run for office, but not to weaken their power by joining a political party. Mercier himself tended to dis-tinguish industrialists as progressive or reactionary depending upon whether or not they had fought at the Front. He made a determined effort to win veterans' groups away from political abstinence and from a preoccupation with pensions and reunions and to transform them into an active political movement devoted to national reform. His ef-forts were aided by the tendency of veterans' groups to cherish author-

---

[49] August Soulier, *L'Instabilité ministérielle sous la troisième république, 1871–1938* (Paris, 1939), pp. 379–380, mentions specifically the organized groups of civil servants, taxpayers, and veterans. The paradox is, of course, that though veterans in the Croix de Feu and UNC attacked all interest groups which pursued materialistic self-defense, other ex-servicemen's groups like the Union Fédérale were among the worst offenders.

[50] *Le Redressement Français: organisation et réformes* (Paris, 1927), p. 6.

[51] "Pour une Politique des anciens combattants," *Nos Plaisirs,* Nov. 28, 1926, pp. 30–31. See also José Germain, "Le Minotaure A. C.," *Paris-Phare,* Dec. 4, 1927, pp. 7–8; *Bulletin,* November, 1926, p. 10.

ity, discipline, and national unity, which often converted them into right-wing political forces.[52]

The UNC, like the Redressement, was founded shortly after the war, specifically to defend veterans' interests. In the mid-1920's its Paris branch, led by the deputy Jean Goy and the municipal councilor Georges Lebecq, started a campaign to draw the national organization into "civic action." [53] Goy collaborated with the Redressement from its inception and in the Chamber he headed a small independent group called the *non-politiques* who were occupied primarily with economic questions. According to Georges Valois, who for several years acted as economic adviser to the Action Française, Goy received a subsidy from Mercier in 1925 to mobilize veterans into a political Front Républicain.[54] Moreover, Mercier was a ranking member of the Parisian UNC and had numerous friends among its leaders.[55]

Officially the national UNC confined itself to defending veterans' benefits until 1933, when, prodded by the Parisian section, it endorsed a broad program of reform—a *redressement national.*[56] In outline, the UNC's program as it emerged in 1934–1935 was very similar to the Redressement's: it attacked Italian-style corporatism, Marxism, and "statism"; and it advocated deflation and the constitutional reforms proposed by Doumergue.[57] To bring order to capitalism and competence to government, the UNC also urged better coordination of professional organizations through a strengthened National Economic Council, plus certain technocratic changes in the parliamentary committee system. It antagonized various left-wing veterans' groups by urging all veterans to accept the principle of pension revision (that is, deflationary cuts).[58] The Redressement Français, too, asked veterans

[52] For the right-wing tendencies of veterans see René Rémond's excellent analysis in "Les anciens Combattants et la politique," *Revue française de science politique,* V (April–June, 1955), 267–290.

[53] See Lebecq's testimony on the UNC's history in *Commission d'enquête du 6 février,* II, 8–38. Its organs were *La Voix du combattant* and *L'UNC de Paris.* On veterans' movements in general see Pierre Frédérix, *État des forces en France* (3rd ed.; Paris, 1935), pp. 170–178.

[54] *Chantiers,* Feb. 10, Mar. 1, 20, and May 9, 1934.

[55] Mercier papers. Although Lebecq did not know Mercier, he said that he "would be very happy to meet him"; see *Commission d'enquête du 6 février,* II, 1848.

[56] *Ibid.,* IV, 8–9.

[57] For the details of the program see *L'UNC de Paris,* June, 1934; *Voix du combattant,* Oct. 6, 20, 27, and Nov. 10, 1934; Jean Goy, *Réforme des institutions, réforme électorale et réforme parlementaire* (Paris, [1935]).

[58] In 1934 when Doumergue attempted a 3 percent cut in veterans' pensions the UNC backed him, but the left-wing Union Fédérale (*Cahiers de l'Union Fédérale,* May 1, 1934) and the Communist ARAC (*Le Réveil des combattants,* Aug. 16–Oct. 15, 1934) objected violently. This Right–Left division over the pension issue almost splintered the general veterans' association, the Confédération Nationale des Anciens Combattants (*Excelsior,* July 9, 1934).

not to violate their sacred trust with those who had fallen, and endanger the nation by obstructing pension reductions.[59] In fact, Mercier's group was but one of many business organizations which were closely allied with the national UNC. As many as thirty groups representing manufacturers, merchants, and taxpayers also cooperated with the UNC, and, according to Lebecq, helped formulate its program.[60] In addition, the UNC was linked with the Croix de Feu, and Lebecq is said to have consulted with the Croix de Feu on February 5 about its plans for the demonstrations.[61]

In the riots on February 6 the Parisian UNC, personally directed by Goy and Lebecq, led the assault against the Chamber from the Place de la Concorde. When asked the UNC's purpose on that evening, Lebecq replied that it sought "to replace a ministry of partisans with a ministry of public safety," and that it was "very happy" with the new cabinet.[62] Unlike some left-wing veterans' groups, such as the Union Fédérale, the UNC, with the official support of its business allies, vigorously backed Doumergue and his reforms throughout 1934. It sent delegations to him in the midst of the November cabinet crisis and offered to demonstrate for his government if necessary.[63] *Le Figaro* (November 6, 1934) reported that these delegations represented "three and a half million veterans, industrialists, and merchants."

The program of the Croix de Feu, though vague, closely resembled those of both the UNC and the Redressement. It is worth note that both Mercier and Colonel de La Rocque were inspired by the example of the same two military heroes, Marshals Lyautey and Foch. Lyautey from his deathbed reportedly commanded La Rocque "to achieve a reconciliation of Frenchmen around the servicemen." [64] The Colonel was

---

[59] *Bulletin,* February, 1933, p. 7.

[60] *Commission d'enquête du 6 février,* II, 1848. Lebecq denied that the Redressement was included, but he acknowledged that other UNC leaders might be acquainted with Mercier's movement. For a list of these business groups see *Le Figaro,* Nov. 6, 1934. Among them were the Confédération Générale des Contribuables, the Confédération des Groupements Commerciaux et Industriels de France, and numerous retailers' and property owners' associations.

[61] Lebecq admitted that he participated in rallies of the Croix de Feu, but, he said, only as a private citizen and not as a representative of the UNC (*Le Populaire,* July 18, 1935) . Georges Riché, a founder and director of the Croix de Feu, told the author (July 8, 1964) that Lebecq had met with La Rocque on the eve of the riots, though La Rocque himself denied that this ever happened; see Édith and Gilles de La Rocque, *La Rocque tel qu'il était* (Paris, 1962) , p. 285.

[62] *Commission d'enquête du 6 février,* IV, 114–115.

[63] See Édouard Herriot's statement in *Jadis: d'une guerre à l'autre, 1914–1936* (Paris, 1952) , II, 468. Also see Goy, *Réforme,* p. 10, and Jacques Fischer, *Doumergue et les politiciens* (Paris, 1935) , pp. 230, 241 ff.

[64] Édith and Gilles de La Rocque, pp. 18–36, 53–55, 132.

hostile to party politics ("We will chase politicians from the national patrimony"), and sought to spread a spirit of reconciliation. He described the Croix de Feu as a movement of the Center: "neither fascist nor socialist," it "knows no enemy other than hate and will reconcile all Frenchmen in respect and love for work, family, and country." [65] He attacked "statism" as a synonym for "waste, disorder, and impotence." [66] His ideas on constitutional reform were typically conservative: degenerate parliamentarianism required a stronger executive and a strict limitation of the Chamber's powers. He also advocated sweeping deflation, including pension revision, along with increased economic discipline, specifically, the elimination of both "politics" and the "oligarchies" from workers' and employers' organizations. Like many Frenchmen in the '30's, the Colonel also spoke of the "decadence of capitalism," but he hesitated to endorse corporatism,[67] and his economic reforms were too mild to disturb many businessmen. Rather, his proposals for tax cuts and for the substitution of "adequate compensation" for the unpopular social insurance law [68] appealed to business interests. Indeed there is evidence that at least during 1934–1935 the Croix de Feu, like the UNC and the right-wing veterans in general, found substantial support in business circles.[69]

After February 6, the Croix de Feu, unlike the UNC and the Redressement, gave the Doumergue government only conditional support—"a temporary dressing on gangrene" as La Rocque called it.[70]

[65] *Croix de Feu, Parti Social Français: tracts politiques, 1934–1939* (Paris, n.d.). For the program of the Croix de Feu also see its organ *Flambeau;* François de La Rocque, *Service public* (Paris, 1934); and *Excelsior,* July 9, 1935.

[66] *Flambeau,* Mar. 2, 1935.

[67] This is also Alexander Werth's view, in *France in Ferment* (London, 1934), p. 280, and it seems more accurate than Matthew Elbow's attempt (*French Corporative Theory,* p. 130), to classify La Rocque as an avowed corporatist. The Colonel's program was mostly platitudes, and what really counted was the mystique.

[68] Comité de Vigilance des Intellectuels Antifascistes, *Les Croix de Feu, leur chef, leur programme* (Paris, 1935).

[69] C.-J. Gignoux, who later headed the CGPF, insisted that the veterans and the leagues were not Fascists, but exasperated Frenchmen who merited praise for their action on February 6 (*Journée industrielle,* Feb. 8, and May 12–13, 1935). The business-oriented *Revue politique et parlementaire* also approved of the right-wing veterans ("Ce que représentent les a. c.," July 10, 1934, pp. 3–9). Some businesses, like the Nicolas company, were accused of pressuring employees to join the Croix de Feu (*J.O. débats,* Dec. 3, 1935, p. 2308). H. Maizy ("Les Groupes antiparlementaires républicains de droite en France de 1933 à 1939," unpublished thesis, Institut d'Études politiques, Paris, 1952) mentions rather vaguely that the high bourgeoisie became interested in the Croix de Feu and the leagues during 1934–1936. Paul Chopine, a disillusioned leader who left the movement in 1934, charged that capitalists like Mercier had recently come into the Croix de Feu; see his *Six Ans chez les Croix de Feu* (Paris, 1935), pp. 155–157.

[70] *Commission d'enquête du 6 février,* IV, 42.

The Colonel was close to Doumergue, but he showed little enthusiasm for his cabinet until November, when he appeared publicly with him and angrily attacked those who had brought his downfall.[71]

Mercier, and perhaps other Redressement leaders as well, privately encouraged the Croix de Feu. To what extent Mercier did so is not precisely known, but it is evident that the Left has distorted the connection. A Communist historian, for example, has recently said that "La Rocque owed his promotion to leadership of the Croix de Feu to his intrigues and to powerful support; first of all to Mercier." [72] This same historian asserts that La Rocque, after leaving the army in 1929, was employed by the Compagnie Générale d'Électricité, where Mercier was a member of the board of directors. However true that may be, the evidence indicates that the Colonel had left the firm and become president-general of the Croix de Feu (1931) before he ever met Mercier.[73] It seems clear that the individual most responsible for La Rocque's ascendancy in the Croix de Feu was not Mercier but Marshal Foch.[74]

Mercier met La Rocque at a luncheon held at the Tour d'Argent on December 15, 1933.[75] At the end of the meal he joined the Croix de Feu and paid a thousand francs for his membership. Mercier joined the movement not to enlist "veterans to die for the dividends of Alsthom and the CPDE" [76] (as one critic charged), but out of sympathy for the movement's general objectives. He did not assist in the direction of the Croix de Feu, finance it, or publicly encourage Redressement members to join it. La Rocque himself denied that the electrical magnate subsidized his organization, and Mercier confirmed this denial.[77] His influence in the Croix de Feu was negligible.[78] In a histori-

[71] On the question of La Rocque's allegiance to Doumergue see Fischer, pp. 190 ff. Paul Creyssel, *La Rocque contre Tardieu* (Paris, 1938), pp. 60–63; Werth, *Which Way France?*, pp. 74, 90–91.

[72] Willard, *Aspects du fascisme*, p. 209.

[73] "Notes," Mercier papers. It was Pierre Azaria, not Mercier, who brought La Rocque into the Cie. Générale d'Électricité (Édith and Gilles de La Rocque, p. 69), which in any event was not part of the Messine syndicate. And in 1932 La Rocque asked Tardieu for a letter of introduction to Mercier; it is unlikely that this would have been necessary if the two had ever met before. See the letter from La Rocque to Tardieu, June 14, 1932, reprinted in Pozzo di Borgo, *La Rocque, fantôme à vendre* (Paris, 1938), pp. 170–171.

[74] Interview with Georges Riché, July 8, 1964.

[75] "Notes," Mercier papers.

[76] Georges Valois, *Chantiers*, Mar. 20, 1934.

[77] "Notes," Mercier papers; La Rocque, *Commission d'enquête du 6 février*, II, 1603–1604.

[78] La Rocques' son Gilles (Édith and Gilles de La Rocque, p. 284) suggests that Mercier wanted to control the Croix de Feu but that his father put him off. Consequently, Gilles writes, Mercier held "hard feelings" toward his father. This contention is contradicted by Mercier, who insisted that he had no contact with La Rocque after the luncheon and did not try to "sponsor" the group ("Notes," Mercier papers).

cal context the significant bond between the two men was their common dedication to national renovation inspired by the war.

In the end La Rocque became uneasy about Mercier's membership,
fearing that it damaged the movement's reputation. After February 6
the left-wing press exploited Mercier's affiliation to smear the veterans
as the shock troops of the "two hundred families," and in March, 1936,
La Rocque sent a director of his organization to request Mercier's resignation. Mercier was surprised and indignant; he resigned but remarked "how stupid" it was to exclude him simply because he was a
grand patron.[79]

If there was a similarity of mystique, purpose, and even specific
goals, and if Mercier joined the Croix de Feu and the UNC, then is it
accurate to call him and the Redressement "Fascists" or "pseudo-
Fascists"? Was there a "Fascist threat" in 1934, as the Left charged, led
by the Croix de Feu and inspired by Mercier and his fellow capitalists,
which planned to replace the republic with a Mussolini-style dictatorship? Certainly the Redressement manifested some of the components
of fascism: wounded patriotism, the "spirit of the trenches," and anti-
parliamentarianism. But it went no further. Mercier and his movement had no taste for the leadership cult, for a party dictatorship, for
private militias or violence, or for corporatism. These businessmen
sought strong government—a Poincaré, a Tardieu, or a Doumergue—but they opposed any form of totalitarianism or worship of
the state. In spite of his revulsion at the politics of the Third Republic,
Mercier still believed in individual liberty—no Fascist would have
said, as he did, that "human liberty is the divine in us."[80] The Redressement believed in rule by the established elites—big business,
high-ranking civil servants, and academicians—and was far from paying
homage to the masses as fascism, "the democratic heresy," did. Perhaps
most significant, the Redressement's political aims were not revolutionary; it advocated constitutional reform to streamline the republic, and
never spoke of trying to bring down the government in order to replace it with a party dictatorship. On the contrary, it wanted to maintain the old ruling order, but in a modernized form. The real proof of
the essentially conservative nature of Mercier and his group is that
they had no political aims that went beyond Doumergue's reforms.

In a similar way a contemporary French historian has argued that
the Croix de Feu lacked many of the ingredients of fascism, and that it
was essentially a conservative movement in the authoritarian, national-

---

[79] Interview with Georges Riché, July 8, 1964, who recalled this conversation. Also
see the letter from Riché to Gilles de La Rocque, May 11, 1962, in Édith and Gilles
de La Rocque, p. 293.

[80] Quoted in *Ernest Mercier: une grande destinée*, p. 81.

ist tradition intent on preserving the existing social order.[81] Certainly
Mercier, Lebecq, and La Rocque did not behave like Fascists after
1934.[82] One must look at other right-wing groups in France like Doriot's Parti Populaire Français to find truly Fascist movements.

In summary, the Redressement directors played a significant role in
the riots of February 6, and they must share, as the president of the
parliamentary investigating committee contended, in the heavy responsibility of all those who excited public opinion to the point of violence.[83] It seems clear, too, that Mercier encouraged and helped interest
at least one of the principal participants, the Paris UNC, in political reform. But there is little evidence to support the interpretation which
argues that "the riots of February 6 were desired and methodically organized by the great magnates of industry and finance on whom the organizations and leagues, which played a decisive role on that day, de-
pend directly or indirectly. . . . The actors of February 6 were only
performers whom others maneuvered." [84] Some businessmen were glad
to see antiparliamentary demonstrations, but this is a far cry from the
existence of a capitalist plot against the republic. Admittedly the Croix
de Feu and the Paris section of the UNC not only acted simultaneously, but were the only major veterans' organizations that marched
on the sixth [85]—Mercier was probably aware of their intentions. But

[81] Rémond, *La Droite en France*, pp. 209–216. See also Raoul Girardet, "Notes sur
l'esprit d'un fascisme français, 1934–1939," *Revue française de science politique*, V
(July–September, 1955) , 529–546. There is also a most revealing remark by La
Rocque explaining that he did not go further on February 6 because he wanted only
"the re-establishment of order"; see Édouard Bonnefous, *Histoire politique de la
troisième république* (Paris, 1956–1965) , V, 212. The relationship between conservatism and fascism in France is investigated, but not resolved, by Robert J. Soucy:
"The Nature of Fascism in France," *Journal of Contemporary History*, I (1966) ,
27–55.

[82] Only Goy became pro-Nazi. In November, 1934, he traveled to see Hitler—an
interview that so incensed the ardent nationalist deputy Franklin-Bouillon that he
challenged Goy to a duel. Lebecq disavowed Goy's trip, and later during the
Occupation remained hostile to the Germans while Goy collaborated; see Xavier
Vallat, *Le Nez de Cléopâtre: souvenirs d'un homme de droite, 1918–1945* (Paris,
1957) , pp. 200, 207. La Rocque after 1936 accepted the transformation of the Croix
de Feu into a rather conventional right-wing political party, the Parti Social
Français.

[83] Laurent Bonnevay, *Les Journées sanglantes de février 1934* (Paris, 1935) , pp. 22,
175, 203.

[84] Michon, *Les Puissances d'argent*, pp. 29–30. Michon claims to offer documentary
proof, but he builds his case on the assumed influence and intentions of Mercier and
other big businessmen. In fact, he bases his argument on the accusations of Georges
Valois, who after his flirtation with the neo-capitalists became their enemy. Michon's
interpretation is repeated by Daniel Guérin, *Front Populaire: révolution manquée*
(Paris, 1963) , pp. 50–51.

[85] Both groups demonstrated for the first time on February 4 and 5, whereas the
other veterans who participated, like the Communists, acted with them only on the
6th. However, the parliamentary investigation decided against the existence of a plot

Mercier did not hold a position of command in either veterans' organization and apparently had little influence in making the decision to demonstrate.

The Redressement and the two veterans' groups did not seek to replace the republic with a Fascist regime, but intended to use the opportunity presented by the Stavisky scandal to force constitutional reform on the Chamber. By implication this meant driving the Daladier government from power and repudiating the left-wing majority in the 1932 parliament. The Redressement industrialists acted not as Fascist sympathizers, however, but as frustrated and angered conservatives seeking to change the manner in which the deputies ruled France. In many ways the sixth of February represented a conservative revolt; a mixture of reformist veterans and businessmen accepted violence to achieve a "national redressement." The UNC and the Croix de Feu, supported by business allies like the Redressement, sought the establishment of strong government by limiting parliamentary power and chastising the deputies, as well as the continuation of deflation and the exaltation of patriotism and social reconciliation. This interpretation of February 6 accounts, of course, for only some of the heterogeneous participants in the crisis, and omits the vital role played by the political leagues. The intentions and views of extremist groups like the Action Française were certainly different from those of these conservatives. Yet it was patriots like Mercier and the veterans, irate conservatives sparked by "the spirit of the trenches," who played a decisive and often misunderstood role in the events of February, 1934.

---

of common action by a vote of 12 to 7 (*Commission d'enquête du 6 février,* IV, 173–176. La Rocque and Lebecq specifically denied any collusion with the Redressement. For a detailed rebuttal of the plot thesis see Beloff, "The Sixth of February," pp. 9–35.

7

The Popular Front
and the Franco-Soviet Pact

THE political developments of 1935 in France were gloomy ones for Ernest Mercier. The Left, closing ranks, began a campaign against the influence of big business; it even proposed the nationalization of the electric power industry. Worst of all, this fast-emerging Popular Front threatened to sweep the approaching elections and introduce a platform that to Mercier seemed revolutionary.

The issue that most directly affected him was, of course, the growing political controversy over the development of electric energy by private enterprise. The fundamental question was whether or not public utility companies had properly developed the nation's natural resources and created an electric power system capable of meeting the needs of the economy. Had hydroelectric resources been adequately utilized, was distribution efficiently coordinated, and was sufficient, inexpensive power readily available? To complicate the issue, there were also charges that international "trusts" secretly controlled and exploited this public service. To attempt to judge the French power industry's performance in these respects would require a detailed technical analysis which is beyond the scope of this study. However, since this controversy directly concerned Mercier, it is necessary to present the issues and make some observations.

Since the non-Communist Left, in particular the CGT, began the debate, its views may best be presented first. As early as 1918 the CGT had stated that the principle of the social ownership of public wealth required nationalization of certain industries.[1] Under the guidance of Léon Jouhaux, who was secretary-general of the CGT, this doctrine was revised and incorporated in 1934 into the trade unions' "plan."

[1] *La Nationalisation industrialisée* (Paris, 1920). For later views of the CGT on nationalization, see J. Dupoil *et al., La Nationalisation des industries-clés,* Conférences de l'Institut supérieur ouvrier, No. 21 (Paris, n.d.) ; Ludovic Zoretti, *Le Plan de la CGT,* Conférences de l'Institut supérieur ouvrier, No. 19 (Paris, n.d.). For descriptions of the CGT's program, see Maurice Byé *et al., Nationalization in France and Italy* (Ithaca, N.Y., 1955), pp. 70–72; Adolf Sturmthal, "Nationalization and Workers' Control in Britain and France," *Journal of Political Economy,* LXI (1953), 51–52.

This plan proposed a "directed economy" as the solution to the depression and recommended the nationalization of all "key industries." It was argued that several key industries, including mining, transportation, metallurgy, chemicals, and electric power, which supplied raw materials rather than manufactured products directly for consumption, actually controlled manufacturers' costs and thus determined the prices that consumers had to pay. Thus the entire cost of living was affected by the price of the kilowatt hour. If these industries were to be nationalized, so the argument went, the whole structure of the economy would be altered, because this "nationalized sector" would be operating not for the profit of individual capitalists but for a more equable distribution of wealth. This plan for nationalization was given considerable support from both the Socialist party and the Catholic trade unions.[2]

The CGT was especially critical of mismanagement in the electric power industry.[3] It accused the leaders of that industry of creating a system which failed to meet the nation's economic needs and served capitalism rather than the general welfare. The major fault of management, according to Jouhaux, was that it neglected the potentialities of hydroelectric power or "white coal," as it was called. France utilized only about one-fifth of its available water power resources, at the same time that it imported great quantities of coal and petroleum to the detriment of the nation's balance of payments. In this debate between "white coal" and "black coal," the Left contended that a greater utilization of hydroelectric power would lower rates because it was inherently less costly to produce than thermal power. Also, it maintained that the high-tension network in France was so rudimentary that Paris was unable to receive large quantities of cheap hydroelectric energy from the Massif Central. And it attacked the power industry as part of "a national energy trust," run by international finance and Anglo-Saxon petroleum interests. Mercier and the Messine syndicate were, of course, singled out for special mention here. Finally, according to the CGT experts, the sheltered, monopolistic character of the industry allowed it to make scandalous profits even during the depression. In short, private enterprise was guilty of exploiting the electric power mo-

---

[2] See Sturmthal, "Nationalization and Workers' Control," pp. 43–46. The Communists, essentially for tactical reasons, rejected nationalization throughout the interwar period and insisted that it should follow, not precede, the proletarian revolution. The Radicals also steadfastly refused to endorse any broad program of nationalization.

[3] CGT, L'Électricité, les resources nationales au service de la nation sous le contrôle de la collectivité (Versailles, 1938).

nopoly at the expense of the consumer and national economic development.

At the trade union congress in Toulouse in March, 1936, which unified the CGT and the Communist CGTU and advanced the cause of the Popular Front, the unions adopted Jouhaux's plan for the immediate nationalization of the distribution of electric power. New tripartite administrative bodies composed of representatives of the state, consumers, and "producers" (technicians and workers) were to supplant the capitalists' boards of directors. Once distribution was controlled, new nationalized hydroelectric centers, "the great hope of the future," would be built to replace the privately owned thermal plants.

Mercier and other leaders of the electric power industry were quick to deny the charges of mismanagement.[4] To the proponents of "white coal," Mercier pointed out that France needed to maintain an equilibrium among its producers of energy and must not sacrifice the coal industry to the development of hydroelectric power; that is, hydroelectric centers not only supplanted thermal plants, which were good customers of the coal industry, but also directly competed with the mines as a source of power. The obvious weakness of Mercier's strangely anti-Saint-Simonian argument is that it sacrificed economic progress to the status quo.

The real issue was which type of electric power was less expensive for France to produce. Mercier challenged the generally held notion that hydroelectric power was cheaper than thermal power, but his argument was not altogether convincing. He stated that the price of a kilowatt hour depended upon geography, that is, the proximity to mines or mountains, and that for Paris the relative costs for the two kinds of power were about equal as of 1930. The expenditures for wages and coal by thermal plants, he calculated, balanced the heavy capital and transmission costs of hydroelectric plants. He had to admit, however, that within fifty years, when capital charges had been paid, the cost of hydroelectric power would be less.[5]

He offered another rebuttal by arguing that the sources of "white coal" had been sufficiently developed and that a substantial thermal capacity was necessary to compensate for the wide seasonal variations in water power. During the mid-1930's the production of hydroelectric power did equal thermal power for the first time and matched it an-

[4] For Mercier's position, see his speeches delivered during 1935–1938 (*Ernest Mercier: une grande destinée*, pp. 270–275).

[5] For all the power plants operated by Électricité de France in 1951–1952, the cost of a kilowatt hour produced by thermal power was roughly four times more than one produced by hydroelectric power; see François Bouchayer, *Les Pionniers de la houille blanche et de l'électricité* (Paris, 1954), p. 127.

nually thereafter.[6] Yet even this fact does not validate Mercier's claim that free enterprise had developed hydroelectric power adequately. By 1939 there were vast untapped sources of "white coal" and the nation suffered from a general deficiency of power.

It seems clear that some of the CGT's charges against the power industry, especially when applied to Mercier and the Messine group, were unjustified. The international connections of the French electric industry, for example, were not unique, nor do they prove that it was run contrary to the national interest. The assertion that "trusts" controlled the industry and exploited consumers was always denied by Mercier and other management officials, and the CGT never offered proof. Nor did the Messine syndicate deserve the Left's censure as a Malthusian monopoly. The performance of Mercier's syndicate up to the depression was more Saint-Simonian than Malthusian, and during the doldrums of the '30's it still displayed more vigor than most of its rivals. The Union d'Électricité had pioneered in modernizing the production and distribution of electricity, and it had initiated the transmission of hydroelectric power from the Massif Central to Paris in 1926. Before the outbreak of the Second World War this company had five hydroelectric stations either in operation or under construction and held the controlling interest in nine others. Approximately one-third of the needs of the Union d'Électricité came from water sources.[7] As a thermal engineer, Mercier tended to exaggerate the virtues of thermal power, but he also led his syndicate toward developing hydroelectric energy.

Furthermore, in defense of the public utility companies, it must be pointed out that their performance was on the whole superior to that of other branches of the French economy during the depression. Electric power was one of the few industries that increased production during the general economic slump.[8] And the failure to develop a sufficient productive capacity and an efficient distribution system was not entirely the fault of private enterprise—the state, after all, was a partner in this sheltered industry, granting concessions, allocating subsidies, and taking a part in fixing rates and in managing mixed companies. Indeed, utility managers often blamed the government for delaying

---

[6] Estimates vary on the ratio of hydroelectric to thermal energy, but one of the most reliable states that 1934 was the first year in which the production of power was equally divided between the two sources (Malégarie, *L'Électricité à Paris,* p. 283). Also see OEEC, *Industrial Statistics, 1900–1959,* pp. 84–86.

[7] "Participations hydroélectriques de UDE," Mercier papers.

[8] *Études et conjoncture: L'Industrie française* (1953), pp. 98 ff.; *Annuaire statistique, rétrospectif* (1961), p. 121.

modernization and expansion.[9] Yet another obstacle was the negative attitude of Frenchmen toward long-term investment; high interest rates tended to hinder the construction of expensive new hydroelectric plants. Finally, the utility managers pleaded with some justification that they faced difficult natural hazards in developing a tightly coordinated and efficient power grid. Water resources in France were concentrated in areas far distant from most industrial centers, and the lack of good, cheap coal made it impossible to follow the British system of small dispersed thermal plants.

The Left was, however, justified in its general criticism that France was deficient in electricity. During the '20's French production of electric energy grew at a slightly faster pace than the other major European nations. But between 1930 and 1939 France fell woefully behind, with a far lower increase in its total production of electricity than any other major Western country.[10] While Germany and Great Britain almost doubled their production of thermal energy during this decade, France remained static. The only increase France recorded was from hydroelectric energy, but here countries with similar water power resources, like Italy, surpassed it. France increased its total productive capacity at a rate of only 3 percent annually, though consumer needs expanded at a rate of 8 percent. On the eve of the Second World War, only a small portion of the available water power resources had been tapped—less than countries with comparable natural resources—and many existing thermal plants were obsolescent. Despite the desire for more and more electric power, interconnections were still inadequate, and only a few railway lines were electrified. The power industry had made handsome profits,[11] but it had done almost nothing to expand the facilities to meet the demand.

The war years brought serious shortages and nearly halted the industry's lagging growth. Thus nationalization was to come in 1946, almost inevitably, after fifteen years of sluggishness and after decades of steady extension of government control. The underlying paradox is how an industry that was more expansive than its European counterparts in the '20's, reversed itself and became one of the most retarded in the

[9] For example, a former Messine manager maintained that the Ministry of Public Works was responsible for postponing renovation of the Gennevilliers center in the '30's; see E. Rauber in *Ernest Mercier*, p. 294.

[10] For data on this problem see OEEC, *Industrial Statistics*, pp. 84–86; *Études et conjoncture: L'Industrie française* (1953), pp. 6–7, 97–100, 142–146; *Annuaire statistique, rétrospectif* (1961), pp. 129–130, 68*–69*.

[11] Malégarie, p. 549; J. Dessirier, "Secteurs 'abrité' et 'non abrité' dans le déséquilibre actuel de l'économie française," *Revue d'économie politique*, July–August, 1935, pp. 1338–1339.

'30's and early '40's. The answer lies in the massive economic collapse France suffered after 1930. The electric power industry reluctantly followed the over-all decline in French industrial production. Management was partly to blame for the industry's underdevelopment, but the government, investors, and possibly even vested interests in the coal industry,[12] were also responsible. Certainly Mercier and the Messine managers were not alone at fault.

The demand for nationalization of the electric power industry was only one aspect of mounting criticism aimed either directly or indirectly at Mercier. One of the most popular themes in the campaign of the Popular Front was an attack on the economic and political power of big business. A vast amount of propaganda appeared from the early '30's on exposing the "trusts," the "two hundred families," and the "capitalist-fascist plot" against the republic. A series of financial scandals, especially the collapse of the Oustric Bank in 1931, aroused public indignation over the practices of corporate finance. Indeed, by 1935 popular sentiment was running strongly against big business and its interference in politics.

The French economy, according to certain left-wing critics, was in the grip of "supercapitalism." [13] They argued that capitalist exploitation had entered a new stage in the twentieth century, symbolized by the appearance of the corporation and its elephantine offspring, the "trust." The board of directors collectively owned a tiny portion of a firm's capital stock, yet they were supposedly able to wield absolute control by means of various financial maneuvers. The managers used this power, according to these polemicists, to extract enormous personal rewards and to offer the stockholders miserly dividends. The small stockholder, the "real" owner, passively accepted the management of the board of directors, ignorant of the fact that the board appropriated the profits of his investment. In short, the "real" owner of the corporation was neither the beneficiary nor the master of his own property.

As a supermanager with an enormous income—the precise amount could only be guessed at—Mercier was often cited as an example of such managerial exploitation. He was, in fact, an extremely wealthy man, though this hardly proves "exploitation." According to his own records, his average annual income in the '30's was close to 2,500,000

[12] Ingvar Svennilson, *Growth and Stagnation in the European Economy* (Geneva, 1954), p. 116.

[13] See Raymond Bouyer, *Le Capitalisme contemporain, fiction et réalité* (Paris, n.d.); Albert Aymé-Martin, *Nos grands Financiers contre la nation* (Paris, 1931); Jules Moch, *Arguments et documents contre capitalisme, crise, déflation* (Paris, 1936).

francs (about $110,000 in terms of the purchasing power of the day) .[14]
Furthermore, boards of directors, at least in the Messine syndicate, did
not wield the authority ascribed to them by the Left.

Popular Front propaganda repeatedly asserted that the entire economy of France was controlled by a small, interlocking directorate, the
almighty "two hundred families," [15] which carefully guarded their interests by means of "agents" or members of a family sitting on boards
of directors. Polytechnicians were supposedly favorite agents of the
"two hundred families." As one writer remarked, "If bankers and high
civil servants form the warp of the boards of directors, the woof is
made by the graduates of the École Polytechnique." [16] Mercier, of
course, was usually depicted as the agent of the Rothschilds. There
was, in the Left's view, a kind of incestuous relationship between corporation managers and bankers. The end result of this interbreeding
was the growth of huge "trusts" which dominated entire branches of
industry and were controlled by a handful of managers and their financial relations. The Communists published detailed charts outlining the
tentacles of this "trust octopus," and one ambitious Socialist attempted
to trace the intricate pattern of relationships that bound the "economic oligarchy" together.[17]

The Popular Front was determined to crush France's "wall of
money," and its campaign against the "economic oligarchy" was organized to attract not only middle-class investors but also small businessmen.[18] A few capitalists were shown as enriching themselves by exploiting the savings and stocks of the many middle-class investors, and the
profits of privately owned, but state-sheltered, public utility corporations were offered as a prime example of big business making fortunes
while small enterprises suffered.[19] Psychologically, the campaign was
bound to be effective, since most Frenchmen suspected big business any-
way. As early as 1928 André Siegfried observed: "Since the priest
ceased to be the most dangerous menace, I think that the main idea of
French democracy now is to prevent the power from falling into the
hands of the business magnate," and on this issue "the small bourgeois

[14] "Les Bénéfices de 22 années de vie industrielle," Oct. 8, 1940, Mercier papers.

[15] See Francis Delaisi, *La Banque de France aux mains des 200 familles* (Paris,
1936) ; CGT, *Actualité du plan* (Versailles, [1936]) , pp. 28–36.

[16] Aymé-Martin, pp. 26–27.

[17] Augustin Hamon, *Les Maîtres de la France.*

[18] Bouyer, pp. 28–29, compares the exposé of modern capitalism to Necker's report
on the bankruptcy of the monarchy.

[19] Henry W. Ehrmann, *French Labor from Popular Front to Liberation* (New
York, 1947) , pp. 13–14, estimates that on the eve of the elections the profits of
utility companies were up 29 percent from 1929, and small enterprises' profits were
down 66 percent.

meets the industrial workman." [20] Shortly before the 1936 elections, a British journalist toured France and found that the attack against the "two hundred families" was "an ever-recurring theme in the election campaign this year, and a theme which has undoubtedly 'caught on.' " [21] In fact, one scholar argues that even owners of small industrial or commercial firms believed the propaganda against the "trusts" though they would not espouse labor's politics.[22]

The other thrust of the Popular Front's campaign aimed at linking the "economic oligarchy" to the Fascist menace. This tactic, chiefly a journalistic one, sought to expose Mercier, Laval, and La Rocque as the leaders of a capitalist-Fascist plot against the republic. Mercier was already under attack for his alleged mismanagement of the electric power industry and for his august role in big business; now he was being attacked for his political activities. The heat of this criticism even scorched the Redressement. During the summer and fall of 1935 the Communists hammered at the theme that the men of the Croix de Feu were capitalist puppets who had been maneuvered into an attempted coup d'état on February 6: "The plans were well conceived. Mercier, Finaly, Rothschild, and their cohorts commanded. La Rocque executed!" [23] According to L'Humanité, Laval was both a Fascist and a capitalist agent—the proof of the latter accusation being, it said, that the Redressement had boasted of having inspired Laval's deflationary program and also that Mercier had spoken of his friendship with Laval.[24] Many left-wing periodicals referred to Mercier as the Fascist financier of the Croix de Feu.[25]

The Left's hostile campaign went on for months, but Mercier found it less alarming than the political situation as it developed in 1935. Throughout that year negotiations advanced toward the establishment of working-class unity, and on July 14, when the Radicals joined the Communists and Socialists in a massive "anti-Fascist" demonstration, it seemed a reality. Finally in January, 1936, the Radicals officially joined the new Popular Front. By this time Mercier was convinced that French political life had split into a bloc of the Left led by the Communists and a bloc of the Right led by the political leagues. With

[20] "The Psychology of French Political Parties," Journal of the Royal Institute of International Affairs, January, 1928, p. 19.

[21] Alexander Werth, Which Way France?, p. 268.

[22] Ehrmann, Organized Business, pp. 28, 53, 117.

[23] L'Humanité, July 23, 1935.

[24] Ibid., July 21 and Aug. 8, 1935. For Mercier and Laval see Bulletin, July, 1935, p. 20.

[25] La Lumière, July 15, 1935, p. 3; Les Documents politiques, December, 1935, p. 551.

such a division, he had no real political alternative. It was inconceivable that he would endorse the Popular Front, but he had become increasingly critical of the violence and dictatorial tendencies of the extreme Right. He clung to the dream of a national rapprochement and attacked the leagues as well as the Left for perverting its symbol, February 6, into an issue of partisan politics.

Faced with this gloomy political situation, Mercier and the other Redressement directors were reduced to making a few suggestions to head off a Popular Front victory and, they thought, civil war between the Communists and the leagues. Champin, for example, announced somewhat wildly that even he, "an old liberal," had lost faith in universal suffrage and recommended its temporary suspension to achieve "radical reform." [26]

Sometime in the fall of 1935, Mercier, after reflecting on the history and the prospects of the Redressement, decided that the organization should be dissolved. The record of the preceding decade was hardly an encouraging one: the movement had enjoyed, at best, a few minor triumphs. Superficially, it remained intact, holding biannual assemblies, sponsoring lectures, and publishing two periodicals, but in fact it had done nothing of importance for years. Its dues-paying membership, which had never gone above 20,000, was static, at best, in the last years.[27] Because of the depression, the lavish subsidies from business had declined, and as Mercier himself said, the movement "survived only through vigorous and continuous effort." [28] Although one official proudly pointed out that the founders of the group still directed it, this fact probably demonstrated a lack of vigor as much as it did stability. In sum, Mercier could not claim many accomplishments after ten years of effort, and he probably recognized that the movement had been deteriorating since the late '20's.

Even worse, there seemed no hope for the future. The rise of the Popular Front had swept away all chance of rule by the Moderates and with the Left in power Mercier and his colleagues could hardly expect any offers to participate in government. Mercier openly admitted that the Redressement could no longer command any political influence. Since the business elite had become suspect to the general public,

---

[26] *Bulletin,* July, 1935, p. 27.

[27] Figures compiled from annual reports published in the *Bulletin* are incomplete:

	1927	1933	1934	1935
Dues-paying members........	10,000	20,000	—	—
Committees in Paris communes.	53	72	75	75
Provincial centers............	82	112	114	114

[28] *Bulletin,* November–December, 1935, p. 11.

thanks to the campaign against the "two hundred families," big business was clearly discouraged from trying to intervene in politics. The Redressement had not been specifically named as one of the paramilitary leagues which the Left had said it would disband, but it seemed expedient to retire. Nor could the industrialists find haven with the Right, for there the partisans of dictatorship seemed to be in the ascendancy. As Mercier said, in this troubled atmosphere of extremism, "the ways of prudence appear closed for the time being." [29] Moreover, the Redressement finally realized that its program was badly out-of-date. *Rationalisation* belonged to the avant-garde of the '20's, not the '30's. Now, the youthful, energetic elements of French society were interested in a planned economy, nationalization, corporatism, even fascism. But the Redressement preferred "to return to the ranks" rather than adopt such radical theories.[30] Thus on November 30, 1935, almost exactly ten years after its creation, the Redressement announced its dissolution.

Roger Mennevée, a left-wing journalist who had devoted a great deal of time to "exposing" the Redressement, offered an explanation for the movement's rise and fall. He believed that it had been founded to "safeguard the particular interests of the oligarchical groups which were basically opposed to any demands for sacrifice by the state." [31] After the electoral victory of the Left in 1924, he said, the Redressement had been formed specifically to defend the oligarchy's economic interests. The defense consisted mainly of sounding the alarm of a Communist danger, and according to Mennevée, it led naturally to the support of antidemocratic and antiparliamentary political groups. Soon the Redressement was allied with the Fascist leagues; it subsidized the Croix de Feu, and fomented the riots of February 6. But in aligning itself with fascism, Mennevée contended, the group discovered to its horror that it had backed the wrong horse. It realized that the Fascist dictators were as much "despoilers" of economic interests as the Communists. This realization shocked the Redressement back into "at least implicitly" supporting democratic institutions, and thus it dissolved itself.

Like a good many left-wing explanations, Mennevée's analysis oversimplifies the facts by indiscriminately applying the Fascist label to all right-wing groups. Mercier's movement, as I have made clear, was never inclined toward fascism, nor did its support of the Croix de Feu mean that it was sympathetic to Fascist ideals since La Rocque's move-

[29] *Ibid.*, p. 12.
[30] Champin, *ibid.*, p. 15.
[31] *Les Documents politiques*, December, 1935, p. 550.

ment was not truly Fascist. Therefore it can hardly be said that disillusionment with fascism brought about the end of the Redressement. Furthermore, Mennevée judges the purpose of the Redressement too narrowly. He distorts the entire history of the movement by stressing defense of economic interests and ignoring the "spirit of the Front" and the crusade for modernization.

A second, more recent, interpretation suggests that Mercier dissolved the Redressement out of fear "that the movement he had wanted authoritarian and anti-communist might become a tool of German subversion." [32] This interpretation, too, is not altogether sound. Mercier himself was militantly anti-Nazi, and it seems unlikely that his movement would openly have departed from its stand of opposition to the Third Reich. There was, to be sure, growing dissension within the movement over Mercier's enthusiasm for a Soviet alliance, but the dissenters did not advocate a rapprochement with Hitler as an alternative, and they showed no signs of becoming apologists for the Nazi cause.

The dissension was apparent, however, and in view of the domestic political situation in France and the general state of decay of the movement, Mercier simply wearied of pursuing the seemingly hopeless task of domestic reform. The sensible course seemed to be to disband the organization altogether and to strike off in a new and more promising direction.

Ever since Hitler's rise to power Mercier had been increasingly concerned with international affairs, and for a brief time under Premiers Flandin and Laval, both personal friends, he had an opportunity to participate directly in the conduct of French diplomacy. Both these heads of state called upon Mercier to use his influence within the business community to aid their foreign policies.

Mercier had been a prominent advocate of a Franco-Italian entente since 1932. One of his close friends was Hubert Lagardelle, who was attached to the French Embassy in Rome. Lagardelle acted as the Redressement adviser on Italian affairs, and from him Mercier derived considerable knowledge of Mussolini and the Fascist state. In December, 1934, when Lagardelle returned to Paris to confer with Laval, then Foreign Minister, he gave a lecture to the Redressement on Franco-Italian relations. The next month Laval went to Rome to work out an agreement with Mussolini which was intended to initiate a general rapprochement.

[32] Ehrmann, *Organized Business,* p. 66.

The Rome agreement was followed by a period of apparently genuine amicability. The two nations exchanged military missions and veterans' delegations, and exhibits of Italian art were held in Paris. Mercier became an active participant in the friendly exchanges when an attempt was made to strengthen economic ties. In March, 1935, a French trade mission met with an Italian group in Rome, but negotiations broke down. To help reactivate the talks, a group of French industrialists, led by Mercier, undertook a tour of Italian industrial centers.[33] Negotiations on the trade proposals were resumed in April at Milan with Mercier and his touring business leaders present, and a provisional commercial agreement was concluded.

Perhaps by intent, these businessmen arrived in Milan on April 12, the day after the opening of the important diplomatic conference at nearby Stresa. The British, French, and Italian heads of state had gathered at this lovely resort to confer on Hitler's recent repudiation of the disarmament clauses of the Versailles treaty. Mercier and one or two others quietly left the Milan conference and went to Stresa, where, Mercier has said, he talked with Flandin and Laval on the evening of the thirteenth. Mercier warned Laval not to take Italy's friendship for granted and suggested that the only way to secure it was for France to head an anti-German coalition.[34] Mercier, with some of his friends, including Lagardelle, also had a long conversation with Mussolini that same evening.[35] Mercier was, of course, pleased at the outcome of the diplomatic conference—the reaffirmation of the Locarno agreement in a show of strength against Hitler—and he returned to Milan satisfied.

The French businessmen soon went on to Rome, where Mercier again met with Mussolini, this time as spokesman for the French tour, and in recognition of his efforts in behalf of Franco-Italian friendship he was awarded the title of Grand Officer of the Crown of Italy.

One student of the diplomacy of appeasement has described pro-

[33] Their host was Count Volpi di Misurata, head of the Confindustria. Mme Mercier accompanied her husband along with many of his friends, including René Mayer, Jacques Level, Auguste Detoeuf, and René Fould.

[34] *Bulletin*, July, 1935, p. 20.

[35] Mussolini was attempting to arrange a loan from France, and it was rumored that Mercier and René Mayer, who represented the Rothschilds, discussed a loan with Italian businessmen at Stresa (Hamon, III, 49). In January when Laval and Mussolini met in Rome it was reported that "Mussolini asked for permission to float an Italian loan in Paris but was told that France could not allow this until Italy put her house in order"; see Straus to Hull, Jan. 16, 1935, *Foreign Relations of the United States, Diplomatic Papers, 1935* (Washington, D.C., 1953), I, 173–175. Mayer, in a letter to the author dated August 31, 1964, denies any knowledge of these financial negotiations.

Italian elements in France in 1935 as "the timid, the deceived, the anti-Bolshevik and the bought," [36] but for Mercier none of these terms seems applicable. He was neither timid nor bought, and by 1935 he was on the verge of becoming an outspoken proponent of a Franco-Soviet alliance. He did admire Mussolini's economic accomplishments,[37] as did a good many other people, but he was not deceived by fascism; he criticized both the dictatorial and corporative aspects of the regime in Italy. And though he was one of the leaders of the pro-Italian faction of the French Right, he was perhaps as much against Germany as he was for Italy. Germany, he believed, was France's greatest enemy, and he was willing to bargain to obtain a friend against what he assumed was a common enemy. When Italy deserted France, Mercier immediately advocated a bargain with the devil himself— Joseph Stalin.

Mercier was also concerned about Rumania, which had become familiar to him during the First World War and in which he had long had business interests. In the spring of 1935 he made a trip to Bucharest, partly to look after his petroleum holdings, partly to visit with old friends, including King Carol, with whom he dined, and assess for himself the condition of Franco-Rumanian relations. It seemed evident to him that France had lost Rumania through indifference and that the trade agreement between Rumania and Germany signed on March 23, 1935, placed Rumanian industry under German control.[38]

The summer brought an early end to the Stresa front. Mussolini alienated the British by preparing for war against Ethiopia. Mercier saw this was another Fascist blunder, but at the same time he hoped that Great Britain would not invoke sanctions against Mussolini and force him into Hitler's camp. In June Britain dealt the crushing blow to the Stresa front by signing a naval agreement with Germany. To Mercier, this was more proof of French domestic weakness—particularly of growing leftist strength and financial instability—which had lost France Great Britain's confidence. Now, obviously, Mercier had to look elsewhere for help in forming an anti-German coalition. The Soviets seemed the only ones left who could hold back Hitler.

Until 1935, largely because of powerful French economic interests who had long memories and deep suspicions, there had been little more than a trickle of trade between France and the Soviet Union. French investors still remembered the disaster of the pre-1914 loans,

[36] Elizabeth R. Cameron, *Prologue to Appeasement, A Study in French Foreign Policy* (Washington, D.C., 1942), p. 150, applies Denis Brogan's remark about pro-Hitler elements to their pro-Italian counterparts.

[37] See his observations on Italy in *L'Usine*, May 16, 1935, p. 27.

[38] See his remarks in the *Bulletin*, July, 1935, p. 24.

which they said had dragged France into war, and which had later been repudiated by the Soviet Union. The rise of Nazism had tended to bring France and Russia together, however, and on May 2, 1935, a mutual-assistance pact was signed in Paris. Two weeks later Premier Laval visited Moscow to reinforce the new accord. One result of these talks was the decision to expand the existing commercial agreement between the two nations, and the Soviet government began to explore the possibility of placing a large order for French technical and military equipment.

Laval turned to Mercier for assistance in winning the French business community's acceptance of closer commercial and diplomatic relations with the Soviet Union, which Mercier had advocated for some time. Mercier was invited by the Soviet ambassador to visit Russia, and in late October, 1935, he flew to Moscow, accompanied by Mme Mercier, M. and Mme Detoeuf, and Pierre Schweisguth, of the Banque Mirabaud. For two weeks the group toured the capital and Leningrad, visited factories, and talked with Red army leaders. Before their departure they attended a formal dinner with Stalin celebrating the November 7 Revolution. Mercier was favorably impressed with Russia's economic achievement and military might, and when the Russians, aware of his position as an unofficial representative of the French government, asked him to tell Laval of their interest in forming a firm military alliance with France, he agreed to do so.

Laval listened to Mercier's offer from the Soviets, and put the matter aside.[39] Mercier then attempted to enlist support for both the expansion of trade with the Soviet Union and for ratification of the mutual-assistance pact which was to come before parliament in February, 1936. On January 29, he addressed a gathering of important civil and military leaders, sponsored by X-Crise, an organization of technocratic-minded businessmen and engineers, most of whom were graduates of the École Polytechnique.[40] Mercier's analysis of the Soviet regime and his proposals for extending economic relations and concluding a military alliance set off a heated debate among the Polytechnicians. Indeed, his extraordinary thesis on Franco-Soviet relations is significant not only as a stage in the development of his thought but also as the start of a controversy that illuminated French views of the Soviet experiment. The lecture was immediately printed and overnight he became the topic of conversation in Parisian society.[41] A few weeks later,

[39] Memorandum, Mercier papers. On Laval's intention to avoid a military agreement with the Soviets, see Paul Reynaud, *Mémoires* (Paris, 1960–1963), II, 155–156.
[40] For a history of this group, see Guy Desaunay, "X-Crise."
[41] *La Flèche,* Feb. 29 and Mar. 7, 1936.

at the height of the debate over ratification, Mercier was the main speaker at a public discussion held at the Sorbonne.

The gist of Mercier's thesis was that the Soviet Union, with its enormous natural resources and its growing industrial might, was fast becoming an important element in the world economy, and within the year 1936 would have to end its former isolationism.[42] Traditionally, Russia supplied Germany with raw materials and bought German industrial products in return, but now the Soviet Union feared that this trade would only help the Nazis build up their war machine. This gave French manufacturers a golden opportunity to stimulate the sluggish French economy by taking advantage of the Nazi–Soviet rift.

The Soviet Union was, he said, an ideal French market. Since Soviet industry concentrated almost exclusively on the production of capital goods, the people were deprived of consumer products. The depressed economic condition of the Russian worker, Mercier believed, constituted a potential threat to the regime, and was part of the economic dilemma that Soviet leaders were faced with: how to raise wages for the underpaid and give them more consumer goods without sacrificing the program of industrialization and risking inflation as well. To make their problem even more difficult, the Nazi threat made defense needs ever more urgent for the Kremlin and precluded the immediate possibility of shifting to the production of consumer goods. Furthermore, even if the Soviet regime did eventually make this shift, the Russian population was growing as fast as its industry, which meant that demand would exceed supply for decades. It was also likely that the manufacture of consumer goods would introduce an element of free choice into the economy which might jeopardize the strict control necessary for completing the long-range economic plans. The only answer to this dilemma was for the Soviet regime to end its policy of economic isolation and to trade abroad for consumer products—products that were the specialty of French manufacturers.

But many French businessmen had serious misgivings about resuming trade with a regime that had cancelled the Tsarist debts, and they feared that the centralized, state-controlled Soviet economy would turn commercial relations to its advantage. Mercier's answer to this was that since the Soviet government, which was responsible for all external commerce, desired friendly relations with the West, it would guarantee the proper execution of all foreign trade. He thought there was no reason to fear Soviet competition, because Russia's natural market was underdeveloped Asia rather than overindustrialized Europe. Nor was

[42] The following section is based on *URSS, Réflexions par Ernest Mercier,* Éditions du Centre polytechnicien d'études économiques, No. 1 (Paris, 1936).

there any likelihood of Russia's dumping exports abroad, because it did not have the necessary economic abundance; and in any event, Europe was capable of defending itself against that eventuality. Indeed, Western free-enterprise had several important commercial advantages over the Soviet Union, chiefly that of its flexible and sophisticated marketing system as contrasted to the ponderous, unimaginative state bureaucracy.

Further to allay the fears of French business—fears he had helped create in the '20's with his anti-Bolshevik campaign—Mercier argued that the Soviet regime was gradually abandoning revolutionary communism. As a result of the tremendous effort and sacrifice that had gone into constructing the new Communist state, the leaders were gradually adopting a more conservative outlook, putting aside, at least temporarily, their goals of international revolution for the more immediate goal of simply preserving their domestic achievement. Indeed—and here Mercier plunged into controversy—the Soviet economy was slowly returning to the ways of capitalism. For example, he pointed out, in order to increase production Stalin had introduced the Stakhanov system of production incentives like prizes and wage rates based on output—Stakhanov having been a notably prodigious worker. Thus the law of increasing productivity had forced the regime to set aside the Marxist doctrine of wage equality. This was, of course, no more than an economic necessity, not willingly resorted to under the Communist system; but it was only part of what necessity would force the regime to do. Mercier also professed to see little difference between the Soviet plant manager and the capitalist employer, since both received higher salaries and exercised authority over their workers, and he pointed to certain developments in Soviet society, such as the efforts made to reconstitute the family, as further indications of a drift from pure Marxism. He emphasized that these changes in Russia did not mean that the Soviet leaders were consciously abandoning or altering their ideals; the Stakhanov system was certainly only a temporary expedient. Whatever their reasons, however, Mercier was convinced that natural economic laws were gradually and permanently driving the Soviet economy away from communism and closer to capitalism.

Mercier made no effort to prove that the Russian people were disillusioned with communism. On the contrary, he seemed to argue its value as a social system for the Russians. Citing Montesquieu, he suggested that no social organization was intrinsically superior to all others, and that "the present state of Russia constitutes undeniable progress for this country over that of the past." [43] It was true that the Soviet

[43] *Ibid.*, p. 104.

regime had obtained such mass acquiescence by official persuasion—
that is, by glorifying the economic achievements and by creating the
impression of equality and freedom from exploitation, and the "hyper-
dictatorial government" also erred in its distortions of truth, in its
camouflaged exploitation of workers, and in its use of secret police and
forced labor. Certainly, he said, there was no reason why Frenchmen,
who were more blessed in every way, should want to imitate the Russians. The Soviet regime persuaded the people to be satisfied with their
poor lot, whereas in France the Left preached "mutual envy" and
spread discontent among a more fortunate populace.

Yet the expansion of trade between France and the Soviet Union
was secondary in Mercier's estimation to the establishment of a solid
political and military alliance. In this, of course, he had to anticipate
objections from the Right, which believed that such a policy overestimated Soviet strength and put France into a position of being
maneuvered by Stalin into fighting his war against Germany. Mercier,
speaking from his own observations, argued that the Soviet Union was
rapidly arming itself and that certainly the Red army had far better mo-
rale and equipment than its Tsarist predecessor. To be sure, the Russians were short on communications and transportation, and if war
came soon logistics would force them to sacrifice a vast amount of territory and industrial plant. For that reason alone, the Soviet regime
needed *time*—five or, better, ten years in which to develop adequate
protection for its tremendous social and economic achievements. Mercier declared that Stalin wanted France to strengthen itself in order to
keep watch on the Rhine; a weak France only tempted Hitler and
might lose everything for the Soviet Union. Thus Mercier suggested
that Stalin should demonstrate his desire for a French alliance by ordering the Comintern to stop its intervention in the internal affairs of
other nations. In short, Mercier was convinced that the Soviet government did not want war of any sort at the moment, and that it believed
a powerful French ally was the key to peace in Europe.

Some persons interpreted Mercier's crusade for closer relations with
the Soviet Union as an act of pure self-interest; [44] a few cynics even suggested that he had gone to Moscow to get business for his companies.
This sort of criticism made Mercier justifiably angry: he insisted that
the extension of trade relations would benefit all French industry, and
there is no doubt that Mercier's aims were not petty ones. A second
kind of criticism interpreted what it termed Mercier's "sharp about-
face" as due to fear of Nazi anti-Semitism. In order to protect his wife,

---

[44] See *La Flèche*, Mar. 22, 1936; "Débat sur l'URSS," *X-Crise Bulletin*,
February–April, 1936, p. 46.

these critics said, and the Rothschilds whom he supposedly represented, and perhaps himself—since rumor had it that he was a Jew—
Mercier became "the most active agent of the Comintern in the midst
of the 'two hundred families.' " [45] Here again, the charges were based
on misconceptions: certainly these critics failed to take into account
Mercier's fears of German power, which motivated his friendship with
the Soviets.

The left-wing press was very skeptical of Mercier's new admiration
of the Soviet Union, and it continued to refer to him as a leader of the
"two hundred families." *L'Humanité* (February 14, 1936) acknowledged his praise for Soviet progress, but commented that some of his
observations were "gratuitous" or "partisan." Georges Valois, in
Nouvel Age (March 5) , warned the Left to beware of the sudden turn-
about of a "man of February 6." Similarly, the independent leftist
paper *La Flèche* (February 29 and March 7) , directed by Gaston Ber-
gery, refused to accept Mercier's conversion, as it said, from fascism
and attempted to expose this "king of electricity" who had donned the
Phrygian cap. *La Flèche* praised Mercier's courageous stand on the
issue of the pact, but suspected that it was only a subterfuge to pressure
Stalin into constraining the French Communist party.

In print at least, no one on the Left was willing to accept Mercier's
opinion that communism was faltering in Russia. Jean-Richard Bloch,
who wrote for *La Flèche* and later for the Communist paper *Ce Soir,*
referred scornfully to "bourgeois dilettantes" who visited the Soviet
Union and when they saw a society hard at work believed that the revolution was in decay.[46] On the contrary, he protested, the Russian
revolution was continuing and the exploitation of man by man was
ending. Bloch declared that the Russian worker was convinced that he
labored not for an employer but for the revolution and for future generations. Mercier's rather lame reply was that exploitation had not
ended when some men still commanded and others obeyed. He agreed
with Bloch that the Russian worker did not feel exploited, but this was
only true because the worker did not really know what was happening
to him. To Mercier, the Stakhanov system was only a subtle form of exploitation by the state.

Other leftist critics like François Moch argued that there was a vast
difference between a French employer and a Soviet plant manager
since the former used others to amass personal gain and power,
whereas the latter, even if he did work for himself, did not exploit oth-

[45] Coston, *Les Financiers qui mènent le monde,* p. 117.
[46] *La Flèche,* Feb. 29, 1936; see also *X-Crise Bulletin,* p. 41.

ers and of necessity labored in the general interest.[47] Moch pointed out that the Soviet system operated for the benefit of consumers and produced no Citroëns or Rockefellers. A Soviet manager, unlike a member of the Comité des Forges, could not direct his plant by personal whim, nor could he reinvest in it himself since all production was subordinated to a general economic plan. Mercier, displaying some real sophistry, contended that Moch's distinction between capitalist employers and Communist managers was more apparent than real: both, he said, received substantially higher salaries than their employees, and in fact the Soviet managers had much more power than their Western counterparts because the Russian working class did not even enjoy the right of protest. Mercier was on somewhat safer ground in his efforts to reconcile capitalist and Communist managers by showing how, from a Saint-Simonian point of view, they were inspired by the same motives. For all managers, including the Communists, "the real motive that drives men to work, risk, and undertake ventures is essentially the same as that which I have reported blossoming in the Soviet Union: the appetite or passion to create, and the joy of serving the general interest." [48] Mercier summed up his response to his left-wing critics by declaring that the Soviet government had deliberately abandoned its Communist ideals for the time being. And it was a "reasonable hypothesis" that "economic necessities" would make a return to pure Marxism "more and more difficult." [49]

But the strongest criticism came from Mercier's colleagues in business. There is no doubt that the vast majority of them found his thesis unpalatable.[50] They were particularly fearful of the revolutionary aspects of the Soviet regime and did not agree at all that it had become more conservative. And there were few employers who were farsighted enough to re-examine their views of the Soviet experience or to accept the truth that a Soviet alliance was a necessity for France.

Some businessmen were most skeptical of trading with the Soviet Union; others seemed particularly worried that Hitler might consider the pact as an attempt at encirclement, which would mean that it would provoke war, not prevent it. The response of Pierre Pucheu expressed just such misgivings.[51] Pucheu was a manager in the steel industry, and was to become a key figure in formulating economic policy

[47] X-Crise Bulletin, pp. 61–63.
[48] Ibid., p. 48.
[49] Ibid., p. 47.
[50] Interviews with various business leaders. On the reaction of fellow employers to his project, see ibid., pp. 41–45, 54–56.
[51] X-Crise Bulletin, pp. 57–60.

at Vichy. He discouraged any hopes French manufacturers might have of opening up a prospective market in the Soviet Union—on the contrary, he warned, this Communist nation constituted a serious economic threat. He thought it could easily shift to the production of consumer goods, and since it had a modern industrial plant, it could pursue a policy of "economic imperialism." Though Pucheu gave the Soviet pact his qualified approval, he criticized Mercier for giving it a dangerous, "anti-German" interpretation, and he offered instead a proposal for international economic cooperation designed to help Hitler solve his domestic problems; this, he hoped, would divest the pact of its aggressive character. In particular he advised extending loans to Germany in exchange for its return to "the European entente." Pucheu, in other words, like many French industrialists who disagreed with Mercier, was inhibited by fear—fear that a strong stand against Hitler might precipitate war, and fear that only the Soviets would benefit from a resumption of trade relations.

Using the means at once most effective and most logical, business— represented by certain powerful financial interests—dashed the trade proposals by refusing credit to manufacturers who were tempted by the Soviet market. When trade with the Soviet Union had first been resumed, most French banks had balked at giving any help to the Communist cause, at least until the Soviet regime agreed to make some attempt to pay off the Tsarist debts.[52]

It was therefore no surprise that Mercier encountered stiff opposition from financial interests when he and other industrialists attempted to obtain credit for a Soviet order that had been pending since early 1935. The Soviet Union offered to pay for a billion francs' worth of French technical and military equipment in short-term government bonds, thus requiring the manufacturers to find credit. First the Bank of France and then other banks refused to cooperate.[53] *La Flèche* (May 16, 1936) later commented: "It is not easy to thwart important policies of the Bank of France and the Comité Général des Assurances, even when half of the Comité des Forges is on your side."[54] Indeed, the issue of Franco-Soviet trade in 1935–1936 revealed a schism within the French business community between the world of finance and certain industrial interests.

[52] See Vincent Auriol's statement reported in *Le Populaire*, Mar. 3, 1936.

[53] See Köster to German Foreign Office, Apr. 26, 1935, German Foreign Office Microfilm (National Archives, Washington, D.C.), serial M196, frames M006133–34.

[54] In a letter to *La Flèche* Mercier stated that he had not solicited the banks himself (June 13 and 20, 1936).

Undaunted, Mercier attempted to circumvent the opposition of high finance by obtaining public credit.[55] The only private financial support these industrialists had been able to locate was that of two relatively small banks, the Banque Louis-Dreyfus and the Banque Séligman. In the fall of 1935, these firms had offered Mercier's group credit for 200 million francs on the condition that they obtain the remaining 800 million from the government. According to a law passed in 1928, the government had the authority to insure up to 80 percent of the value of an exporter's sale if it served the national interest. The legislation had been enacted for the purpose of helping export firms obtain reasonable credit rates from private sources by having the state act as a guarantor, but the Laval government and Mercier's consortium were apparently trying to alter the role of the state in this instance from a guarantor to creditor, to the extent of 800 million francs. In December, 1935, Georges Bonnet, the Minister of Commerce, officially requested the public Caisse des Dépôts to advance the Mercier–Dreyfus–Séligman consortium 800 million francs. However, a few days later the directors of the Caisse des Dépôts upset this financial maneuver by rejecting the government's plea.

Despite this rebuff Mercier's consortium continued to seek government credit for the trade project. As a result, during the Chamber's debate over ratification of the pact in February, 1936, representatives of high finance raised the issue of the Soviet purchases to discredit the scheme. Foreign Minister Flandin tried to exclude the orders from the discussion as being irrelevant. But Comte Charles de Lasteyrie, a spokesman for the banks, proposed a resolution to prevent the government from rendering any financial assistance whatsoever for the expansion of Franco-Soviet economic relations until the Soviet government agreed to indemnify the French holders of Tsarist securities.[56] He approved the action of the directors of the Caisse des Dépôts and insisted that those interests which sought trade with the Soviet Union should do so at their own risk. The French press further clouded the matter by misrepresenting the Soviet orders as another Russian attempt to float a loan in conjunction with a political agreement. The Soviet ambassador himself felt called upon to deny the rumors that a loan was connected with the pact, and to say that the Soviet government had not yet officially approved the trade project.[57] Ultimately finance had

[55] On this attempt see the well-informed article in *La Flèche,* May 16, 1936. There was also a revealing discussion of the scheme in a finance committee hearing reported in both *Le Populaire* and *L'Humanité* (Feb. 29, 1936).

[56] *Le Temps,* Feb. 12 and 13, 1936; *Le Populaire,* Mar. 3, 1936.

[57] *Le Temps,* Feb. 11, 1936.

its way: the government wavered in the face of opposition, and the project died in committee.

Though the Chamber eventually ratified the pact, the vote revealed the deep division among conservatives over the proper policy to follow in order to pacify Hitler.[58] It took Germany's reoccupation of the Rhineland in March, 1936, to draw the Right together in the Senate in support of ratification. Mercier's own victory was only partial, since the trade scheme had been effectively killed by the banks, and Laval had put aside close military cooperation.[59]

This political foray was barely over when the Popular Front won its victory at the polls. Mercier, assuming that the victorious Left would begin its rule by fulfilling its campaign promises to curb the power of the "two hundred families," quietly resigned a number of his directorships before the new government could demand that he do so.[60] This is not to say that he considered Premier Blum and the Socialists his enemies, for Mercier enjoyed their respect and in some cases their friendship.[61]

Mercier of course realized that one who had been denounced however mistakenly, as a leader of the "two hundred families" could hardly be expecting a receptive audience for his ideas during these days of high hope for a Socialist utopia. Obviously, he was no longer going to be consulted as he had been under Flandin and Laval, and even his name was suspect. For these reasons, he decided to publish his views on the Popular Front anonymously, in a book entitled *Résurrection française*.[62]

Résurrection française (the title of course recalls the Redressement Français) revealed very little change in Mercier's views. He assessed responsibility for the rise of the Popular Front by blaming the Right and the Center for their failure to champion social progress. He also criticized both the Moderates and the Radicals for their feuds which divided the Center. But the party most responsible was the Socialist

---

[58] See Charles A. Micaud, *The French Right and Nazi Germany, 1933–1939* (New York, 1943) , pp. 67–84.

[59] Even after the failure of his trade scheme Mercier continued to campaign for a revival of commerce with the Soviet Union. See his proposal to the International Chamber of Commerce in April, 1936, reprinted in *Ernest Mercier*, pp. 197–202.

[60] Mercier to Stein, Nov. 16, 1936, Mercier papers.

[61] Vincent Auriol, the Minister of Finance in Blum's cabinet, would later eulogize: "Occasional heated arguments, far from making Ernest Mercier my enemy, made him my friend—his great intelligence, his untiring, far-reaching activity, his generosity, and the breadth of his vision made me prize his friendship more dearly each day" (Auriol to Mme Ernest Mercier, Oct. 6, 1158, Mercier papers) .

[62] *Résurrection française, erreurs politiques et vérités humaines* (Paris, 1937) . According to the editor, the book was published anonymously in order to focus attention on the ideas rather than on the author.

party, which had fundamentally changed France by replacing the spirit of fraternity with the notion of class struggle. Mercier admitted that the Socialists had provided the necessary impetus for social reform against the inertia of the Center and Right, but he detested the way in which the party, by propagating the materialistic Marxist myth, incited the poor with the promise of an equal distribution of wealth. "Today the endemic sickness of Frenchmen is envy," he wrote. "It is a passion that is never satisfied, and once it is loosed it knows no limits; it is public enemy number one." [63] In sum, the Popular Front was the consequence of general social inertia, the divisions among non-Marxist political parties, and Socialist propaganda.

In his own defense, Mercier rejected the Socialists' accusation that employers were largely responsible for the backward social-economic situation which led to the eruption of discontent in 1936. On the contrary, he said, employers had been so harassed by the disorder of the post-1914 era and by the "incoherent" and "malevolent" economic policies of inept politicians that they had little energy left for their social and public duties. But even under these conditions, Mercier asserted, certain enlightened businessmen (meaning those who had been at the Front during the war) had not only inspired some reforms but were preparing fundamental social and economic advances when the strikes occurred in the spring of 1936. Mercier was here obviously stretching his argument, for there was almost no social progress in France during the '20's and the early '30's—and certainly none that was directly inspired by businessmen. As for the Popular Front, Mercier thought that it had introduced social reform recklessly, though he admitted that social inertia had contributed to the disturbances of 1936.[64] He advised the parliamentary Right to halt its tactic of accelerating such measures so as to discredit them sooner. It would be impossible to reverse the Popular Front's program, he warned, once it had been adopted.

Not surprisingly, Mercier's enthusiasm for the Soviet Union showed signs of having waned with the coming of the Popular Front and the spread of agitation among labor. In *Résurrection française* he even held Moscow to blame for engineering the formation of the Popular Front and leading the strikes of May and June, 1936, in order to train the masses in revolution and to menace the Blum government. In fact, he thought the Communists could have seized power on June 11–12 when the government had nearly lost its authority and the public

---

[63] *Ibid.*, p. 140.

[64] He was also quoted as saying that the forty-hour week introduced by the Popular Front was "a reckless plunge into the unknown"; see Werth, *Which Way France?*, p. 331.

seemed passive—but the Soviet ambassador had "ordered" a return to work. Rather than so blatantly intervening in French internal affairs, Mercier said, Moscow would far better have turned its attention to improving its diplomatic relations with London and Paris. It is noteworthy that the concern Mercier showed here over Moscow-inspired agitation increased rather than diminished after the publication of the book; by November, 1937, he was expecting a Red revolution in Paris —or so, at any rate, it has been said by Eugène Deloncle, the leader of the anti-Communist secret society called the Cagoulards.[65]

For the most part, however, *Résurrection française* was less concerned with evaluating the Popular Front than with suggesting reforms that might still save the nation from chaos. Mercier urged the working class to relegate the Marxist myth to the museum and concentrate on improving themselves as individuals: the only answer to the ultimate problem of human purpose, he said, was self-realization. Happiness was derived not from the Marxist chimera of an equal distribution of wealth, but from the enjoyment of true equality—that is, the enjoyment of individual freedom.

He also reiterated his disgust with "mass politics" and urged the restoration of leadership by "the elite." The masses, he said, were governed by "blind passion" rather than by reason, and when men gathered in crowds at Red Square or in Nuremberg they assumed a new character and seemed capable of only crude reactions. In France, the will of the masses as expressed through universal suffrage had become sacred; it was regarded as the fount of wisdom, but in truth it had destroyed good government. The fact that needed recognition, Mercier insisted, was that government should act not according to "the will of the majority" but "in the interest of the majority." [66] He also reasserted his belief that the nation should be directed by an elite of talent: that is, a nonpolitical elite drawn from all society and selected not by fortune or even technical skill but simply by the ability to lead. He defined this elite as an "aristocracy of sentiment"—leaders who countered hate with love, envy with sympathy, and timidity with resolution. This definition was something of a change from his earlier one, in which the elite had represented the concrete ideals of success in business, but after his early failures he seemed satisfied with a vague and rather sentimental definition. His elite now was distinguished only by talent and love.

Yet the central message of Mercier's book was a plea for a resurrec-

---

[65] See Deloncle's testimony in J.-R. Tournoux, *Pétain et de Gaulle* (Paris, 1964), pp. 395–396.
[66] *Résurrection française*, p. 128.

tion of the spirit of fraternity. Once again he recalled the "spirit of the trenches," which still had not overcome the petty hatreds of party politics. The main problem confronting the nation was how to create a mood and a spirit that would bring understanding among Frenchmen. The best way, he thought, was to "break with corrupt contemporary politics—professional politics, the political game, the hypocritical comedy which is acted under our very eyes. Prevent a tiny, but influential minority from perpetuating the disorder off which it lives." [67] In short, with the Popular Front in power, Mercier's only recourse seemed to amount to pleas for a moral revolution. He said a pious prayer for Frenchmen to forget their old quarrels and to be spiritually reborn as those who had experienced the Great War had been reborn. But as one reviewer of the book observed, "What an admirable program! But who is the divine prophet who could persuade his listeners to apply it?" [68]

Mercier's book was more or less indicative of his position from 1936 on; he who had been the leading businessman-reformer of the '20's gradually retreated from public affairs while other employers, shocked into action by the stunning victory of the Popular Front, set about trying to organize the business community and give it a workable philosophy. Some of them, following the path blazed by Mercier, set up study groups. One of the most important of these included Auguste Detoeuf, Mercier's former colleague in the Redressement Français, and several other employers from the electrical industry. Detoeuf's group, known by the name of its review, *Nouveaux Cahiers,* was mainly interested in industrial relations and "vocational organization," and though it was of course familiar with Mercier's earlier experiment and approved of his civic-mindedness and patriotism, it had no desire to emulate his tactics and become a political pressure group.[69] Another one of the new movements, more militant than Nouveaux Cahiers, was the Comité de Prévoyance et d'Action Sociale.[70] This group, led by Germain-Martin, one of the founders of the Redressement and a former Minister of Finance, acted as an anti-Communist, anti-CGT propaganda center for small businessmen. It worked closely with the CGPF. Between 1936 and 1939 this organization became a militant defender of business interests; it advanced corporative ideas and often engaged openly in political activity. Still another study group was formed by several former Redressement leaders, including Mercier, along with

[67] *Ibid.,* p. 177.

[68] Henri Mazel in *Mercure de France,* Aug. 1, 1937, p. 505.

[69] Based on interviews with former leaders of the Nouveaux Cahiers, Henry Davezac, May 8, 1961, and Guillaume de Tarde, May 5, 1961. See also Ehrmann, *Organized Business,* pp. 46–49.

[70] See its organ, *L'Élan social.*

other prominent industrialists and academicians. This group was known as the Comité Technique pour la Réforme de l'État.[71] The head of the organization was Jacques Bardoux, one of the founders of the Redressement, and its program of technocratic political reform was a carbon copy of its predecessor of the '20's, except that this time the government to be cleansed was the Popular Front. The technocrats called for a "Fourth Republic," free of party politics, and armed with a strong executive and an independent administration. They even recommended making the new republic more "Athenian" by adding a score of the nation's elite to the Senate. The "defeat" dealt business by the Popular Front also brought about the complete renovation of the leadership and philosophy of the CGPF and led to the establishment of a new organization, the Comité Central de l'Organisation Professionnelle, which experimented with corporative reforms.

Mercier was not, of course, the direct inspirer of these business reform movements of the late '30's, and aside from the Comité Technique he was not particularly concerned with them, but they certainly bore a similarity of purpose to his Redressement. And it was the Redressement that had first proposed the idea that businessmen ought to participate in civic affairs. After 1940, this tendency toward organization and engagement in public life among French businessmen was to gather momentum.

There is only fragmentary evidence on Mercier's career between the Popular Front period and the war. His attention was apparently focused on foreign affairs—in particular, on speeding the French armament program and on consolidating an alliance system with the nations of eastern Europe. He protested against French inaction when Germany reoccupied the Rhineland in 1936, and he called the abandonment of Czechoslovakia at Munich "a kind of suicide." [72]

When Germany annexed Bohemia in the spring of 1939 and international tension grew, Mercier returned to the public forum. In a lecture delivered in April he stated that the world had one great problem—to restrain Germany from beginning a war.[73] If Hitler could be kept from aggression, he argued, war might be avoided. It was only a matter of time before the Nazi structure would collapse from its own inner tensions. Mercier stressed the internal opposition to persecution and "Spartanism," and confidently analyzed the economic mistakes of the

---

[71] For the program of the Comité Technique see two works by Jacques Bardoux: "La Réforme de l'état," *Revue des deux mondes*, Mar. 15, 1935, pp. 268–286, and *La France de demain, ni communiste, ni hitlérienne: un plan* (Paris, [1937]) .

[72] Mercier recalled his protest in *La France devant son destin* (Paris, 1939) , p. 7.

[73] *Ibid.*, pp. 9–14.

Nazis. He attacked appeasement as an extremely dangerous policy since it might persuade Hitler that the West was weak and tempt the Third Reich into action before the regime collapsed from internal stress.

Mercier still maintained that only a Franco-Soviet alliance would ultimately deter Hitler from aggression. (By 1939 the Popular Front no longer seemed dangerous, and Mercier was again quite willing to champion friendship with the Soviet Union.) "A solid system of eastern alliances supported by Russia" could, he said, stop the approaching catastrophe, but this required "purging France of foreign political agitators, in particular the Russians"; he was convinced that the Soviet leaders themselves would "appreciate this virile attitude." [74]

This same speech also contained one other important message: a plan for European unity. Not surprisingly, it was a distinctly French plan, by which France would be the center of one power bloc and a federated Germany the center of another. The French bloc would include the "liberal nations" of continental Europe (including Italy) and much of Africa, and would be supported also by Great Britain and the United States. Germany, "restored to its true historical character, which is federative and not Prussian," would lead the nations most closely akin to it. Then, after fifteen years or so, "the incoherent and impractical Europe of closed nationalities" could be transformed into "a coordinated Europe tending ultimately toward a federal form." [75] The leading spirit would, of course, be "the ideal of France," which, as the guardian of the values of Western civilization, had an international mission to fulfill. Its destiny was to lead Europe out of the current crisis toward peace. Its "moral superiority" was its great advantage over Nazism.

Perhaps the real significance of Mercier's views on international relations was this vision of France's place in the modern world. He believed that France was still a great power endowed with a special mission of moral leadership. Of course not all French business leaders agreed with him. Indeed, a striking comparison can be made with the attitudes of Auguste Detoeuf. Unlike Mercier, Detoeuf did not think that France should play the role of "a directing nation"; it was, he thought, simply one nation among many other nations.[76] Frenchmen seemed to think they alone had won the Great War. But if France were really "a great nation," it would not have trembled for fifteen years before a disarmed Germany, and it would have made a generous peace

[74] *Ibid.*, p. 7.
[75] *Ibid.*, p. 32.
[76] "Blasphémes," *Nouveaux Cahiers*, Apr. 1, 1938, p. 3.

with the Weimar Republic. The crucial years were long past: "Our loss of rank, our humiliation in terms of power, dates from long ago, dates from that period before the war when German and American industry crushed our industry. . . . With regard to material force we will be what we are—a second-class country." [77]

Mercier, of course, could scarcely disagree on the latter point, but whereas he reacted by urging that France modernize her industry and thus regain her true position among nations, Detoeuf recognized the virtues of the traditional French economy. Frenchmen simply had to make the choice between happiness and power: if they wanted to regain their former rank as a world power, they would have to forsake all the traditional virtues, especially their individualism, for discipline and organization. Frenchmen could not hope to compete when they worked forty hours a week and Germans worked sixty, when one people argued and the other obeyed, when one had few children and the other forbade celibacy. The problem was one of ambivalence:

> Deep in our hearts we have chosen, but we act, we shall act as if we have not chosen. We want to appear as a leader of Europe, refusing opportunities for peace because of false prestige, preserving a colonial domain disproportionate to our power, assuming the posture of a braggart which might one day involve us in the war we detest. Let us at least have the courage to choose the only role that we can for our nation, that of remaining France. A France more modest perhaps on the material plane, but greater on the intellectual and moral plane.[78]

Thus during the Munich crisis, while Mercier attacked appeasement as suicidal, Detoeuf stressed the moral guilt Frenchmen felt for treating Germany so harshly after the war. He saw nothing humiliating in "yielding" to Germany, and called the desire of Frenchmen to "make the law for Europe" simply "a form of vanity." [79]

It is risky to attempt any generalizations about attitudes within the business community toward this issue of France's place in the modern world. Nevertheless, the clearly expressed views of Mercier and Detoeuf suggest the significance of this problem. It is possible that many businessmen shared Detoeuf's belief that France was no longer a great power. Indeed, if this attitude was prevalent, it would help explain the French policy of appeasement during the '30's. Yet neither the Nouveaux Cahiers nor the Redressement won a wide following; this may

[77] *Ibid.*, p. 4.
[78] *Ibid.*, p. 3.
[79] "Pour la France et pour la liberté," *Nouveaux Cahiers,* Nov. 1, 1938, p. 1.

indicate that other businessmen did not recognize the need for either modernization or "adjustment." That is, perhaps most businessmen, unlike Detoeuf or Mercier, did not face the crucial fact that other nations had outstripped France in physical power. If this is true, then the mistake of the French business community was that it ignored its nation's dilemma and chose to drift until 1940 when the German army proved France's weakness.

8

The Closing Drama

THE GERMAN OCCUPATION AND THE LIBERATION

A T THE OUTBREAK of the war in 1939 Mercier offered his services to the Ministry of Armaments hoping to utilize the experience he had gained in 1917–1919, but the government rejected his overture. This rebuff was followed by a series of graver disappointments and afflictions that made the war years a personal ordeal.

The battle of France in the spring of 1940 brought in its wake four million refugees and widespread suffering among the civilian population. To many of these needy countrymen Mercier's managerial skills proved to be of immense help. On May 23, Camille Chautemps, speaking for the government, acted upon the request of the American ambassador and asked Mercier to help organize the distribution of American Red Cross aid.[1] Within two weeks, largely through Mercier's efforts, the Secours Américain aux Victimes de la Guerre was formed, joining the forces of the American and French Red Cross, the Secours National, and the French public utility industry.

In early June when the French government left Paris for the south, Mercier was advised by friends in the administration to follow along. He realized that his militant anti-Nazi record would place his life in jeopardy if the invading armies reached the capital, but it was not fear of the Germans that convinced Mercier to leave. Rather, his duties as head of the CFP and as a director of Red Cross relief required him to remain in contact with the government. He therefore joined the hordes of people jamming the roads leading from Paris. Abruptly, Mercier changed his mind and turned back to Paris to offer his services to the army defending the city. But the commanding officer turned him away, and he reluctantly resumed his drive to Bordeaux.

A few days later, the first American Red Cross ship arrived in the harbor at Bordeaux with medical supplies, and two days after that, on

[1] This account is based on interviews with Mme Ernest Mercier, June 24, 1964, and Joseph Thuillier, July 10, 1964; and also *L'Oeuvre de la Croix-Rouge Américaine en France et le Secours Américain aux Victimes de la Guerre, 1940–1944* (Paris, 1945).

June 22, France capitulated. Had he wished to do so, Mercier could easily have joined the thousands of refugees who were sailing for the safety of foreign ports. Disregarding the dangers to himself and his Jewish wife, he decided to stay and returned to Paris. Mercier believed it was his duty to safeguard the French electrical and petroleum plant as best he could and to continue his relief work.

After the armistice the German authorities forced the American Red Cross to use the port of Marseilles and to limit its activities to unoccupied territory in southern France. In the midst of the chaos that followed the fighting, the water, gas, and electric power companies used their organization to help distribute food, clothing, and medical supplies throughout this part of France. All through the fall and winter of 1940–1941 the public utility companies, partly with their own funds, provided information on local refugee problems, stored supplies, and dispensed aid. In April, 1941, after many months of directing this relief, Mercier traveled to Marseilles for an official ceremony attended by Admiral Leahy, the American ambassador at Vichy. The ceremony honored Mercier and the other French and American leaders who had organized the relief program.[2]

The Pétain government at Vichy, which had been established shortly after the cessation of hostilities in the summer of 1940, seemed to Mercier, the proud veteran of the Great War, no more than an "armistice regime" born out of a humiliating military defeat. And even though in many respects Vichy embodied Mercier's own reforming ideals, and indeed included many of his business associates and friends from the defunct Redressement, Mercier himself had no part in it. Pétain himself had been associated with the Redressement, and his closest adviser on social and economic affairs was Lucien Romier, long a spokesman for the Redressement.[3] Raphaël Alibert, Hubert Lagardelle, and numerous other former Redressement leaders and supporters also held important posts in the new government,[4] and a number of

[2] Before the occupation of southern France in 1942 halted its work, the Secours Américain had distributed 300,000 tons of American supplies to French children and war victims. Mercier received the American Red Cross silver medal of merit for his work.

[3] Alfred Mallet wrote that for three years during the war Romier was "the Marshal's most influential adviser"; see *Pierre Laval* (Paris, 1954–1955), II, 51. Also see Henri du Moulin de Labarthète, *Le Temps des illusions* (Brussels, 1946), pp. 149–150, 372. Romier was anti-German and anti-totalitarian; he left Vichy in early 1944, sick and disillusioned, and died soon after.

[4] Alibert served at Vichy as Minister of Justice during 1940, acted as adviser to Pétain, and helped in the attempt to draft a new constitution. In a letter to the author (Feb. 6, 1962), Alibert explained that he had seen Pétain at Redressement meetings, but they had never spoken; their relationship did not begin until October

top managers from the Messine group and the CFP were directly concerned with economic affairs at Vichy.

The over-all aims of the Vichy regime closely resembled those once espoused by the Redressement. Indeed, Pétain would have preferred to describe his program as a "Redressement français" or a "Rénovation nationale" rather than a "Révolution nationale" as it came to be called.[5] It is difficult, however, to assess the Vichy program precisely, since the regime was so heterogeneous or pluralistic in character. Historians do not agree on the classification of the different groups of reformers who governed France between 1940 and 1944.[6] Of the numerous factions, only two—the Vichy conservatives and the technocrats—are relevant here. The former, who championed the National Revolution of 1940–1941, represented the official program of reform at Vichy and had much in common with Mercier and his supporters. Both the National Revolution and the Redressement sought to replace the politicians who ruled France under the Third Republic with the "conservative elites"—that is, with high civil servants, businessmen, and military leaders. Both wanted to rid the government of the corrupt parliamentarians and bring in the healthy, uncontaminated social forces of the nation. Both believed that under the republic party politics, interest groups, and socialism had made good government impossible. Indeed, the privileged groups, which had been deprived of political power by universal suffrage and the Left, sought to re-establish their rule. More generally, the National Revolution and the Redressement both believed in the ideals of fraternal reconciliation of classes, the restoration of the family, and the revival of civic duty.

On the subject of economic reform, the two movements also had much in common. The Vichy conservatives, after throwing out the old political parties, sought to replace the existing individualistic society with a "communal" or "organic" social order. This corporative vision was to be achieved by limiting the functions of the state and by distributing power to traditional economic and social authorities. Thus employers from each industry were grouped together into Comités d'Organisation (CO) where their representatives worked closely with

---

9, 1937, when they met through a common friend. Lagardelle was Minister of Labor in 1942. Émile Mireaux was Secretary of State for Education and Fine Arts in 1940, and Achille Mestre also participated in trying to frame the Vichy constitution during 1942–1943. General Laure was Pétain's biographer and a member of his personal staff, and General Debeney accompanied the Marshal to Sigmaringen in 1944.

[5] Robert Aron, *Histoire de Vichy, 1940–1944,* p. 205.

[6] See Stanley Hoffmann, "Aspects du régime de Vichy," *Revue française de science politique,* VI (January–March, 1956), 44–69. Cf. Aron, *Vichy,* pp. 196–217.

government officials in controlling production, allocating raw materials, and setting prices. Eventually the quasi-corporative CO became the preserve of big business and gave rise to a kind of self-government by employers. Earlier the Redressement directors, especially Mercier, had been suspicious of corporatism because it seemed tainted with self-seeking professionalism and might surreptitiously increase rather than decrease state intervention. Yet they too had longed for the benefits that the new CO offered: national economic organization, collaboration between business leaders and government officials, and rule by a technical elite. These advantages were to overcome their doubts about participating in the CO.

In only one superficial respect did the defunct Redressement and the National Revolution diverge. Mercier's movement had been dominated by big business and the ideal of industrial modernization, whereas the Vichy government—more reactionary at least officially— aimed at restoring the balanced character of the French economy. Publicly, Pétain supported the ideal of National Revolution by denouncing the "trusts" and by dissolving the strongholds of big business like the CGPF and the Comité des Forges. In practice, however, it was the technocratic managers from big business who actually ran the Vichy economy.[7]

Indeed, part of the significance of the Vichy experiment in the evolution of modern France is that it marked the emergence of the technocrats. Here, for the first time, a clique of managers and officials imbued with the spirit of the Polytechnique and devoted to the Saint-Simonian philosophy of "industrialism" were the nation's *de facto* economic rulers.[8] One of these men was Yves Bouthillier, the Minister of Finance from 1940 to 1942 and a former Messine manager. These technocrats were denounced as leaders of the mysterious "Synarchy"—said to be a secret, conspiratorial society bent on the seizure of political power and the establishment of a new "French empire" run by technocrats.[9] The Synarchy was largely a romantic myth, and such a view exaggerates the interconnections among the Vichy technocrats, who in fact shared lit-

[7] The notion that the Vichy regime pursued an "anti-capitalist" policy is dismissed as false in Léon Liebmann, "Entre le mythe et la légende: 'l'anti-capitalisme' de Vichy," *Revue de l'Institut de sociologie*, No. 1 (1964), 109–148.

[8] This discussion is based on studies by Henry Ehrmann, *Organized Business in France*, pp. 58–90; Guy Desaunay, "X-Crise," pp. 159–166; Jean-Pierre Callot, *Historie de l'École Polytechnique*, pp. 228–231.

[9] The technocratic spirit of the Fifth Republic has tended to revive this myth. For a recent "exposé" of the Synarchy and the "two hundred technocrats" who supposedly now rule France in place of the defunct "two hundred families," see Henry Coston, *Les Technocrates et la Synarchie*, Lectures françaises, numéro spécial (Paris, 1962).

tle more than similar economic objectives and a common point of view.

The technocratic outlook also pervaded the new economic organizations at Vichy, the Comités d'Organisation. Like Mercier, the managers who presided over the CO had lost confidence in traditional economic individualism and the free market, and turned to direction by a technical elite. Many of these reformers went further than Mercier and fully embraced the corporative vogue. What was most striking about the personnel of the large CO, however, was the prominence of Mercier's managerial team. The presidents of the all-important electric power, gas, and aluminum CO were Roger Boutteville, Joseph Thuillier, and Raoul de Vitry—all top managers in the Messine group. Auguste Detoeuf, Mercier's colleague at Alsthom, headed the electrical manufacturing CO, and Mercier's partner at the CFP, Robert Cayrol, headed the CO for liquid fuels.[10] The role of these modernizing managers was not missed by the old-style employers, who soon attacked the CO and the return of "the mandarins of our Third Republic . . . the pseudo-bureaucrats, the Polytechnicians, the *inspecteurs des finances,* the former members of the Conseil d'État, all abstract, dogmatic theoreticians." [11] The Vichy Comités d'Organisation were the first instance of rule by the "new men," but the obstacles of war and occupation made their efforts far from successful.

In all this, however, Mercier had no part. He encouraged his managerial colleagues to accept the presidencies of several of the CO, but he refused Bouthillier's request that he too participate.[12] Why he chose to remain aloof is not altogether clear, but apparently his scruples were patriotic: he wanted nothing to do with the "armistice regime" that had surrendered to the Germans.[13] Rather than cooperate with the Vichy government, and thus with the Germans, Mercier hoped to withdraw altogether from public life and confine himself to his managerial duties.

He soon discovered there was no security in withdrawal. In September, 1940, a law regulating corporation management (a law still in force) was enacted. Bouthillier, the Minister of Finance, was the au-

[10] Centre d'information interprofessionnel, *Liste des Comités d'organisation* (Paris, 1942). Another of Mercier's managers, Jules Meny, preceded Cayrol in the liquid fuel CO, but he was deported in 1943.

[11] Eugène Schueller, *La Révolution de l'économie,* pp. 125–126.

[12] Claude Willard (*Quelques Aspects du fascisme en France avant le 6 février 1934,* p. 217) is incorrect when he asserts that Mercier served in the Comités d'Organisation.

[13] See "Vita," Mercier papers; interviews with Roger Boutteville, May 19, 1961, and Jean Buisson, Aug. 1, 1964. M. Buisson served with the technocrats at Vichy and is a close friend of the Mercier family.

thor of this legislation which struck at "supermanagers" like Mercier by strictly limiting the number of board memberships a person could hold at any one time and making the board of directors personally liable for the management of a corporation. Bouthillier defended this law for advancing the National Revolution: it was to strip big business of its "old instrument of domination," the existing lax corporation law, in order to win it to the CO and the cause of economic organization.[14] Mercier believed that Bouthillier had formulated the law out of personal pique against him—perhaps because he refused to cooperate with the new government [15]—but it is certainly possible that the zealous Bouthillier, who had a reputation for fanaticism, enacted the measure simply to further the CO. Whatever the reason, Mercier was forced to resign a score of his positions in late 1940 including the presidency of the CFP, leaving him only his posts in the Messine group. From then on he was totally estranged from the Pétain regime.

A far more serious trouble was the one posed by Mercier's alleged Jewish ancestry. Rumors that he was a Jew had long existed. They had been encouraged when he married Mme Reinach, and they were kept alive by newspaper stories of the world of Jewish high finance, in which supposedly Mercier had all sorts of secret connections, especially with the Maison Rothschild. Allegations of this sort were commonplace even among Mercier's own acquaintances, though he was known to be a Protestant and neither he nor his wife was committed to any religion.

In the fall of 1940 these rumors erupted in a vicious campaign against Mercier in the French anti-Semitic press. One Paris paper that operated as part of the German propaganda machine suggested that Mercier's mother was the daughter of a rabbi of Constantine and also revived the charge that he was an agent of the Rothschilds.[16] It demanded that he relinquish his managerial positions so as to make it impossible for the Rothschilds, who had fled France, to control the French economy from abroad. The campaign spread and soon other papers attacked Mercier for his prewar warnings against Nazi Germany and for his activities in behalf of a Franco-Soviet alliance. In July, 1941, *Le Matin* and other papers reported that Mercier had been placed under surveillance by the Vichy government.[17] The report proved to be only a rumor, but it encouraged the slanderers. On July

---

[14] Yves Bouthillier, *Le Drame de Vichy* (Paris, 1950–1951), II, 301–303.

[15] "Vita," Mercier papers.

[16] Henry Coston in *La France au travail*, Nov. 27, 1940. Coston repeated these charges in his book *La Finance juive et les trusts* (Paris, 1942), p. 58.

[17] See *Le Matin* of July 24, 1941.

31 a leading anti-Semitic weekly, *Au Pilori,* took Vichy officials to task for being so lenient with Mercier and his wife. Mercier, the paper said, had "one foot in the Jewish clan, the other in the Protestant clan"; he was fond of Radical Socialists and Freemasons, and once even had "a hired flirtation with the Communists." The conclusion was that if Mercier was not himself a Jew, or at least a half-Jew, "he is worthy of being one."

Mercier's reply to this malicious campaign, which even exposed him to the threat of blackmail, was to protest directly to Fernand de Brinon, the Vichy representative in Paris.[18] Brinon issued a public denial that Mercier was under surveillance.[19] Mercier then secured the services of Jacques Charpentier, the head of the French bar association and an outspoken critic of anti-Semitism, to institute libel suits against the slanderers. These suits effectively put a stop to the libel, but Occupation authorities decided to exploit the press campaign for their own purposes. The Gestapo called on Mercier and accused him of having openly stated his anti-German sentiments in a letter that had come into their possession. They searched his office in vain for proof that he had written the letter. As they were leaving, Mercier defiantly told them not to come again. But now he sensed that he was in real danger. The Commissariat Général aux Questions Juives in Paris requested that he submit proof of his "pure Aryan" ancestry. This was not easy to do in wartime, especially since his mother had been born in Dorpat, but he did it.[20] Still the harassment continued, with German as well as Vichy authorities demanding proof. Time and again they called upon him to submit evidence that his four grandparents were "Aryans." Then in 1942 the Commissariat initiated proceedings to confiscate his house and property. When he protested, the Commissariat hastily said that there had been a "clerical error." [21]

Arrest now seemed imminent for both Mercier and his wife. Mme Mercier had earlier left Paris for the comparative safety of the Vichy zone, but she had returned when German troops extended the occupation to all France in late 1942. Throughout this time Mercier continued to direct the Messine group from Paris, fully aware that Occupation authorities considered him an avowed anti-Nazi and at least a

[18] According to a letter from Mercier to Gustave Mercier, Aug. 6, 1941, and "Notes," Mercier papers, one of his slanderers offered to keep quiet, for a price.

[19] Mercier to Brinon, July 24, 1941, and Brinon to Mercier, July 27, 1941, Mercier papers.

[20] See Mercier to De Faramond, Oct. 30, 1941, Mercier papers. De Faramond was a director of the Commissariat.

[21] Mercier to De Faramond, Apr. 15, 1942, and De Faramond to Mercier, Apr. 29, 1942, Mercier papers.

Jewish fellow-traveler, if not a Jew himself. After the total occupation, the danger grew worse, and finally, on August 10, 1943, the Gestapo came to his home in suburban Neuilly with orders to deport him as a hostage. By a stroke of good fortune, Mercier happened to be in the hospital with blood poisoning, and the Germans, thinking that their prey was fatally ill, gave up the chase. The same day a score of high civil servants were arrested at their offices, including Mercier's son-in-law Wilfred Baumgartner, and his successor at the CFP, Jules Meny. Neither Baumgartner nor Meny was a Jew, but like Mercier they were regarded as enemies of collaboration. Baumgartner survived his deportation to Buchenwald, but Meny never returned from Dachau.

For some reason, there had been no warrant for Mme Mercier's arrest—indeed, she survived the Occupation unharmed. Mercier recovered from the blood poisoning, only to be immobilized with a slipped disc. His wife slowly nursed him back to health, and during his convalescence he began working with the French Resistance.

Since the armistice, Mercier had met regularly with a small group of professional men who, like him, were anti-collaborationist and anti-Vichy. The leader of the group was Jean de Traz, an engineer; the eminent architect Auguste Perret and the well-known writer André Siegfried also belonged, and there were also two lawyers, a judge, an engineer, and a Polytechnician.[22] At first the group of nine merely exchanged views, but by 1942 they had begun to turn their discussions into action and were collecting intelligence to relay to Free French headquarters in London via the Underground. As soon as Mercier was well, he began attending the clandestine meetings and taking part in the work of the group; he was, of course, in a position to give valuable information about vital power lines in the Paris region. As with many Resistance groups, the precise nature of the work can only be guessed at, but it was of sufficient importance to earn the approval and encouragement of General de Gaulle a year before the Liberation.[23]

As the fighting swept across France in 1944 Mercier did his best to keep the Parisian power system in operation and free from permanent

[22] Besides Mercier, Perret, and Siegfried, the other members of this Resistance group were Maurice Garnier, Robert Georges-Picot, Maurice Picot-Fégard, M. Peyron, and Félix Sartiaux. This account is based on a memorandum (June, 1945, Mercier papers) and a letter to the author from Mme Jean de Traz (Aug. 8, 1964). The activities of this little-known group were all the more impressive considering the poor record of business in the Resistance (see Ehrmann, *Organized Business*, p. 95). These men may perhaps be the unidentified leaders in the public utility industry who assisted the Resistance after 1942; see Arthur Calmette, *L' "O.C.M.," Organisation Civile et Militaire, histoire d'un mouvement de résistance de 1940 à 1946* (Paris, 1961), p. 76.

[23] Memorandum, June, 1945, Mercier papers.

damage. Bombings and shortages made his task extremely difficult. When the Allies entered Paris on August 25, they immediately dispatched an American army engineer to go to the rue de Messine and work out with Mercier plans to restore utilities service to the Paris area.

While the Allied armies continued their drive eastward, Mercier received a call from the provisional government to represent France at an important international business meeting.[24] Since Mercier was untainted by collaboration, and also was one of the few prominent businessmen active in the Resistance, he was in good standing with de Gaulle's government. As head of a small delegation Mercier flew from liberated Paris in November, 1944, via an American army transport. After long delays en route they arrived in Rye, New York, five days late. Various American business groups had organized this international business conference for the purpose of making "a preliminary survey of the economic basis of peace." [25] Ostensibly the principal topic under discussion was the reconstruction of world trade, though many delegations had come simply to plead for American loans.

Mercier's report to the conference on France's economic situation was not at all encouraging. He gloomily predicted that the war would cost the French a 30 percent reduction in their standard of living for a decade.[26] To assist France in the task of reconstruction and modernization, he asked for help in putting the transportation system and ports back in operation. Not surprisingly, as a former proponent of the Pan-Europe idea, Mercier also endorsed proposals for Western economic integration.

He had intended to read a prepared speech on two issues that were to provoke great controversy in postwar France: nationalization and planning. Owing to his late arrival at the conference, the speech was canceled, but it is nonetheless a valuable statement of Mercier's economic thought at the last stage of its long metamorphosis. The tone of the speech is one of a certain acceptance of the inevitability of the nationalization of the electric power industry, along with a measured defense of private enterprise. He criticizes state ownership for introducing extraneous considerations, such as politics or budgetary problems, into a business operation, and he is particularly fearful that nationalization may destroy the most dynamic element of private enterprise,

[24] "Compte-rendu sommaire de la délégation française," Dec. 26, 1944, Mercier papers; Ernest Mercier, La Conférence de Rye (Paris, 1945).
[25] From the official brochure entitled "The Story of the International Business Conference, November 10–18, 1944."
[26] "Le Commerce international après la guérre," Mercier papers.

managerial authority. If nationalization does become "indispensable," he insists that the managers (including himself) be given "the responsibility and risk" of control, or otherwise they will soon become timid bureaucrats.[27]

As for economic planning, Mercier here shows himself to be in the vanguard of technocratic planners who have flourished in postwar France. The necessity of long-range, flexible planning, he says, is "indisputable." And any economic plan, though it should allow as much freedom as possible for private initiative, can only be achieved "under the direction and initiative of the state." He even suggests vaguely that planning will overturn "the traditional relationship between the state and industry" and make the latter "one of the essential ways in which the state expresses itself." Mercier's passion for economic renovation had finally led him into accepting government planning for France. (He later noted that of all the delegates at the conference, American businessmen seemed the least receptive to his views on planning and the most hostile to systematic government intervention.) Significantly, in 1946 Mercier's two partners at the Union d'Électricité and the CFP, Roger Boutteville and Robert Cayrol, were to preside over the special electricity and oil commissions that helped elaborate the first economic plan for France.

After Germany's defeat in the spring of 1945 the awful physical and human destruction left by the war once again stirred interest in replacing the European state system with some form of international federation. Mercier clung to his ambiguous position of supporting a European federation, but excluding Germany from the union. In a private letter written in July, 1945, he restated his view that a unified Germany was "too big for Europe." [28] The innate aggressiveness of Germans, their unwillingness to abide by the rules, and their economic advantages would in the end disrupt any attempt to build a true "United States of Europe." The only solution was to erect a West European customs union which centered on France and the Benelux countries and was "associated" with Great Britain, Italy, and Spain. But even the effort to build such a modest customs union, Mercier believed, would have to overcome the incompetence of French political leaders in economic affairs. For proof of this incompetence one had only to look at the "foolish" domestic policies of the provisional government and the ridiculous deliberations of parliament: "every time the Consultative Assembly gathers to discuss a serious question like economics or North

[27] "Maintenance of Private Industries," Mercier papers.
[28] Mercier to unknown correspondent, July 12, 1945, Mercier papers.

Africa, its benches contain only a handful of members. The evil is thus pervasive."

Mercier had come through the war with a clean record, but the sins of the business community as a whole inevitably reflected upon him, and in the Fourth Republic he never regained his former position, though he was named to the Council of the Legion of Honor in 1945. Along with most other businessmen, he was blamed for the defeat, and scorned for collaboration. As one scholar wrote of the early postwar period, "The government no less than the man in the street was convinced that the employers' record during the most difficult hours of the country had been at best undistinguished, in many cases despicable." [29] Left-wing leaders in the liberation era generally shared the view of a noted Socialist who condemned French business for seeking the defeat in 1940, and for collaborating with the Germans.[30]

Far more distressing to Mercier than this popular disgust with big business was the ugliness of the campaign for nationalization. Proponents of nationalization, playing on the collaborationist theme, used such phrases as "a sanction against the traitors," and the CGT said it would "smash the malevolence of the Vichy bunglers." [31] The triumphant resistance movement also revived the old cry that nationalization would free French democracy from the immoral "trusts." Both General de Gaulle and the National Resistance Council denounced "monopolies" and "special interests" and called for extensive nationalization.[32] Once again, the Socialists and Communists spoke of the "economic Bastilles" and charged that the "trusts" controlled much of the press, exploited their friends in the high civil service, corrupted deputies and elections, and on occasion, used their economic power to destroy unacceptable cabinets.[33] The Communists argued that only nationalization could eliminate the possibility of another capitalist counterattack like that which had followed the Popular Front.

The electric power industry was one of the key targets in the 1944–1946 campaign for nationalization. Critics argued that a few, semimonopolistic syndicates, in particular the Messine group, exploited the choice portion of the industry and left the less profitable

---

[29] Ehrmann, *Organized Business*, p. 103.

[30] Jules Moch, *Guerre aux trusts, solutions socialistes* (Paris, 1945), p. 13.

[31] Georges Lefranc, *Les Expériences syndicales en France de 1939 à 1950* (Paris, 1950), pp. 291–293. On the motivation for nationalization also see Sturmthal, "Nationalization and Workers' Control in Britain and France," pp. 44–45.

[32] See Maurice Byé, *Nationalization in France and Italy*, pp. 74–75; Moch, *Guerre aux trusts*, pp. 10–11.

[33] Benoît Frachon, *La Bataille de la production, nouvelle étape du combat contre les trusts* (Paris, 1946), p. 94; Moch, *Guerre aux trusts*, pp. 12–15.

remnants to thousands of small, uncoordinated, inefficient companies.[34] Another common complaint was that hydroelectric power had been insufficiently developed, and that, in general, a Malthusian outlook had retarded progress and allowed other nations to surpass France in both the production and the consumption of electricity. It was further argued by the Left that a rapid expansion of hydroelectric power would require enormous capital far beyond the capacity of private industry.[35] It is true, as I have noted earlier, that in the decade of the '30's France fell behind in the development of electric power, but the responsibility for the record was not all management's, and certainly not all Mercier's or that of his modernizing colleagues. In the passion for immediate and radical change after the Liberation, careful distinctions were seldom made, however, and Mercier was usually spoken of as one head of the awful "hydra" that was responsible for all of the ills of the power industry.

Mercier was stung by what seemed to him the ingratitude that his countrymen displayed in their fervor for nationalization, and his initial reaction was a vigorous defense of the power industry's record. At a general assembly of the Union d'Électricité in May, 1945, he praised the bold achievements of the corporation, which, he pointed out, had been accomplished in spite of restrictive legislation.[36] He argued that the company had developed modern thermal supercenters, and that when hydroelectric power became available the company had immediately utilized it. He insisted that the Messine corporations were joined mainly by technical rather than financial ties and therefore did not constitute a "trust." [37] But, he said, he would accept reform if it were equitable to the stockholders, and if it conformed to the national interest.

When it became clear that nationalization was inevitable, Mercier did what little he could to shape the reform so as to avoid "an economic disaster" for France. In January, 1946, he expressed his hope that there might be some way to avoid transforming "an alert, vigorous

[34] Moch (*Guerre aux trusts,* p. 72) estimates that five large syndicates accounted for 74 percent of the total production and that five others were responsible for 16 percent, leaving only 10 percent for the remaining hundred or more small companies. At the end of the war the number of private electric companies engaged in production was 154, in transmission 86, and in distribution 1150; see Byé, *Nationalization,* p. 164. The role of the Messine syndicate is described in an article entitled "Nationalization of French Supply," *The Electrician,* Dec. 21, 1945, p. 690.

[35] See Frachon, pp. 180–181, 215; *L'Année politique 1946* (Paris, 1947), pp. 67–69.

[36] For a verbatim report of this speech see *Les Documents politiques,* fascicule 6 (1945), pp. DV-10 to DV-16.

[37] In the Preface to a book by Malégarie, *L'Électricité à Paris,* Mercier wrote bitterly: "If they had been trusts, they would have defended themselves better and would have been more respected."

industry into a dreadful, ponderous public administration." [38] He also supported a project offered to the Constituent Assembly by the conservatives which, following the prewar British system, organized private enterprises under state control rather than expropriating them outright.[39] All the aims of the nationalizers, Mercier insisted, could be achieved under such a plan without the "incomprehensible folly" of destroying more than two thousand private companies.[40]

The law of April 8, 1946, which nationalized the electric power and gas industry in effect destroyed Mercier's career. During the Vichy regime he had been forced to resign his directorships in the petroleum industry. Now, except for posts in a few small enterprises and in the holding company of Lyonnaise des Eaux which were not nationalized, he lost his major managerial positions in the utilities field. The nationalization law applied only to companies producing more than 12 billion kilowatt hours a year, but this included both the Union d'Électricité and the CPDE.

The seemingly vindictive and unjust attacks on management that accompanied nationalization were what most astonished Mercier; that nationalization would come was more or less a foregone conclusion, but the bitterness of the condemnation was, he said, the greatest disappointment of his life.[41] Certainly many contemporary leaders of the French electrical industry agree with Mercier that the polemics against private enterprise were unfair and that the timing and method of reform were unwise. At the final general assembly of the Union d'Électricité in May, 1946, Mercier, indicating his submission to nationalization, advised those who intended to continue working under the new system to keep public service as their primary goal. He allowed himself the pleasure of a final denunciation of the "vacillating" and "absurd" leadership of politicians, and stated that the nation's future rested with apolitical technicians.[42] And when some young, admiring engineers paid their respects to their retiring president, Mercier gave them advice from his own experience: "Love your profession, your engineering trade, because it is a grand and noble occupation. The Union d'Électricité is no more. So be it. Serve its successor with

---

[38] *Les Documents politiques,* fascicule 1 (1946), p. EF-3.

[39] For a description of this proposal see *L'Année politique 1946,* p. 68.

[40] Speech to stockholders of Lyonnaise des Eaux, Feb. 4, 1946, Mercier papers.

[41] Interview with Mme Ernest Mercier, June 19, 1964. An example of these unjustified attacks was the accusation by *L'Humanité* (Nov. 30, 1946) that Mercier had ordered the sabotage of hydroelectric plants and that he was a German collaborator. This charge was so blatant that Mercier began a libel suit, but he dropped it when the paper stopped its polemics.

[42] *Les Documents politiques,* fascicule 5 (1946), p. EF-2.

the same consideration and devotion. As for me, I shall return to what I was many years ago—an engineer like yourselves." [43]

Mercier was then sixty-eight years old. His managerial career was over, but he was not yet ready to retire. Since 1945 he had been president of the French branch of the International Chamber of Commerce, reconstituted with his help, and he continued in that office for another two years. He was also invited by his friend the Marquis de Vogüé, in 1946, to sit on the board of the Suez Canal company. He participated in several international conferences on the development of world power resources and the peaceful application of atomic energy, amassing in these years an extraordinary number of friends throughout the world of business. But it was the navy that made him happiest by welcoming him into the Académie de Marine in 1951—and gave him occasion to smile when it mistakenly called him back to active duty at the age of seventy.

Yet, as Mercier loved to repeat, he thought of himself primarily as an engineer. Relieved of his other duties, the old Polytechnician donned his blue coveralls and returned to research. For many years he had been interested in improving electric turbines, and in the laboratory he once more was able to capture the excitement of creating, as he had known it in the early days of the Messine group. His discoveries earned him numerous awards and distinctions.[44] But his wartime illnesses had seriously weakened him and during 1954–1955 cancer destroyed his health. The tired Saint-Simonian was still busy with his research when he died on July 10, 1955.

[43] *Ernest Mercier: une grande destinée*, pp. 254–255.

[44] In 1947–1948 he received awards from the Académie des Sciences, the Société des Ingénieurs Civils de France, and the Société d'Encouragement pour l'Industrie Nationale.

9

Conclusion

THE CAREER of Ernest Mercier foreshadows a significant historical development in modern France and in other advanced industrial countries—the rise of the technical-managerial elite.[1] H. Stuart Hughes has written recently that France's "ultimate future" belongs to "the modernizers—the enlightened businessmen and civil servants."[2] The technocratic spirit with its dedication to efficiency, modernity, and expertise grew only sporadically during the first decades of the twentieth century, but it has flourished since the Second World War in both French industry and the government bureaucracy. French business managers have recently been evaluated as the most technocratic in Europe,[3] and apolitical technicians direct the economic planning commission and hold important ministerial posts. The new prestige and power of the technocrat has prompted some to describe the Fifth Republic as the "republic of engineers." There is, as a result, growing discussion of the virtues and dangers of technocracy for France.[4]

[1] A good survey of the role of managerial elites as an international phenomenon is *Management in the Industrial World: An International Analysis,* eds. Frederick Harbison and Charles A. Myers (New York, 1959). "Technocracy and the role of experts in government" was a subject of discussion at the Fifth World Congress of the International Political Science Association, held at Paris in September, 1961. See especially the paper delivered by Roger Grégoire, which summarizes the various national reports. The trend since the Second World War from parliamentary democracy to "expertocracy" in western Europe is analyzed by Karl D. Bracher, "Problems of Parliamentary Democracy in Europe," *Daedalus,* Winter, 1964, pp. 179–198.

[2] H. Stuart Hughes, "Gaullism in the Mirror of History," in *An Approach to Peace and Other Essays* (New York, 1962), pp. 148–149.

[3] Granick, *The European Executive,* pp. 72 ff.

[4] An extraordinary amount of literature has appeared since the Second World War in France on the problem of technocracy. Much of this discussion has been prompted by moral or philosophical concern over a society increasingly dominated by *technique.* One such study is Jacques Ellul, *The Technological Society.* Jean Meynaud has written two excellent works, *Technocratie et politique* and *La Technocratie, mythe ou réalité?* on the issues raised by the technocrats' accession to political power. The Ellul and Meynaud volumes also contain extensive bibliographies. For a brief introduction to the issues see Jacques Billy, *Les Techniciens et le pouvoir* (Paris, 1963). The best history of the technocratic movement in France between 1930 and 1960 is Philippe Bauchard, *Les Technocrates et le pouvoir* (Paris,

The origins of this movement toward technocratic rule are clearly revealed through Mercier's career. The backwardness of the French industrial plant, which the First World War had exposed, shocked Mercier and his fellow neo-Saint-Simonians. Most of these enlightened managers were products of the École Polytechnique or the other *grandes écoles* of engineering which fostered technocratic ideas. In Mercier's day these neo-Saint-Simonians directed many large companies in the modern sector of the economy, especially in those semipublic industries that hovered between private and government control. The obstacles Mercier faced in his crusade to win the nation's leadership to the standard of economic and political modernization revealed the stubborn resistance in French society to such change. The failure of the Redressement Français disclosed the prevailing Malthusianism and the political apathy within the business community, even among the managerial elite, during the interwar years. Despite the resistance to modernization, the neo-Saint-Simonians enjoyed a brief moment of influence in the late '20's. The depression, however, shattered their hopes. During the '30's business leaders concentrated on surviving rather than modernizing, although there was growing discussion of technocratic ideas.[5] The defeat of 1940 suddenly brought the technocrats, especially Mercier's managerial clique and many of the former Redressement supporters, into power at Vichy. After the war nationalization removed Mercier from command, but the managerial cadres he formed and the other technocratic heirs of the neo-Saint-Simonians extended their influence in business and government.

As the technicians and managers have risen to become the elite in modern industrial society, their character, training, and attitudes assume greater significance. Daniel Bell has summarized the issue: "Just as the industrial worker (although not the majority of the early capitalist society) created the social problems of the past hundred years, so the new technical classes will set the problems of the new decades. Their recruitment, their education, their culture, their élan, their de-

---

1966). George Friedmann's article in the symposium *Industrialisation et technocratie* (Paris, 1949) provides a succinct history of technocratic doctrine. In 1957 a number of prominent French leaders organized a technocratic study group somewhat reminiscent of the Redressement Français called the Centre d'Études Prospectives. Its organ is the periodical *Prospective*.

[5] A number of avant-garde reviews like *Plans*, *L'Homme nouveau*, and *L'Ordre nouveau* appeared in the early '30's. In their pages young intellectuals, like Robert Aron, expressed their contempt for the materialism and uniformity fostered by American-style capitalism, yet they also experimented with technocratic schemes. See Jean Touchard, "L'Esprit des années 1930: une tentative de renouvellement de la pensée française," *Tendances politiques dans la vie française depuis 1789* (Paris, 1960), pp. 89–120.

sires, become crucial for the health and growth of the society. And inevitably the social politics of a country . . . will revolve about them." [6] Since Ernest Mercier was a great pioneering technocrat, his biography provides insight into the mentality of this new directing elite in France.

One of Mercier's shortcomings as a reformer was his political naïveté. The Redressement Français was an amateurish experiment in political action that was doomed to failure by its founder's refusal to enter the political arena openly. The movement's distinguished leadership, material resources, and propaganda machine were largely ineffectual because it neither commanded any votes itself nor controlled any parliamentarians. Mercier waited in the anteroom, reforms in hand, expecting the rulers of the Third Republic to invite him into the council chamber. In general, he believed that both political parties and ideologies were artificial and unnecessary for good government. His disregard for political ideology almost cost him his life during the war when, despite his differences with the Nazis, he remained on the job. Mercier discovered that he could not rid the republic of politics, and in the end he felt unjustly victimized by the politicians who swept away his managerial authority during the Liberation.

Mercier's political activity also supports the contention that the technocratic mentality may be fervently elitist and antidemocratic. His ultimate political goal approached a Saint-Simonian state where experts ruled independently of democratic controls. His pressure group denounced universal suffrage, party politics, and the parliamentary system as they functioned under the Third Republic. During the crisis atmosphere of the early '30's, the Redressement industrialists encouraged authoritarian movements, and therefore they bear considerable responsibility for the riots against the Chamber on February 6, 1934. And after the defeat of 1940 most of Mercier's circle participated in the effort by the Vichy regime to "cleanse" France of parliamentary politics. Mercier's political biography suggests that without a strong, effective government the technocrat is likely to embrace authoritarian or antidemocratic alternatives. This is not to argue that the technocratic tradition in modern France has been purely authoritarian in its politics. Contemporary Saint-Simonians like Jean Monnet or Pierre Mendès-France, who is a devoted parliamentarian, represent a contrary and truly democratic technocratic tendency. The vital, though unresolved, issue is which type of technocracy will predominate—that of Mercier or Mendès-France?

[6] "The Future of the Left," *Encounter*, May, 1960, pp. 59–61.

There was also a certain callousness about Mercier's mechanistic approach to human problems. His plea for social reform reflects his basic humanitarianism. Yet he also seemed unmindful of the heavy cost in human suffering required by his plans for modernization. The apostle of change lacked charity for those sinners wedded to tradition.

Considering Mercier as a model of the modern French technocrat, one sees that his merits outweigh such defects. He was above all a selfless Saint-Simonian who sought to create, to build, and to improve the human situation. For Mercier it was both man's "royal privilege" [7] and his duty "to create better conditions of existence, to create more order and more harmony, [and] to aid the march of progress." [8] The source of Mercier's reforming zeal was not a desire for personal power or wealth but an altruistic dedication to the public welfare. His managerial and technical skills combined with this Saint-Simonian energy made him one of the great builders of modern France.

In addition, most of Mercier's views on streamlining French institutions should be encouraging to the student of technocracy. He was among the vanguard of employers who fought for social reform. He tried to reconcile labor and management through a combination of good will, concrete reform, and prosperity. The evolution of Mercier's economic thought also parallels the important trend toward economic expansion and national planning in twentieth-century France. Mercier, who was little concerned with the method of disciplining the economy to attain rapid growth, moved gradually away from the ideal of laissez-faire capitalism. At first he proposed regulating competition by industrial concentration and producers' agreements. Later he adopted certain corporative notions and finally embraced economic planning by business and government. It is likely that Mercier would have endorsed even nationalization in 1946 as a means of advancing economic modernization if it had been instituted without polemics against him. His enlightened economic views also included a keen interest in European unity. Mercier championed the cause of a customs union long before the rest of the French business community accepted the need for economic integration. He looked beyond economic unity and dreamed of a European political federation, though he found it difficult to include Germany in his dream. In domestic politics his campaign to streamline the state anticipated the technocratic reforms of the Fourth and Fifth Republics. He also made one of the first efforts to organize French businessmen and engage them in public affairs. De-

[7] Speech to the Association Amicale des Anciens Élèves de l'École Polytechnique, May 15, 1949, Mercier papers.

[8] Mercier, *Albert Petsche,* p. 54.

spite the shortcomings of the Redressement Français, Mercier's example did not go unnoticed. After 1936 there were numerous imitators, and during the war Vichy launched an ambitious effort to reorganize French business. There have been indications that since 1945 French employers have shown more interest in national life. Sensitive employers, like the Jeunes Patrons, have begun to search for new ways to justify their authority and to acknowledge their social responsibilities.[9]

The France Ernest Mercier wanted was a Saint-Simonian France. Should his technical-managerial class gain power, it may be the France of the future. This new France would be more dynamic, more productive, more European-minded, and more strongly governed than the old France. But it might also be a France ruled by an elite of technocrats who may be indifferent to democracy and who hold progress as their only goal. If Ernest Mercier is a model of the modern technocrat, he gives Frenchmen some cause for concern, but much more reason for hope.

[9] See the articles by François Bourricaud, "Contribution à la sociologie du chef d'entreprise, le 'Jeune Patron,'" *Revue économique*, November, 1958, pp. 896–911, and "'Malaise patronal,'" *Sociologie du travail*, III (1961), 221–235. One student of French business history has recently written that the employer of today is "much more humane, much more open, much more dynamic" than his predecessors; see Roger Priouret, *Origines du patronat français* (Paris, 1963), p. 235.

Appendix

THE MANAGERIAL POSITIONS
OF ERNEST MERCIER c. 1935 *

ELECTRIC POWER AND UTILITIES
President

Lyonnaise des Eaux
Nord-Lumière
Union d'Électricité

Vice-President

Sté. Marocaine de Distribution d'Eau, de Gaz et d'Électricité
Cie. Parisienne de Distribution d'Électricité
Union Hydro-Électrique
Union pour l'Industrie et l'Électricité

Member of Board of Directors

Cie. Nationale du Rhône
Cie. Parisienne de Chauffage Urbain
Électricité du Nord-Est Parisien
Énergie Électrique du Littoral Méditerranéen
Énergie Électrique du Maroc
Forces motrices de la Truyère
Ouest-Lumière
Sté. Andelysienne d'Électricité
Sté. de Gérance et d'Exploitation d'Entreprises Électriques
Sté. des Chutes de Banca
Sté. Générale de Force et Lumière
Sté. Régionale de Transport de Gaz
Sud-Lumière
Union Électrique et Gazière de l'Afrique du Nord
Versaillaise de Tramways Électriques et de Distribution d'Énergie

* This list of Mercier's positions was compiled from: the Mercier papers; *Annuaire de l'Union des Syndicats de l'Électricité, édition 1935–1936; Ernest Mercier: une grande destinée; Les Documents politiques,* February, 1935, pp. 79–80.

ELECTRICAL MANUFACTURING
President

Alsthom (Sté. Générale de Constructions Électriques et Mécaniques)

Member of Board of Directors

Cie. Générale d'Électricité
Cie. pour la Fabrication des Compteurs et Matériel d'Usines à Gaz
Sté. Alsacienne de Constructions Mécaniques

POWER FINANCE
President

Union Financière pour l'Industrie Électrique

Member of Board of Directors

Sté. Financière Électrique
Sté. Financière pour le Développement des Services Publics

PETROLEUM
President

Cie. Française des Pétroles
Cie. Française de Raffinage
Cie. Navale des Pétroles
Omnium International des Pétroles
Steaua Française

Member of Board of Directors

Franco-Roumaine des Pétroles Colombia
Iraq Oil Company
Steaua Romana
Union des Pétroles de Martigues

BANKS
Member of Board of Directors

Banque de Paris et des Pays-Bas
Crédit Commercial de France
Crédit National

OTHERS
Member of Board of Directors

Cités-Jardins de la Région Parisienne
Exploitation des Schistes Bitumineux d'Autun
Péchiney (Cie. des Produits Chimiques et Électro-Métallurgiques, Alais,
    Froges et Camargue)
Penhoët (Sté. des Chantiers et Ateliers de Saint-Nazaire)
Sté. Anonyme de Publications et d'Éditions
Sté. Internationale de Régie Co-Intéressée des Tabacs au Maroc
Union Immobilière Hoche

Bibliography

NOTE ON SOURCES

The basic published source for the career of Ernest Mercier is the memorial volume prepared after his death by his widow—*Ernest Mercier: une grande destinée*. Although this work contains only a few excerpts from Mercier's writing that are not available elsewhere, it is valuable for some enlightening essays by his business associates, friends, and relatives. Mercier's ideas and activities are recorded in his many books and articles, and in the publications of his pressure group.

Mercier's private papers are presently in the possession of his widow. They are by no means complete. Much had already been scattered or lost before I had the privilege of seeing them in the summer of 1964. The most important documents I arranged to have reproduced, and they are now deposited in the Hoover Institution on War, Revolution, and Peace. These consist largely of his speeches, vitae, business memoranda, early drafts of his writings, family records, and memorabilia written after his death by friends. There are, unfortunately, only fragments of his voluminous correspondence. His papers also include an important, confidential autobiography of some sixty pages which Mercier wrote in 1941 for the use of his lawyer in a slander case. There are two other items of note in this collection: a short biography written by Mercier's brother Maurice, and an unpublished history of the Redressement composed by Henri Cacaud in 1955. In addition, a few of Mercier's letters are available in the papers of Louis Loucheur.

The activities of the Redressement can be traced in some detail through its publications, in particular through its monthly *Bulletin*. This periodical is available at the Bibliothèque Nationale and is on microfilm at the University of Illinois Library. The former library has all the Redressement's publications cited here except for the newspaper, the *Région parisienne*. Roger Mennevée's review, *Les Documents politiques*, provides considerable information about the evolution of Mercier's organization, but it must be used with great care. Mennevée's archives, which may be of some general scholarly interest, have recently been acquired by the library of the University of California at Los Angeles. The official files of the Redressement remain to be examined—if they are still intact.

On the general topic of modern French business the most valuable guides are Henry W. Ehrmann's *Organized Business in France* and the comprehensive *Le Monde des affaires en France de 1830 à nos jours*. The response of the business community to public affairs during the interwar period can be traced in several periodicals: *La Journée industrielle, Le Capital, L'Information,* the *Bulletin quotidien, Le Réveil économique, L'Usine,* the *Revue industrielle,* and the *Bulletin* of the CGPF. Left-wing periodicals such as *La Flèche, La Lumière,* and *Les Documents politiques* which specialized in exposing the political power of big business are useful, but hardly reliable, sources. Biographical data for businessmen before the Second World War are meager. Indeed, only a handful of modern French business leaders have found their biographers. Therefore the historian is forced to rely upon the highly biased, and often inaccurate, studies by Augustin Hamon, Albert Aymé-Martin, Émmanuel Beau de Loménie, and Henry Coston. Since the war, biographical sources have vastly improved with the publication of *Who's Who in France,* the *Annuaire Desfossés,* the *Bottin Mondain,* and the periodical *Entreprise.*

The history of the electric power industry has not been explored except for the narrow and rather dated studies by Charles Malégarie, Jacques Doreau, and Albert Renaud. An invaluable guide is *Economic Conditions in France* which contains the reports of Sir Robert Cahill, the British commercial counsellor in Paris. The origins of the hydroelectric power industry are presented by François Bouchayer. Data on specific power companies can be found in the electrical industry's *Annuaire,* the *Annuaire Chaîx,* the work by J. Tchernoff, and in the studies by the British Electrical and Allied Manufacturers' Association. Periodicals like the *Revue générale d'électricité* and the *Revue d'économie politique* provide regular comment on the industry's evolution.

The history of the French petroleum industry has received much more attention. The most useful studies are by Edgar Faure, Guillaume de Labarrière, Étienne Dalemont, and Jean Rondot.

For the literature on the problem of technocracy in France see note 4 in the Conclusion.

My most valuable sources for this biography were the personal interviews and correspondence with the following businessmen, political leaders, academicians, writers, and friends of Ernest Mercier: Raphaël Alibert, Ludovic Barthélemy, Émmanuel Beau de Loménie, Roger Boutteville, Jean Buisson, Jacques Chastenet, Richard de Coudenhove-Kalergi, Paul Dauphin, Henry Davezac, Prince J. L. Faucigny-Lucinge, José Germain, Claude-J. Gignoux, François Goguel, Stanley Hoffmann, Alfred Lambert-Ribot, François Legueu, Pierre Massé, René Mayer, Mme Ernest Mercier, Victor de Metz, René de Montaigu, René Rémond, Georges Riché, Guillaume de Tarde, Joseph Thuillier, Mme Jean de Traz, Pierre Waline.

This bibliography is divided into the following major categories: manuscripts, published writings of Mercier, publications of the Redressement Français, government documents, books and articles consulted, and periodicals consulted.

MANUSCRIPTS

Loucheur, Louis. *Papers.* Hoover Institution on War, Revolution, and Peace, Stanford University.
Mercier, Ernest. *Papers.* See Note on Sources.

MAJOR PUBLISHED WRITINGS OF ERNEST MERCIER
(chronological order)

The "Union d'Électricité" and the Gennevilliers Station. Translated by C. M. Popp. Paris, 1922.

"Quelques Réflexions sur l'organisation des distributions d'électricité de la région parisienne," *Revue générale de l'électricité*, XX (July 10, 1926), 42–43.

La Production et le travail. Cahiers du Redressement Français, Series I, No. 14. Paris: SAPE, 1927.

"Les Conséquences sociales de la rationalisation en France," in *L'Aspect social de la rationalisation.* Cahiers du Redressement Français, Series I, No. 10. Paris: SAPE, 1927.

"Réflexions sur l'élite," *Revue des deux mondes,* February 15, 1928, pp. 882–895.

Albert Petsche, 1860–1933. Paris: Martial, 1933.

La Crise et l'élite. Paris: La Cause, 1933.

"Considérations sur une politique nationale de l'énergie," *L'Usine,* May 16, 1935.

"Débat sur l'URSS," *X-Crise Bulletin,* February–April, 1936, pp. 34–69.

URSS, Réflexions par Ernest Mercier. Éditions du Centre polytechnicien d'études économiques, No. 1. Paris: CPEE, 1936.

"Un grand Industriel français préconise le commerce avec la Russie. . . . ," *L'Économie internationale,* April 1936, pp. 4–6.

Résurrection française, erreurs politiques et vérités humaines. Paris: Fasquelle, 1937.

La France devant son destin. Paris: Fasquelle, 1939.

La Conférence de Rye. Paris: SPID, 1945.

Le Cycle équipression et la turbine à gaz. Paris: La Société, 1947.

Address in *Bulletin de l'Association des Anciens Élèves de l'École Polytechnique,* July, 1949, pp. 43–48.

Excerpts in *Ernest Mercier: une grande destinée.* Paris: Éditions SEFI, 1958.

THE *REDRESSEMENT FRANÇAIS*
(a) *Official Publications*

Bulletin mensuel, 1926–1935.

Charles-Bellet, L. *La Bataille du franc, réflexions d'un producteur.* 2nd ed. Paris: Éditions du Redressement Français, 1928.

Compte rendu de l'Assemblée générale du 14 décembre 1927. Paris: le Redressement Français, 1927.

Hirsch, Julius. *La Rationalisation de la production.* Paris: le Redressement Francais, 1927.

Le Redressement Français: organisation et réformes. Paris: le Redressement Français, 1927.

La Région parisienne, 1927–1935.

Romier, Lucien. *Le Redressement Français: idées très simples pour les Français.* Paris: KRA, 1928.

(b) *The Cahiers of the* Redressement Français: *First Series (1927)*
National Education

1. *L'Éducation nationale:* René Hubert and E. Geoffroy
2. *Une Éducation moderne:* Paul Desjardins and Paul Hunziker
3. *L'Éducation physique:* Forsant and D'Clippet
4. *Nos Études supérieures:* J. Lefas, Prof. J-L. Faure, and Bruhat

Production and Labor

5. *Agriculture:* M. Augé-Laribé, P. Garnier, and M. Bitouzet
6. *Matières premières et forces naturelles:* P. Parent, L. Marlio, and P. Lemy
7. *La Réorganisation industrielle:* A. Detoeuf
8. *Organisons la production:* Devinat, Mme Thumen, and Raoul Bigot
9. *L'Artisanat:* J. Delage
10. *L'Aspect social de la rationalisation:* E. Mercier, J. Zamanski, and E. Picard
11. *Distribution et consommation:* P. François, E. Picard, Poisson, and H. Duhem
12. *Voies et communications modernes:* Bordes, Gustine, H. Cangardel, Girardeau, and Blum
12. *Échanges commerciaux:* P. Elbel, F. Delaisi, Bernard Lavergne, A. Bommelaer, and Pierre Lyautey
14. *La Production et le travail:* E. Mercier

Social Questions

15. *Le Problème de logement:* J. Lévêque and J-H. Ricard
16. *L'Urbanisme:* H. Prost and G. Monsarrat
17. *L'Hygiène sociale:* Mme Brunschwig, Dr. Evrot, Dr. Queyrat, Mlle Hardouin, Mme Gonse-Boas, Dr. Sand, and Charles Lallemand
18. *L'Hygiène à l'atelier:* Wurtz
19. *La Natalité et la famille:* J. Lefas, F. Boverat, Abbé Viollet, and C. Bonvoisin
20. *Les Centres sociaux: l'enseignement ménager:* Mlle Bassot, Diemer, and Mlle de Robien
21. *L'Utilisation des loisirs et l'éducation populaire:* J. Guérin-Desjardins, J-H. Adam, R. Georges-Picot, and Charles Lallemand
22. *Les Assurances sociales:* P. Frantzen
23. *L'Immigration ouvrière en France:* W. Oualid
24. *L'Organisation de la vie sociale:* R. Dautry

Administrative Organization

25. *La Réforme parlementaire*
26. *La Réforme judiciaire*
27. *La Réforme administrative*
28. *Les Lois militaires*

Financial Questions

29. *L'Organisation financière:* E. Giscard d'Estaing, Émile Mireaux, Maurice Kellersohn, M. Ladie, and De Saint-Pulgent

International Questions

30. *Une Diplomatie moderne:* J. Bardoux and Allary

Colonial Questions

31. *La Production des colonies:* Édouard Payen, Ladreit de Lacharrière, and Germenot
32. *La Mise en valeur de notre domaine colonial:* Lejeune, Daudet, Charbonnel, Édouard Payen, and Germenot
33. *La France Nord-Africaine:* Gustave Mercier

Summary
34. *Le Congrès de l'organisation*
35. *Voeux et solutions*

(c) The Cahiers of the Redressement Français: *Second Series*

1. *Politique extérieure:* Reports of the study committees (1932)
2. *Monnaie et budget:* R. Wolffe (1932)
3. *Pour la Sécurité de la politique financière:* Henri Cacaud (1932)
4. *La Revendication allemande de l'égalité des armements:* Augustin Léger (1932)
5. *Les Bases de la politique extérieure de la France* (1933)
6. *La Politique italienne dans l'Europe centrale et orientale:* Jacques Ancel (1933)
7. *L'Allemagne sous la dictature de Hitler:* Albert Rivaud (1933)
8. *Le Japon, la Chine et la Mandchourie:* Albert Rivaud (1933)
9. *Le Réarmement allemand:* General Debeney (1933)
10. *L'Obsession de la guerre en Allemagne:* Albert Rivaud (1933)
11. *La Défense aérienne du territoire:* General Laure (1934)
12. *L'Europe centrale et Hitlérisme:* Étienne Fournol (1934)
13. *Le Problème autrichien:* Marcel Dunan (1934)
14. *La Politique extérieure du cabinet d'Union nationale:* Jacques Ancel, Albert Mousset, and Maurice Ordinaire (1934)
15. *Le Centre-Est Européen et l'action de la France à la fin de 1934:* Jacques Bardoux, General Debeney, Albert Mousset, and Henry Rollin (1935)
16. *La Crise de l'Afrique du Nord, le péril et les remèdes* (1935)
17. *La Guerre en Extrême-Orient est-elle prochaine? est-elle fatale?* René Saint-Pierre and M. Balet (1935)
18. *Les Intentions de l'Allemagne:* Albert Rivaud (1935)

(d) *Subsidized Periodicals* *

Minerva, 1925–1928.
Le Monde colonial illustré, 1926–1935.
Le Muscle, 1927–1928.
Nos Plaisirs, 1926–1927.
La Revue industrielle, 1926–1935.
La Vague rouge, 1927–1931.

GOVERNMENT DOCUMENTS

France. Assemblée nationale. Annexe au procès-verbal de la séance du 8 août 1947, *Rapport fait au nom de la commission chargée d'enquêter sur les événements en France de 1933 à 1945.* 9 vols. Paris, 1951.
——. Chambre des députés. *Journal officiel de la République française, Débats parlementaires* and *Documents parlementaires.*
——. Treizième législature, session extraordinaire de 1925. *Procès-verbaux de la commission d'enquête sur les conditions dans lesquelles le comité de l'Union des Intérêts Économiques est intervenu dans la dernière campagne électorale.* No. 2098. Paris, [1925].

---

* Dates represent the life span of the periodical, or in the case of the last two items, the period of the Redressement's influence.

France. Treizième législature, session de 1928. *Procès-verbaux de la commission d'enquête sur les pétroles.* No. 5449. Paris, 1928.

———. Quinzième législature, session de 1934. Annexe au procès-verbal de la séance du 17 mai 1934, *Rapport général fait au nom de la commission d'enquête chargée de rechercher les causes et les origines des événements du 6 février et les jours suivants, ainsi que toutes les responsabilités encourues.* 4 vols. Paris, 1934.

Germany. German Foreign Office Microfilm. Serial M196. National Archives, Washington, D.C.

United States. Department of State. *Foreign Relations of the United States, Diplomatic Papers, 1935.* Washington, D.C., 1953.

BOOKS AND ARTICLES CONSULTED

"A bas la rationalisation," *La Révolution prolétarienne,* October 15, 1928, pp. 275–281.

Abetz, Otto. *Histoire d'une politique franco-allemande, 1930–1950.* Paris: Delamain et Boutelleau, 1953.

L'Afrique à travers ses fils: Ernest Mercier. Paris: Librairie orientaliste, 1944.

Albert, Charles. *L'État moderne: ses principes et ses institutions.* Paris: Librairie Valois, 1929.

L'Année politique 1946. Paris: Éditions du grand siècle, 1947.

Annuaire chaix: les principales sociétés par actions. Saint-Ouen, 1922–1936.

Annuaire de l'Union des Syndicats de l'Électricité. Paris, 1920–1936.

Aron, Raymond. *Immuable et changeante: de la IVe à la Ve république.* Paris: Calmann-Lévy, 1959.

Aron, Robert. *Histoire de Vichy, 1940–1944.* Paris: Fayard, 1954.

———. *Une grande Banque d'affaires: la Banque de Paris et des Pays-Bas.* Paris: Éditions de l'épargne, 1959.

L'Avenir de la république. Paris: Librairie Valois, 1927.

Aymé-Martin, Albert. *Nos grands Financiers contre la nation.* Paris: Librairie de la revue française, 1931.

Baldy, Edmond. *Les Banques d'affaires en France depuis 1900.* Paris: Librairie générale de droit, 1922.

Barbier, Pierre. "L'Énergie électrique," in Jacques Bondet (ed.), *Le Monde des affaires en France de 1830 à nos jours* (Paris: Sté. d'Édition de dictionnaires et encyclopédies, 1952).

Bardoux, Jacques. *La France de demain, ni communiste, ni hitlérienne: un plan.* Paris: Recueil Sirey, [1937].

———. "La Réforme de l'état," *Revue des deux mondes,* March 15, 1935, pp. 268–286.

Bauchard, Philippe. *Les Technocrates et le pouvoir.* Paris: Arthaud, 1966.

Baum, Warren C. *The French Economy and the State.* Princeton, N.J.: Princeton University Press, 1958.

Beau de Loménie, Émmanuel, et al. "Les 'Gros,'" *Crapouillot,* No. 16. Paris, 1952.

———. *La Mort de la troisième république.* Paris: Éditions du Conquistador, 1951.

———. *Les Responsabilités des dynasties bourgeoises.* 4 vols. Paris: Denoël, 1947–1963.

Bell, Daniel. "The Future of the Left," *Encounter,* May, 1960, pp. 57–61.

Beloff, Max. "The Sixth of February," in James Joll (ed.), *The Decline of the Third Republic,* St. Antony's Papers, No. 5 (London: Chatto and Windus, 1959).

Bérenger, Henry. *Le Pétrole et la France.* Paris: Flammarion, 1920.

Berg, Peter. *Deutschland und Amerika 1918–1929: über das Deutsche Amerikabild der Zwanziger Jahre.* Lübeck: Matthiesen, 1963.

Bettelheim, Charles. *Bilan de l'économie française, 1919–1946.* Paris: Presses universitaires, 1947.

Billy, Jacques. "Les X dans les affaires," *Entreprise,* November 24, 1962, pp. 47–61.

———. *Les Techniciens et le pouvoir.* Paris: Presses universitaires, 1963.

Bonnefous, Édouard. *Histoire politique de la troisième république.* Vols. IV and V. Paris: Presses universitaires, 1960–1965.

Bonnet, Pierre. *La Commercialisation de la vie française du premier empire à nos jours.* Paris: Plon, 1929.

Bonnevay, Laurent. *Les Journées sanglantes de février 1934.* Paris: Grevin, 1935.

Bouchayer, François. *Les Pionniers de la houille blanche et de l'électricité.* Paris: Librairie Dalloz, 1954.

Bouglé, C. "Le Bilan du Saint-Simonisme," *Annales de l'Université de Paris,* September–October and November–December, 1931, pp. 446–463, 540–556.

Bourbonnais, Marc. *Le Néo Saint-Simonisme et la vie sociale d'aujourd'hui.* Paris: Presses universitaires, 1923.

Bourgin, Georges, *et al. Manuel des partis politiques en France.* Paris: Rieder, 1928.

Bourgoin, P. "La Rationalisation," *Revue de France,* November 15, 1929, pp. 269–294.

Bourricaud, François. "Contribution à la sociologie du chef d'entreprise, le 'Jeune Patron,'" *Revue économique,* November, 1958, pp. 896–911.

———. "'Malaise patronal,'" *Sociologie du travail,* III (1961), 221–235.

Bouthillier, Yves. *Le Drame de Vichy.* 2 vols. Paris: Plon, 1950–1951.

Bouvier-Ajam, Maurice. *La Doctrine corporative.* 4th ed. Paris: Recueil Sirey, 1943.

Bouyer, Raymond. *Le Capitalisme contemporain, fiction et réalité.* Paris: Centre confédéral d'éducation ouvrière, n.d.

Bracher, Karl D. "Problems of Parliamentary Democracy in Europe," *Daedalus,* Winter, 1964, pp. 179–198.

Brady, Robert. *Business as a System of Power.* New York: Columbia University Press, 1943.

———. *The Rationalization Movement in German Industry.* Berkeley: University of California Press, 1933.

British Electrical and Allied Manufacturers' Association. *Combines and Trusts in the Electrical Industry.* London, 1927.

———. *The Electrical Industry in France, Industrial and Economic Progress.* London, 1925.

Brunner, Christopher. *The Problem of Oil.* London: Ernest Benn, 1930.

Burgess, Eugene W. "Management in France," in Frederick Harbison and Charles A. Myers (eds.), *Management in the Industrial World: An International Analysis* (New York: McGraw-Hill, 1959).

Burnham, James. *The Managerial Revolution*. New York: John Day, 1941.

Byé, Maurice, *et al. Nationalization in France and Italy*. Ithaca, N.Y.: Cornell University Press, 1955.

Cahill, Sir Robert. *Economic Conditions in France*. Department of Overseas Trade. London: His Majesty's Stationery Office, 1922–1934.

Callot, Jean-Pierre. *Histoire de l'École Polytechnique, ses légendes, ses traditions, sa gloire*. Paris: Presses modernes, 1958.

Calmette, Arthur. *L'"O.C.M.," Organisation Civile et Militaire, Histoire d'un mouvement de résistance de 1940 à 1946*. Paris: Presses universitaires, 1961.

Cameron, Elizabeth R. *Prologue to Appeasement, A Study in French Foreign Policy*. Washington, D.C.: American Council on Public Affairs, 1942.

Capitant, René. "La Crise et la réforme du parlementarisme en France," *Jahrbuch des Öffentlichen Rechts der Gegenwart*, XXIII (1936), 1–71.

"Ce que représentent les a.c.," *Revue politique et parlementaire*, July 10, 1934, pp. 3–9.

Centre d'Information Interprofessionnel. *Liste des Comités d'organisation*. Paris, 1942.

Chastenet, Jacques. *Histoire de la troisième république*. Vols. V and VI. Paris: Hachette, 1960–1962.

Chevallier, J.-J. *Histoire des institutions politiques de la France moderne, 1789–1945*. Paris: Dalloz, 1958.

Chopine, Paul. *Six Ans chez les Croix de Feu*. Paris: Gallimard, 1935.

Churchill, Winston. *The World Crisis*. Vol. I. New York: Scribners, 1923.

Comité de Vigilance des Intellectuels Antifascistes. *Les Croix de Feu, leur chef, leur programme*. Paris, 1935.

Confédération Générale du Travail. *Actualité du plan*. Versailles, [1936].

———. *La Nationalisation industrialisée*. Paris: Édition de la CGT, 1920.

———. *L'Électricité, les resources nationales au service de la nation sous le contrôle de la collectivité*. Versailles, 1938.

Coston, Henry. *La Finance juive et les trusts*. Paris: Jean Renard, 1942.

———. *Les Financiers qui mènent le monde*. Paris: Librairie française, 1955.

———. *Les Technocrates et la Synarchie*. Lectures françaises, numéro spécial. Paris, 1962.

Cottier, Jean-Louis. *La Technocratie, nouveau pouvoir*. Paris: Éditions du Cerf, 1959.

Coudenhove-Kalergi, Richard N. *Crusade for Pan-Europe: Autobiography of a Man and a Movement*. New York: Putnam, 1943.

Creyssel, Paul. *La Rocque contre Tardieu*. Paris: Sorlot, 1938.

Croix de Feu, Parti Social Français: tracts politiques, 1934–1939. Paris, n.d.

Crozier, Michel. *The Bureaucratic Phenomenon*. Chicago: University of Chicago Press, 1964.

Dalemont, Étienne. *L'Économie pétrolière*. Edited by P. H. Frankel. Paris: Librairie de Médicis, 1948.

———. *Le Pétrole*. Paris: Presses universitaires, 1963.

Dantin, Charles. *Le Réseau de distribution de l'Union d'Électricité et la centrale de Gennevilliers près de Paris*. Paris: Vaugiraud, 1931.

Delaisi, Francis. *La Banque de France aux mains des 200 familles*. Paris: Comité de vigilance des intellectuels antifascistes, 1936.

———. *Oil: Its Influence on Politics*. Translated by C. Leonard Leese. London: Allen and Unwin, 1922.

Delefortrie-Soubeyroux, Nicole. *Les Dirigeants de l'industrie française*. Collection "Recherches sur l'économie française," No. 6. Paris: Colin, 1961.

DeNovo, John A. *American Interests and Policies in the Middle East, 1900–1939.* Minneapolis: University of Minnesota Press, 1963.

Denuc, J. "Structure des entreprises," *Revue d'économie politique,* LIII (January–February, 1939), 220–263.

Desaunay, Guy. "X-Crise, Contribution à l'étude des idéologies économiques d'un groupe de polytechniciens durant la grande crise économique, 1931–1939." Unpublished thesis, Université de Paris, 1965.

Dessirier, J. "Secteurs 'abrité' et 'non abrité' dans le déséquilibre actuel de l'économie française," *Revue d'économie politique,* July–August, 1935, pp. 1330–1358.

Detoeuf, Auguste. *Propos de O. L. Barenton, confiseur, ancien élève de l'École Polytechnique.* Paris: Éditions du Tambourinaire, 1960.

Doreau, Jacques, *Rapports entre l'état et les sociétés de production–transport–distribution de l'énergie électrique.* Thesis, Université de Paris. Paris: Imprimerie du Montparnasse, 1928.

Dubly, Henri-Louis. *Vers un Ordre économique et social, Eugène Mathon, 1860–1935.* Paris, 1946.

Dubreuil, Hyacinthe. *Standards: le travail américain vu par un ouvrier français.* Paris: Grasset, 1929.

Duchemin, René-P. *Organisation syndicale patronale en France.* Paris: Plon, 1940.

Dupoil, J., et al. *La Nationalisation des industries-clés.* Conférences de l'Institut supérieur ouvrier, No. 21. Paris, n.d.

Dussauze, Elizabeth. *L'État et les ententes industrielles.* Paris: Librairie technique et économique, 1938.

Earle, Edward Mead (ed.). *Modern France, Problems of the Third and Fourth Republics.* Princeton, N.J.: Princeton University Press, 1951.

———. "The Turkish Petroleum Company: A Study in Oleaginous Diplomacy," *Political Science Quarterly,* XXXIX (June, 1924), 265–279.

Ehrmann, Henry W. *French Labor from Popular Front to Liberation.* New York: Oxford University Press, 1947.

———. *Organized Business in France.* Princeton, N. J.: Princeton University Press, 1957.

Elbow, Matthew H. *French Corporative Theory, 1789–1948: A Chapter in the History of Ideas.* New York: Columbia University Press, 1953.

Ellul, Jacques. *The Technological Society.* Translated by John Wilkinson. New York: Knopf, 1964.

l'Espagnol de la Tramerye, Pierre. *The World Struggle for Oil.* Translated by C. Leonard Leese. New York: Knopf, 1924.

Faure, Edgar. *La Politique française du pétrole.* Paris: Éditions de la nouvelle revue critique, 1938.

Fels, Comte de. "Le Redressement Français," *Revue de Paris,* May 1, 1926, pp. 5–19, and July 15, 1926, pp. 241–257.

Fischer, Jacques. *Doumergue et les politiciens.* Paris: Le Jour, 1935.

Flandin, Pierre-Étienne. "Le Problème social," *Revue de Paris,* February 1, 1928, pp. 497–509.

Foerster, Friedrich Wilhelm. *L'Europe et la question allemande.* Translated by Henri Bloch and Paul Rocques. Paris: Plon, 1937.

Fohlen, Claude. *La France de l'entre-deux-guerres.* Paris: Casterman, 1966.

Frachon, Benoît. *La Bataille de la production, nouvelle étape du combat contre les trusts.* Paris: Éditions sociales, 1946.

Frédérix, Pierre. *État des forces en France.* 3rd ed. Paris: Gallimard, 1935.

Friedmann, Georges. "Les Technocrates et la civilisation technicienne," in Georges Gurvitch (ed.), *Industrialisation et technocratie* (Paris: Colin, 1949).

Gagnon, Paul. "French Views of the Second American Revolution." *French Historical Studies,* II (Fall, 1962), 430–449.

Gasquet, Georges de. *L'Industrie française de raffinage du pétrole.* Aix-en-Provence: La Pensée universitaire, 1957.

Géraud, André. "The Coming French Elections," *Foreign Affairs,* VI (January, 1928), 217–230.

Gignoux, Claude-J. *L'Économie française entre les deux guerres, 1919–1939.* Paris: Éditions économiques et sociales, [1942].

———. *L'Industrie française.* Paris: Boivin, 1952.

Girard, Alain. *La Réussite sociale en France, ses caractères—ses lois—ses effets.* Institut national d'études démographiques, Cahier No. 38. Paris: Presses universitaires, 1961.

Girardet, Raoul. "Note sur l'esprit d'un fascisme français, 1934–1939," *Revue française de science politique,* V (July–September, 1955), 529–546.

Giscard d'Estaing, Edmond. "Le Néocapitalisme," *Revue des deux mondes,* August 1, 1928, pp. 673–688.

Goguel, François. *La Politique des partis sous la III⁰ république.* 3rd ed. Paris: Éditions du Seuil, 1958.

Goy, Jean (rapporteur). *Réforme des institutions, réforme électorale et réforme parlementaire.* Union Nationale des Combattants, XVI⁰ congrès national de Brest, 6 au 9 juin, 1935. Paris, [1935].

Granick, David. *The European Executive.* Garden City, N.Y.: Doubleday, 1962.

Grégoire, Roger, *et al.* "Technocracy and the Role of Experts in Government." Papers presented at the Fifth World Congress, International Political Association, Paris, 1961.

Guérin, Daniel. *Front Populaire: révolution manquée.* Paris: Julliard, 1963.

Guierre, Maurice. *Robert Cayrol, 1883–1959: de la mer au pétrole, l'unité d'une vie.* Paris: Éditions Perceval, 1960.

Hamon, Augustin. *Les Maîtres de la France.* 3 vols. Paris: Éditions sociales internationales, 1936–1938.

Hayes, Carlton J. H. *France, a Nation of Patriots.* New York: Columbia University Press, 1930.

Herbette, François. *L'Expérience marxiste en France, 1936–38.* Paris: Librairie de Médicis, 1960.

Herriot, Édouard. *Jadis: d'une guerre à l'autre, 1914–1936.* Vol. II. Paris: Flammarion, 1952.

Hessabi, Mehdi. *Le Pétrole en Irak.* Paris: Jouve, 1937.

Hewins, Ralph. *Mr. Five Per Cent: The Biography of Calouste Gulbenkian.* London: Hutchison, 1957.

Hoffmann, Stanley. "Aspects du régime de Vichy," *Revue française de science politique,* VI (January–March, 1956), 44–69.

Homberg, Octave. *Les Coulisses de l'histoire: souvenirs, 1898–1928.* Paris: Fayard, 1938.

Hubert, René. "Le Problème du pétrole devant le parlement," *Revue politique et parlementaire,* CXLIII (June 10, 1930), 376–396.

Hughes, H. Stuart. "Gaullism in the Mirror of History," in *An Approach to Peace and Other Essays.* New York: Atheneum, 1962.

Institut National de la Statistique et des Études Économiques. *Annuaire statistique de la France, rétrospectif.* Paris: Imprimerie nationale, 1961.

———. *Études et conjoncture,* numéro spécial: *L'Industrie française.* 1953.

[International Business Conference, Rye, N.Y.]. "The Story of the International Business Conference, November 10–18, 1944." Official brochure.

Jouvenel, Bertrand de, and Rotter, René. "Le Trust de l'énergie," *La Flèche,* February 1, 1936.

Kindleberger, Charles. "The Postwar Resurgence of the French Economy," in Stanley Hoffmann *et al., In Search of France* (Cambridge, Mass.: Harvard University Press, 1963).

Labarrière, Guillaume de. *La Compagnie Française des Pétroles: les sociétés de pétrole à participation de l'état dans divers pays.* Brest: Imprimerie commerciale et administrative, 1932.

Lagardelle, Hubert. *Mission à Rome, Mussolini.* Paris: Plon, 1955.

Lalance, Auguste. *Mes souvenirs, 1830–1914.* Paris–Nancy: Berger-Levrault, 1914.

Lamirand, Georges. *Le Rôle social de l'ingénieur.* Paris: Desclée, 1937.

Landes, David S. "New-Model Entrepreneurship in France and Problems of Historical Explanation," *Explorations in Entrepreneurial History,* XV (Fall, 1963), 56–75.

La Rocque, Édith and Gilles de. *La Rocque tel qu'il était.* Paris: Fayard, 1962.

La Rocque, François de. *Service public.* Paris: Grasset, 1934.

Laroque, Pierre. *Les Rapports entre patrons et ouvriers.* Paris: F. Aubier, 1938.

Laufenburger, Henry. "La Production industrielle," *Revue d'économie politique,* LIII (June–August, 1939), 1182–1231.

Launay, Jacques de (ed.). *Louis Loucheur: Carnets secrets, 1908–1932.* Brussels: Éditions Brepols, 1962.

Lecordier, Gaston. "Le Mouvement patronal," *Chronique sociale de France,* LCIII (January–February, 1949), pp. 67–84.

Lefranc, Georges. *Les Expériences syndicales en France de 1939 à 1950.* Paris: Aubier, 1950.

Leroy, Maxime. *Les Techniques nouvelles du syndicalisme.* Paris: Garnier, 1921.

Lewinsohn, Richard. *L'Argent dans la politique.* Paris: Nouvelle Revue française, 1931.

Liebmann, Léon. "Entre le mythe et la légende: 'l'anti-capitalisme' de Vichy," *Revue de l'Institut de sociologie,* No. 1 (1964), 109–148.

Longrigg, Stephen. *Oil in the Middle East: Its Discovery and Development.* London: Oxford University Press, 1954.

Lyautey, Louis-Hubert. "Du Rôle social de l'officier," *Revue des deux mondes,* March 15, 1891, pp. 443–459.

Lyautey, Maréchal de France, par les anciens de son équipe. Cahiers Charles de Foucauld. Vichy, 1954.

Magondeaux, Odette de. *Les Ententes industrielles obligatoires et le corporatisme en France.* Paris: Librairie générale de droit, 1937.

Maizy, H. "Les Groupes antiparlementaires républicains de droite en France de 1933 à 1939." Unpublished thesis, Institut d'études politiques, Paris, 1952.

Malégarie, Charles. *L'Électricité à Paris*. Paris: C. Béranger, 1947.

Mallet, Alfred. *Pierre Laval*. 2 vols. Paris: Amiot-Dumont, 1954–1955.

Marlio, Louis. "Les Ententes industrielles," *Revue de Paris*, February 15, 1930, pp. 823–852.

———. "L'Industrie électrique," *Revue des deux mondes*, November 15, 1931, pp. 331–362.

Mason, E. S. "Saint-Simonism and the Rationalization of Industry," *Quarterly Journal of Economics*, XLV (August, 1931), 640–683.

Mendès-France, Pierre. *A Modern French Republic*. Translated by Anne Carter. New York: Hill and Wang, 1963.

Mennevée, Roger. "L'Organisation réactionnaire internationale en France: du 'Bureau Politique International' au 'Redressement Français,' " *Les Documents politiques, diplomatiques et financiers*, October and November, 1926, pp. 451–454, 465–479.

———. "Les Journaux du 'Redressement Français,' " *Les Documents politiques, diplomatiques et financiers*, January and February, 1927, pp. 28–29, 77.

———. "Le 'Redressement Français' et l'oligarchie internationale," *Les Documents politiques, diplomatiques et financiers*, June, 1927, pp. 243–244.

———. "Les nouvelles combinaisons du 'Redressement Français,' " *Les Documents politiques, diplomatiques et financiers*, November, 1927, pp. 437–438.

———. "Un Organisme antimaçonnique occulte: le 'Redressement Français,' " *Les Documents politiques, diplomatiques et financiers*, December, 1927, pp. 489–492.

———. "Les Influences oligarchiques dans la politique française," *Les Documents politiques, diplomatiques et financiers*, December, 1932, pp. 769–775.

———. "Le 'Redressement Français' dans le pré-fascisme français," *Les Documents politiques, diplomatiques et financiers*, April, 1934, pp. 176–178.

———. "Un important événement politico-oligarchique: la dissolution du 'Redressement Français,' " *Les Documents politiques, diplomatiques et financiers*, December, 1935, pp. 549–566.

———. "M. Maurice Petsche, ministre des finances, biographie familiale," *Les Documents politiques, diplomatiques et financiers*, January, 1950, pp. 3–22.

"Ernest Mercier, 1878–1955," *Revue générale de l'électricité*, October, 1955, pp. 471–473.

Meynaud, Jean. *Technocratie et politique*. Études de science politique, No. 2. Lausanne: Imprimerie Bellanger, 1960.

———. *La Technocratie, mythe ou réalité?* Paris: Payot, 1964.

Micaud, Charles A. *The French Right and Nazi Germany, 1933–1939*. New York: Duke University Press, 1943.

Michon, Georges. *Les Puissances d'argent et l'émeute du 6 février*. Paris: Comité de vigilance des intellectuels antifascistes, 1934.

Miquel, Pierre. *Poincaré*. Paris: Fayard, 1961.

Moch, Jules. *Arguments et documents contre capitalisme, crise, déflation*. Paris: Librairie populaire, 1936.

———. *Guerre aux trusts, solutions socialistes*. Paris: Éditions de la liberté, 1945.

———. *Socialisme et rationalisation*. Brussels: l'Eglantine, 1927.

Mohr, Anton. *The Oil War.* London: Hopkinson, 1926.

Moreau, Émile. *Souvenirs d'un gouverneur de la Banque de France, histoire de la stabilisation du franc, 1926–1928.* Paris: Librairie de Médicis, 1954.

Morin, R. "Conseils d'administration," *Revue de France,* March 15, 1929, pp. 378–382.

Mottez, Bernard. "Le Patronat français vu par les Américains," *Sociologie du travail,* III (1961), 287–293.

Moulin de Labarthète, Henri du. *Le Temps des illusions.* Brussels: Diffusion du livre, 1946.

"Nationalization of French Supply," *The Electrician,* December 21, 1945, p. 690.

L'Oeuvre de la Croix-Rouge Américaine en France et le Secours Américain aux Victimes de la Guerre, 1940–1944. Paris, 1945.

Ogburn, William F., and Jaffé, William. *The Economic Development of Post-war France, A Survey of Production.* New York: Columbia University Press, 1929.

Organization for European Economic Cooperation. *Industrial Statistics, 1900–1959.* Paris: Publications de l'OECE, 1960.

Pepinier, R. "Houille noire et houille blanche," *La Revue industrielle,* April, 1935, pp. 143–144.

Perrot, Marguerite. *La Monnaie et l'opinion publique en France et en Angleterre de 1924 à 1936.* Cahiers de la Fondation nationale des sciences politiques, No. 65. Paris: Colin, 1955.

Peyerimhoff, Henri de. "Les Formules modernes d'organisation économique," *Revue des deux mondes,* March 15, 1929, pp. 439–458.

Pinon, René. "Les nouvelles Conceptions de l'état," *Revue économique internationale,* October, 1929, pp. 7–30.

Pirou, Gaëtan. *Les Doctrines économiques en France depuis 1870.* 3rd ed. Paris: Colin, 1934.

———. *Essais sur le corporatisme.* Paris: Recueil Sirey [1938].

Pizanty, Mihail. *Petroleum in Rumania.* Bucharest: Rumanian Economic Institute, 1930.

Pollock, James K. *Money and Politics Abroad.* New York: Knopf, 1932.

Pozzo di Borgo. *La Rocque, fantôme à vendre.* Paris: Sorlot, 1938.

Prévost, Marcel. "Polytechnique: idées et souvenirs," *Revue de France,* December 15, 1930, pp. 577–596; January 1, 1931, pp. 53–68; January 15, 1931, pp. 264–285.

Priouret, Roger. *Origines du patronat français.* Paris: Grasset, 1963.

Rémond, René. *La Droite en France de 1815 à nos jours.* Paris: Aubier, 1954.

———. "Explications du 6 février," *Politique,* July–December, 1959, pp. 218–230.

———. *La Vie politique en France de 1870 à 1940.* Institut d'études politiques, 1959–1960. Paris [1960].

———. "Les anciens Combattants et la politique," *Revue française de science politique,* V (April–June, 1955), 267–290.

Renaud, Albert. *Les Entreprises électriques et les collectivités.* Bordeaux: Éditions Delmas, 1935.

Reynaud, Paul. *Mémoires.* 2 vols. Paris: Flammarion, 1960–1963.

Romier, Lucien. "La Disgrâce du capitalisme," *Revue des deux mondes,*

February 15, 1933, pp. 876–891; March 1, 1933, pp. 110–124; April 1, 1933, pp. 643–656; June 1, 1933, pp. 648–661.

———. *Si le capitalisme disparaissait*. Paris: Hachette, 1933.

———. *Who Will Be Master, Europe or America?* Translated by Matthew Josephson. New York: Macaulay, 1928.

Rondot, Jean. *La Compagnie Française des Pétroles: du franc-or au pétrole-franc*. Paris: Plon, 1962.

Rousiers, Paul de. *Les grandes Industries modernes*. Vol. I. Paris: Colin, 1927.

Roussy de Sales, R. de. "Un Mouvement nouveau aux États-Unis: 'La Technocratie,'" *Revue de Paris*, March 15, 1933, pp. 432–443.

Rowland, John, and Basil, Second Baron Cadman. *Ambassador for Oil: The Life of John, First Baron Cadman*. London: Herbert Jenkins, 1960.

Sauvy, Alfred. *Histoire économique de la France entre les deux guerres, 1918–1931*. Paris: Fayard, 1965.

Sawyer, John E. "The Entrepreneur and the Social Order, France and the United States," in William Miller (ed.), *Men in Business: Essays in the History of Entrepreneurship* (Cambridge, Mass.: Harvard University Press, 1952).

Schneider, Eugène. "A propos des Assurances sociales," *Revue des deux mondes*, May 15, 1933, pp. 427–440.

Schueller, Eugène. *La Révolution de l'économie*. Paris: Denoël, 1941.

Sharp, Walter. *The French Civil Service: Bureaucracy in Transition*. New York: Macmillan, 1931.

Siegfried, André. "The Psychology of French Political Parties," *Journal of the Royal Institute of International Affairs*, January, 1928, pp. 12–28.

Soucy, Robert J. "The Nature of Fascism in France," *Journal of Contemporary History*, I (1966), 27–55.

Soulier, Auguste. *L'Instabilité ministérielle sous la troisième république, 1871–1938*. Paris: Recueil Sirey, 1939.

Sturmthal, Adolf. "Nationalization and Workers' Control in Britain and France," *Journal of Political Economy*, LXI (1953), 43–79.

———. "The Structure of Nationalized Enterprises in France," *Political Science Quarterly*, LXVII (1952), 357–377.

Suarez, Georges. *De Poincaré à Poincaré*. Paris: Éditions de France, 1928.

Svennilson, Ingvar. *Growth and Stagnation in the European Economy*. Geneva: United Nations Economic Commission for Europe, 1954.

Tarde, Guillaume de. *Lyautey, le chef en action*. 3rd ed. Paris: Gallimard, 1959.

Tchernoff, J. *Ententes économiques et financières*. Paris: Recueil Sirey, 1933.

Thibaudet, Albert. *Les Idées politiques de la France*. Paris: Stock, Delamain et Boutelleau, 1932.

Touchard, Jean, et al. *Histoire des idées politiques*. Vol. II. Paris: Presses universitaires, 1959.

———. "L'Esprit des années 1930: une tentative de renouvellement de la pensée politique française," in *Tendances politiques dans la vie française depuis 1789* (Paris: Hachette, 1960).

Tournoux, J.-R. *Pétain et de Gaulle*. Paris: Plon, 1964.

Toynbee, Arnold J., and Boulter, V. M., eds. *Survey of International Affairs, 1935*. Vol. I. London: Oxford University Press, 1936.

Les Trusts contre la France. Paris: *L'Humanité*, n.d.

Vallat, Xavier. *Le de Cléopâtre: souvenirs d'un homme de droite, 1918–1945.* Paris: Quatre Fils Aymon, 1957.

Valois, Georges. *L'État syndicale et la représentation corporative.* Paris: Librairie Valois, 1927.

————. *L'Homme contre l'argent: souvenirs de dix ans, 1918–1928.* Paris: Librairie Valois, 1928.

————. *Un nouvel Âge de l'humanité.* Paris: Librairie Valois, 1929.

Ventenat, Marcel. *L'Expérience des nationalisations.* Paris: Librairie de Médicis [1947].

Verdurand, A. "L'Homme d'affaires et la France," *Revue hebdomadaire,* December, 1927, pp. 339–341.

Veuillot, François. *La Rocque et son parti comme je les ai vus.* Paris: Plon, 1938.

Vignaux, Paul. *Traditionalisme et syndicalisme: essai d'histoire sociale, 1884–1941.* New York: Éditions de la maison française, 1943.

Weber, Eugen. *Action Française: Royalism and Reaction in Twentieth-Century France.* Stanford: Stanford University Press, 1962.

Welter, G. *La France d'aujourd'hui, agriculture–industrie–commerce.* Paris: Payot, 1927.

Werth, Alexander. *France in Ferment.* London: Harper, 1934.

————. *Which Way France?* New York: Harper, 1937.

Willard, Claude. *Quelques Aspects du fascisme en France avant le 6 février 1934.* Paris: Éditions sociales, 1961.

Wolfe, Martin. *The French Franc Between the Wars, 1919–1939.* New York: Columbia University Press, 1951.

Wolff, Robert. *Économie et finances de la France, passé et avenir.* New York: Brentano's, 1943.

Zamanski, Joseph. *Forces nouvelles.* Paris: SPES, 1933.

Zoretti, Ludovic. *Le Plan de la CGT.* Conférences de l'Institut supérieur ouvrier, No. 19. Paris, n.d.

PERIODICALS CONSULTED *

L'Action française, 1927–1935.

Annuaire de l'Union des Syndicats de l'Électricité, 1927–1936.

L'Avenir, 1927.

Bulletin bi-mensuel de la CGPF, 1925–1927.

Bulletin quotidien, 1925–1935.

Les Cahiers bleus, 1928–1932.

Les Cahiers de l'Union fédérale, 1934–1935.

Les Cahiers des droits de l'homme, 1927–1935.

Le Canard enchaîné, 1927–1930.

Le Capital, 1927–1935.

Chantiers coopératifs, 1934.

Courrier des pétroles, 1923, 1927, 1930.

Le Crapouillot, 1950–1952.

Les Documents politiques, diplomatiques et financiers, 1920–1950.

Electrical World, 1925–1946.

* Dates represent the years I have examined rather than the run of the periodical.

The Electrician, 1925–1946.
Entreprise, 1953–1961.
Excelsior, 1934–1935.
Le Figaro, 1926–1928.
Le Flambeau, 1929–1935.
La Flèche, 1934–1936.
La France au travail, 1940–1943.
Le Gaulois, 1927.
Le Grand Guignol, 1925–1927.
Groupe Cortambert, Bulletin de liaison, 1959–1960.
L'Humanité, 1927–1939.
Le Journal, 1927–1931.
La Journée industrielle, 1927–1935.
La Lumière, 1927–1935.
Nouveaux Cahiers, 1937–1940.
L'Oeuvre, 1927–1928.
Paris-Phare, 1926–1931.
Pax, 1926–1928.
Petroleum Times, 1920–1935.
Le Peuple, 1927–1936.
Au Pilori, 1941–1943.
Le Populaire, 1926–1936.
Production nationale et expansion économique, 1926–1927.
Prospective, 1959–1961.
Le Réveil des combattants, 1934–1935.
Le Réveil économique, 1925–1928.
La Révolution prolétarienne, 1927–1934.
Revue d'économie politique, 1925–1939.
Revue de France, 1925–1935.
Revue de Paris, 1925–1935.
Revue des deux mondes, 1925–1935.
Revue générale de l'électricité, 1925–1955.
Revue hebdomadaire, 1927–1928.
Revue mensuelle de l'UIMM, 1927–1929.
Revue politique et parlementaire, 1925–1939.
Le Temps, 1926–1936.
La Tribune des fonctionnaires, 1927–1936.
L'UNC de Paris, 1932–1935.
L'Usine, 1927–1936.
La Voix du combattant, 1934.
X-Crise Bulletin, 1930–1936.

Index